SO-DTM-837

THE PLACE OF THE TOSEFTA IN THE
HALAKHAH OF FORMATIVE JUDAISM

SOUTH FLORIDA STUDIES IN THE HISTORY OF JUDAISM

Edited by
Jacob Neusner
Bruce D. Chilton, Darrell J. Fasching, William Scott Green,
Sara Mandell, James F. Strange

Number 156
The Place of the Tosefta in the
Halakhah of Formative Judaism
What Alberdina Houtman Didn't Notice

by
Jacob Neusner

THE PLACE OF THE TOSEFTA IN THE HALAKHAH OF FORMATIVE JUDAISM

What Alberdina Houtman Didn't Notice

by

Jacob Neusner

Scholars Press
Atlanta, Georgia

HIEBERT LIBRARY
FRESNO PACIFIC UNIV.-M. B. SEMINARY
FRESNO, CA 93702

THE PLACE OF THE TOSEFTA IN THE HALAKHAH OF FORMATIVE JUDAISM

What Alberdina Houtman Didn't Notice

by
Jacob Neusner

©1998
University of South Florida

Publication of this book was made possible by a grant from the Tisch Family Foundation, New York City. The University of South Florida acknowledges with thanks this important support for its scholarly projects.

Library of Congress Cataloging in Publication Data
Neusner, Jacob, 1932–
    The place of the Tosefta in the halakhah of formative Judaism :
what Alberdina Houtman didn't notice / by Jacob Neusner.
        p.   cm. — (South Florida studies in the history of Judaism ;
no. 156)
    Includes bibliographical references.
    ISBN 0-7885-0454-1 (alk. paper)
    1. Tosefta. Shevi'it—Criticism, interpretation, etc.
2. Tosefta. Bava kamma—Criticism, interpretation, etc.
3. Tosefta. Shabbat—Criticism, interpretation, etc. 4. Houtman,
Alberdina. Mishnah and Tosefta. 5. Mishnah—Comparative studies.
6. Tosefta—Comparative studies. I. Title. II. Series.
BM508.5.S33N48   1998
296.1'231—dc21   98-15588

Printed in the United States of America
on acid-free paper

TABLE OF CONTENTS

Preface

In the present monograph, I conduct a systematic *Auseinandersetzung* with a recent Dutch dissertation, that of Alberdina Houtman, accepted at the University of Utrecht, entitled, *Mishnah and Tosefta. A Synoptic Comparison of the Tractates Berakhot and Shebiit.* Tübingen, 1996: J.C.B. Mohr (Paul Siebeck). 225 pp. and her *Mishnah and Tosefta. A Synoptic Comparison of the Tractates Berakhot and Shebiit.* Appendix Volume. *Synopsis of Tosefta and Mishnah Berakhot and Shebiit.* Tübingen, 1996: J.C.B. Mohr (Paul Siebeck). 92 pp. I describe and review her work in Chapter One, identifying the critical issue at which my current research intersects with hers, the matter of the substance of the halakhah, which in my view she simply ignores. In Chapter Two I go over my presentation of the same documentary problem that she treats, as in 1992 I set forth matters.[1] In Chapters Three through Five I present fresh research that bears upon the problem that she has raised, the data that she simply did not notice.

Specfically, Alberdina Houtman ignores that documents not only exhibit interesting formal traits but also make statements. And these statements bear meaning, so that we may ask which of them presupposes another of them, or where among the documents we find the most basic, the most consequential statements, and where we find only the results of principles set forth in some other writing. Consequently, if we wish to examine the relationships between kindred writings, we have to pay attention not only to style but substance. We have also to address the logic that governs the law, identifying statements that take priority, those that come later, in the unfolding of the sense of the halakhah.

Let me spell out how these obvious truths pertain to Houtman's problem: Mishnah-Tosefta, and Tosefta-Mishnah relationships. We have to ask whether the law of the Tosefta rests upon the logic set forth in the Mishnah or vice versa. Along these same lines have to identify the generative problematics of the halakhah and determine where the governing conceptions of what precipitates the exegesis of the law first surface, the Mishnah, the Tosefta, the Yerushalmi, or the Bavli. When we do, we may compare not only the forms of documents — the superficial

---

[1] *The Tosefta. An Introduction.* Atlanta, 1992: Scholars Press for South Florida Studies in the History of Judaism.

traits of program and the like — but the interior construction of the halakhah. Then we may identify where, within that contruction, the contribution of the several documents finds its place.

I regret to report that to none of these questions of a halakhic character does Houtman pay attention. As I explain in Chapter One, she decided to make her mark by utilizing the computer in her research. She thought that computer research was required to permit reading the Mishnah against the base-line of the Tosefta as much as the Tosefta against the base-line of the Mishnah. But when it comes to matters of the halakhah and its logic and animating principles, computers cannot replace intellect, but acumen and perspicacity govern and shape taste and judgment. Neglecting that fact yields a genuinely silly monograph.

When I read her dissertation on the relationship of the Tosefta and the Mishnah, I was (and still am) in the midst of work of my own, in which I was interested in setting forth a systematic statement of the repertoire of the halakhah of formative Judaism, the Mishnah, the Tosefta, the Yerushalmi, and the Bavli. The halakhah was to be viewed as a single seamless statement. In other words, I had in mind a meta-documentary inquiry into the unfolding of the halakhah from its basic principles to its secondary and tertiary levels of development, the whole views as a logical, not a formal problem. This corpus of writings I examined not as a set of discrete literary entities but as a continuous exposition of the law of a given topic. Accordingly, I determined to set aside the issues of documentary relationships and focus only on the presentation, by the documents read in sequence, of topical disquisitions of halakhah.

What I noticed, and what readers will see for themselves in Chapters Three through Fix, was two facts.

First, the Mishnah's statement of the halakhah always is the one that fundamental to the exposition of the halakhah seen as a seamless system, the Tosefta's merely illuminating. The one pronounces the foundations of the halakhah, not just the topics but the principles that govern, the other clarifies the pronouncement. The Tosefta then amplifies and extends the Mishnah's halakhah and richly instantiates it, but rarely offers a halakhic principle at the fundamental character of the Mishnah's statement of the halakhah. Now that is a trait of the two documents that emerges only when we focus upon the substance of the halakhah, its logic and problematic. Treating the halakhic discourse as unitary and not fragmented into documents, I found that I could identify the Mishnah's contribution to the halakhah, viewed systematically, by its characteristics of logic and intellect, that is, by the basic and generative character of its statements. The Tosefta's contribution to the halakhah was equally susceptible of characterization. Viewed in the context of the topic of the halakhah and its systematic (not documentary) exposition, the Tosefta's statements did not precipitate inquiry but only amplified it, responding to a program of logical exposition of topics not present but presupposed in its own halakhic program.

Second, it turns out, by an examination of not the point of origin of a statement but of the content of the halakhic statements, seen side by side, but in any sequence (the Tosefta first, then the Mishnah, or even the Bavli first, then the Tosefta, then the Mishnah), by appeal to the characteristics of thought that register in what is said, we can readily place the several statements into the documents that follow the sequence, [1] the Mishnah, then [2] the Tosefta. What the Tosefta says often presupposes the principles set forth in the Mishnah, but what the Mishnah says rarely, if ever, presupposes prinricples (herementucs, exegetics) set forth in the Tosefta; that statement of logical relationships of the substance of the law can be evaluated only in a close reading of the details of the law in the seamless manner just now indicated. Then, when, in Chapters Three through Five, for one of the two tractates Houtman covers, Shebi'it, and two large ones in addition, we patiently review the halakhic pronouncements of the Mishnah, Tosefta, Yerushalmi, and Bavli, we see the conceptual priority of the Mishnah in the halakhic process.

There is a specific test that repeatedly yields that result. In those tractates that expound the law in response to a set of questions of a fundamental character that I call, the generative problematics, where do we find the statement of that generative problematics? It is in the Mishnah, and so far as I have found to date, only in the Mishnah's statement of the halakhah. And, that fact established, we dismiss as silly the exercise of reading the Tosefta on its own, not in relationship to the Mishnah. That exercise requires that we pretend we have no Mishnah, but we do, and the rest follows. And that, as I say, is what Alberdina Houtman never noticed. I think it is because she never looked.

It remains to explain the choice of tractates set forth in Chapters Three through Five. I deal with one of the two that she has selected, Shebi'it, and two others, but not the other tractate, Berakhot, that she examines. That is because, for the purposes of this *Auseinandersetzung* with Dr. Houtman, tractate Berakhot contributes no useful evidence. There I am not able to identify generative conceptions at the foundations of the law, critical tensions around which the halakhah takes shape. In the halakhah of Shebi'it the full failure of her enterprise becomes clear. That is where the logical priority of the Mishnah's contribution to the definition of the halakhah becomes blatant. When we identify the generative problematics of that halakhah, we find ourselves whollyl within the Mishnah's sector. In Chapters Four and Five I include Baba Qamma and Shabbat further to show that the Mishnah states the generative problematic of the halakhah, and that the Tosefta does not.

Let me place into the context of my *oeuvre* this large-scale exercise of *Auseinandersetzung* carried out with a rather minor and amateurish monograph. In responding in a systematic way to the mistakes of colleagues, past and present, I accept the agenda of learning defined by others. I carry on the exercise in three forms. First, I review nearly every scholarly monograph and book that appears in the field in which I work, the formative age of Judaism with special reference to its history, literature, religion, and theology. I have collected these reviews in various anthologies. Second, I respond in detail in articles and even in systematic inquiries of my own to interesting criticism set forth by others. That is so, in particular, when the criticism strikes me as reasonable and worth intellectual energy; I do not waste time on trivialities, whether people or books. In addition, third, when the occasion presents itself, I have devoted entire monographs to the ideas of others, their particular theses, whether books or dissertations or monographs or mere articles, that have struck me as worth sustained attention. That is not because I think the theses are plausible or even important, but because methodological problems — whether of definition or procedure — strike me as worth of more than casual discussion. Therefore the blunders of others have provided the stimulus to think in an orderly and careful way about the problems at hand.

In the line of prior monographs of that classification, the present work takes its place. The earlier ones include these:

> *Canon and Connection: Intertextuality in Judaism.* Lanham, 1986: University Press of America. *Studies in Judaism* Series.

> *Midrash as Literature: The Primacy of Documentary Discourse.* Lanham, 1987: University Press of America *Studies in Judaism* series.

> *Judaic Law from Jesus to the Mishnah. A Systematic Reply to Professor E. P. Sanders.* Atlanta, 1993: Scholars Press for South Florida Studies in the History of Judaism.

> *Are There Really Tannaitic Parallels to the Gospels? A Refutation of Morton Smith.* Atlanta, 1993: Scholars Press for South Florida Studies in the History of Judaism.

> *Why There Never Was a "Talmud of Caesarea." Saul Lieberman's Mistakes.* Atlanta, 1994: Scholars Press for South Florida Studies in the History of Judaism.

> *The Documentary Foundation of Rabbinic Culture. Mopping Up after Debates with Gerald L. Bruns, S. J. D. Cohen, Arnold Maria Goldberg, Susan Handelman, Christine Hayes, James Kugel, Peter Schaefer, Eliezer Segal, E. P. Sanders, and Lawrence H. Schiffman.* Atlanta, 1995: Scholars Press for South Florida Studies in the History of Judaism.

Are the Talmuds Interchangeable? Christine Hayes's Blunder.
Atlanta, 1996: Scholars Press for South Florida Studies on the
History of Judaism.

As the titles indicate, I have chosen to respond to weighty challenges not in a casual, let alone in an offhand and political manner, but by a close reading of the writing of others and a sustained, rational response thereto. This is done in a public forum, and I have always accorded to those I criticize the same forum for their replies. So far there has been none, here or elsewhere. Silence, in the halakhah, is tantamount to the act of admission and concession.

But that is not my purpose; I learn from my errors and compose each succeeding project as an exercise in improving the preceding one. Poor work by others will not endure, whether or not I contribute to its demise. Asking other peoples' questions in my own way permits me to assess the methods I have devised for the analytical study of Rabbinic Judaism in its formative age. At the same time I am able to test my results by comparing them to those of others who have worked on the same problems but in different ways. And, finally, I am able to set into the context of others' interests results of my own, which ought to enrich the scholarly enterprise. In particular, that alerts co-workers to the pertinence to their work of my own. That is what makes the work worth the effort.

The University of South Florida provides not only a Research Professorship but also a large Research Grant, which support my work. I give thanks for both. Bard College does the same. Both centers of higher learning bring me into everyday collaboration with colleagues of exceptional acumen, good will and intellect, and I learn from them day by day. For me nothing could be the same without them.

JACOB NEUSNER
UNIVERSITY OF SOUTH FLORIDA & BARD COLLEGE

1

What Alberdina Houtman Didn't Notice

Alberdina Houtman, *Mishnah and Tosefta. A Synoptic Comparison of the Tractates Berakhot and Shebiit.* Tübingen, 1996: J.C.B. Mohr (Paul Siebeck). 225 pp.

Alberdina Houtman, *Mishnah and Tosefta. A Synoptic Comparison of the Tractates Berakhot and Shebiit.* Appendix Volume. *Synopsis of Tosefta and Mishnah Berakhot and Shebiit.* Tübingen, 1996: J.C.B. Mohr (Paul Siebeck). 92 pp.

The basic flaw in Dr. Houtman's monograph, which I shall spell out with some care, is simple. She has the odd notion that we may invent a condition contrary to fact and then conduct research to prove that that condition describes the fact. How would we read the Tosefta if we did not have the Mishnah? Would it make sense? Yes, it would, she concludes. But so what? For we do have the Mishnah, and its traits continue to make all the difference in forming a theory of the Tosefta. That in sum is why I find Houtman's book simply silly, answering a question one may ask only in complete indifference to established facts — speculation run amok and without any purpose at all.

Houtman wishes to show that we may read the Tosefta as a free-standing document, as though there were no Mishnah. (She does not doubt that the contrary also is the case.) Since she wants to know whether she may read the Tosefta as if the Mishnah did not exist, she does just that. She finds the Tosefta mostly intelligible, and she is happy with the arrangement of the Tosefta, which she sees as well ordered in its own terms. So if there were no Mishnah, the Tosefta would serve for the same purpose, the presentation of the law.

But, alas, we cannot make things up as we go along and call the result "scholarship." In fact we do have the Mishnah, and no plausible theory of the

Tosefta can be formulated in contradiction to that fact. Not only so, but Houtman as much as admits that fact. Much of the evidence by her own analysis indicates that the Tosefta must be read in relationship to the Mishnah. That is because, she admits, the Tosefta is comprised by various types of material, some of it free-standing, some not but dependent on the Mishnah, and some of it citing the Mishnah in so many words. Further, some of it is arranged in intelligible composites, some of it set forth in composites that derive cogency only from their relationship to the Mishnah (but that is something else that Houtman does not notice). In producing these results of hers, moreover, she recapitulates work complete and in print twenty years ago, part of which she knows but has not understood, part of which she does not appear even to have examined at all.

Apart from wanting to pretend that the facts are other than what they are — to imagine a world in which we had no Mishnah but only the Tosefta, or no Tosefta but only the Mishnah — Houtman engages in yet another fantasy. She wishes to ignore the substance of the documents and concentrate on the form. That explains why at no point does she ask about the relationship, as to logic and premise, between the law set forth in the Mishnah and the law set forth in the Tosefta. Had she done so, she would have noticed, time and again, that the Mishnah's formulation of the halakhah invokes a principle that is logically prior to, and that is presupposed by, the Tosefta's formulation of the corresponding halakhah. But to do so, she would have had to study the halakhah of the documents — pay attention to matters of substance. She would, in other words, have had to enter into, to master the interiorities of the halakhah. Apart from her power to paraphrase what is clear in the text itself, however, she shows no halakhic acumen or perspicacity. That is why she can treat the Mishnah and the Tosefta as simply co-equal statements.

But had she looked at the sequence of statements of a halakhic character on a given topic (from the Mishnah to the Tosefta to the Yerushalmi to the Bavli, or, if she liked, from the Tosefta to the Mishnah and so on), she would have noticed that the Mishnah consistently sets forth what is logically, halakhically primary and fundamental, the Tosefta consistently amplifies, instantiates, and extends the Mishnah's generative halakhah, the Yerushalmi adds only little halakhah but much analysis, and the Bavli, less halakhah but still more analysis. For the Tosefta, Yerushalmi, and Bavli set forth only new details about the halakhic topic with its interior logic that the Mishnah has defined in its basic characteristics. The subsequent documents carry forward the exposition. As a matter of fact the halakhic structure — topics, problematics — emerges nearly whole and complete in the Mishnah, to be refined and amplified and complemented later on, but never to be vastly reconstructed as to its generative categories. Reading the Tosefta outside out of relationship with the Mishnah — as if we had no Mishnah — as Houtman does proves possible only if we ignore all questions of content, as Houtman, alas, has done. Scholarship that simply ignores the substance of the texts that are studied exhibits nihilism. Like others of the arid Goldberg-Schäfer School,[1] by ignoring the substance of the documents in favor of their formal traits, Houtman treats with contempt the religion, Judaism, that values the contents, the substance of these documents, not only the formal problems they manifest.

A single, brief instance, shows that the Mishnah declares the law, the Tosefta gives the reasons, clarifies the details, and otherwise complements and supplements the Mishnah's statements. In the present case the two Talmuds add no halakhah whatsoever, though their analysis of the Tosefta's clarification of the Mishnah proves compelling. We deal with Mishnah-tractate Berakhot 8:1ff., given in bold-face type, and Tosefta's complement, in regular type:

M. 8:1 In reciting the sequence of blessings for wine and the Sabbath, one blesses over the wine, and afterward one blesses over the day.

T. 5:25 The reason is that it is [the presence of the cup of] wine [at the table] that provides the occasion for the Sanctification of the Day to be recited. The benediction over the wine is usual, while the benediction for the day is not usual [and that which is usual takes precedence over that which is infrequent].

M. 8:2-4 In preparing to recite the Grace after the Meal, they mix the cup and afterward wash the hands. He dries his hands on the cloth and lays it on the pillow. They wash the hands, and afterward they clean the house."

M. 8:5 The sequence of blessings at the end of the Sabbath is: Light, and spices, and food, and *Habdalah*.

T. 5:29 One who enters his house after the end of the Sabbath recites the benediction over the wine, the light, the spices and [then] recites [the] *Habdalah* [benediction]. And if he has but one cup [of wine], he sets it aside until after the meal and strings together all [these benedictions] after it [i.e., after the benediction for the meal]. One recites *Habdalah* at the end of the Sabbath, and at the end of festivals, and at the end of the Day of Atonement, and at the end of the Sabbath [which immediately precedes] a festival, and at the end of a festival [preceding] the intermediate days of the festival. One who is fluent [or, accustomed to doing so] recites many *Habdalot* [i.e., enumerates many kinds of separations in his *Habdalah* benediction, e.g., "Praised be Thou, O Lord . . . (1) who separates

---

[1] I refer to the chapter on Arnold Maria Goldberg and Peter Schäfer in *The Documentary Foundation of Rabbinic Culture. Mopping Up after Debates with Gerald L. Bruns, S. J. D. Cohen, Arnold Maria Goldberg, Susan Handelman, Christine Hayes, James Kugel, Peter Schaefer, Eliezer Segal, E. P. Sanders, and Lawrence H. Schiffman.* Atlanta, 1995: Scholars Press for South Florida Studies in the History of Judaism.

the holy from the profane, (2) who separates Israel from the nations, (3) who separates light from darkness...,", and one who is not fluent recites one or two.

If we read the Tosefta as though there were no Mishnah, we should have no formidable problems in understanding the Tosefta. But, as we see, that begs the question. We do have the Mishnah¡, and we do have ample evidence that the framers of compositions located in the Tosefta responded to the contents of the Mishnah. Contrary to Dr. Houtman's preference, we really do have to pay attention to the contents of the texts, not only to their formal traits. And, alas, her interminable, mindless paraphrase — X says this, Y says that — does not suffice.

The upshot is simple. As I shall show in detail, Dr. Houtman's monograph exhibits three disqualifying flaws.

First, she recapitulates the results of already-published research without realizing it, a mark of poor scholarship.

Second, she ignores all questions of history and context. She does not prove that the framers of compositions and composites in the Tosefta did not have the Mishnah in hand. She takes a simpler route. She simply posits a condition contrary to fact — the Tosefta read without the Mishnah — and then *tout court* conducts a massive exercise in illustrating the result of a premise contrary to fact

And, third, she treats this fantasy-exercise as though it were real, happily concluding that we can, indeed, read the Tosefta as a free-standing document. That presents no surprise to her. That is the point at which her remarkable disinterest in the halakhah exacted a very heavy price: her dissertation was ruined, her thesis destroyed, by what she did not notice. So, we must conclude, *iqqar haser min hassefer:* her dissertation forms an exercise in vacuity. What is true is not new, and what is new is not true. For that, in the Netherlands (and German) universities in Theology, they give you a Ph. D.

I.

THE PROBLEM OF MISHNAH-TOSEFTA RELATIONSHIPS

In completed research of my own,[2] I maintained that the Tosefta forms a problem in the unfolding of the writings of Judaism, since its importance lies in its relationship to three other documents, the Mishnah, which came earlier, and the

---

[2] The main results are summarized in Chapter Two, below. They emerged out of *A History of the Mishnaic Law of Purities*. Leiden, 1974-1977: Brill. I-XXII; *A History of the Mishnaic Law of Holy Things*. Leiden, Brill: 1979. I-VI; *A History of the Mishnaic Law of Women*. Leiden, Brill: 1979-1980. I-V; *A History of the Mishnaic Law of Appointed Times*. Leiden, Brill: 1981-1983. I-V; *A History of the Mishnaic Law of Damages*. Leiden, Brill: 1983-1985. I-V. My graduate students of that period did the work on the Mishnaic Law of Agriculture. The detailed analysis of Mishnah-Tosefta relationships for the whole of the Mishnah and the Tosefta therefore has been in print from 1974. Houtman not once refers to any of these forty-three volumes, not even *A History of the Mishnaic Law of Purities*.

Talmud of the Land of Israel and the Talmud of Babylonia, which were completed later on. The Tosefta does not present a system of its own, as does the Mishnah, nor does it present both an inherited system and one of its own, as do both Talmuds. Rather, like a vine on a trellis, the Tosefta rests upon the Mishnah, having no structure of its own; but it also bears fruit nourished by its own roots. A small fraction of the Tosefta's contents can have reached final formulation prior to the closure of the Mishnah, but most of the document either cites the Mishnah verbatim and comments upon it, or — the Mishnah in hand — can be fully and completely understood only in light of the Mishnah even though the Mishnah is not cited verbatim. The Tosefta's materials, some formed into cogent composites, most incoherent and cogent not among themselves but only in relationship to the Mishnah, serve as the Mishnah's first commentary, first amplification, and first extension — that is, the initial Talmud, prior to the one done in the Land of Israel by ca. 400 and the one completed in Babylonia by ca. 600.

The Tosefta, defined in relationship to the Mishnah — a process Houtman undertakes, as we shall see — contains three types of materials, two of them secondary to, therefore assuredly later than,the Mishnah's materials, the third autonomous of the Mishnah and therefore possibly deriving from the same period as do the sayings compiled in the Mishnah.

The first type of materials contains a direct citation of the Mishnah, given in this translation in italics, followed by secondary discussion of the cited passage. That type of discourse certainly is post-Mishnaic, hence by definition Amoraic, as much as sayings of Samuel, Rab Judah, and R. Yohanan, are Amoraic.

The second sort of materials depends for full and exhaustive meaning upon a passage of the Mishnah, although the corresponding statements of the Mishnah are not cited verbatim. That sort of discussion probably is post-Mishnaic, but much depends upon our exegesis. Accordingly, we may be less certain of the matter.

The third type of passage in the Tosefta stands completely independent of any corresponding passage of the Mishnah. This is in one of two ways. First, a fully-articulated pericope in the Tosefta may simply treat materials not discussed in a systematic way, or not discussed at all, in the Mishnah. That kind of pericope can as well reach us in the Mishnah as in the Tosefta, so far as the criterion of

---

Leiden, 1977: Brill. XXI. *The Redaction and Formulation of the Order of Purities in the Mishnah and Tosefta.* I should have thought that a computer-search would have lead her to a work on Mishnah-Tosefta relations that speaks of "redaction and formulation." That is why I have to dismiss her scholarship as incompetent. As I shall point out presently, her Doktor-Väter could not save her, since neither one of them works on Rabbinic Judaism, with reference to the religion, theology, and halakhah of the writings of that Judaism. They undertook to direct research on a subject to the scholarly literature of which they have never contributed. That is not uncommon in Judaic studies in Europe, which is in the hands of generalists, but this is an extreme case.

literary and redactional theory may come to apply. Second, a well-constructed passage of the Tosefta may cover a topic treated in the Mishnah, but follow a program of inquiry not dealt with at all in the Mishnah. What the statements of the Tosefta treat, therefore,,may prove relevant to the thematic program of the Mishnah but not to the analytical inquiry of the framers of the Mishnah. Such a passage, like the former sort, also may fit comfortably into the Mishnah. If any components of the received Tosefta derive from the second century, that is, the time of the framing of the Mishnah, it would be those of the third type.

In proportion, a rough guess would place less than a fifth of the Tosefta into this third type, well over a third of the whole into the first. In all, therefore, the Tosefta serves precisely as its name suggests, as a corpus of supplements — but of various kinds — to the Mishnah.

The Tosefta depends upon the Mishnah in yet another way. Its whole redactional framework, tractates and subdivisions alike, depends upon the Mishnah's. The Mishnah provides the lattice, the Tosefta, the vines. The rule (though with many exceptions), is that the Tosefta's discussion will follow the themes and problems of the Mishnah's program, much as the two Talmuds' treatments of the passage of the Mishnah are laid out along essentially the same lines as those of the Mishnah. The editorial work accordingly highlights the exegetical purpose of the framers of both the two Talmuds and the Tosefta. The whole serves as a massive and magnificent amplification of the Mishnah. In this regard, of course, the framers of the Tosefta may claim considerably greater success than those of the two Talmuds, since the Tosefta covers nearly all the tractates of the Mishnah, while neither Talmud treats more than two-thirds of them (and then not the same two-thirds).

But the Tosefta's redactors or arrangers tend to organize materials, within a given tractate, in line with two intersecting principles of arrangement. First, as I said, they follow the general outline of the Mishnah's treatment of a topic. Accordingly, if we set up a block of materials in the Tosefta side-by-side with a corresponding block of those of the Mishnah, we should discern roughly the same order of discourse. But, second, the Tosefta's arrangers also tend to lay out their materials in accord with their own types. That is to say, they will tend

(1) to keep as a group passages that cite and then comment upon the actual words of the Mishnah's base-passage, then

(2) to present passages that amplify in the Tosefta's own words opinions fully spelled out only in response to the Mishnah's statements, and, finally,

(3) to give at the end, and as a group, wholly independent and autonomous sayings and constructions of such sayings.

When Houtman says the Tosefta follows an intelligible pattern, her judgment is not based on a classification of the traits of the compositions formed into composites such as yields the result just now set forth. It is another thing she does not notice. True enough, I stress that that redactional pattern may be shown only to be a tendency, a set of non-uncommon policies and preferences, not a fixed rule. But when we ask how the Tosefta's editors arranged their materials, it is not wholly accurate to answer that they follow the plan of the Mishnah's counterparts. There will be some attention, also, to the taxonomic traits of the units of discourse of which the Tosefta itself is constructed. That is why two distinct editorial principles come into play in explaining the arrangement of the whole. Even when she stumbles into a solid insight, Houtman misses its point.

When we turn from the definition of the Tosefta and of its editorial and redactional character to the contents of the document as a whole, the Mishnah once more governs the framework of description. For the Tosefta, as is already clear, stands nearly entirely within the circle of the Mishnah's interests, rarely asking questions about topics omitted altogether by the Mishnah's authors, always following the topical decisions on what to discuss as laid down by the founders of the whole. For our part, therefore, we cannot write about the Tosefta's theology or law, as though these constituted a system susceptible of description and interpretation independent of the Mishnah's system. At the same time, we must recognize that the exegetes of the Mishnah, in the Tosefta, and in the two Talmuds, stand apart from, and later than, the authors of the Mishnah itself.

Accordingly, the exegetes systematically say whatever they wish to say by attaching their ideas to a document earlier than their own, and by making the principal document say what they wish to contribute. The system of expressing ideas through re-framing those of predecessors preserves the continuity of tradition and establishes a deep stability and order upon the culture framed by that tradition.

II.
HOUTMAN'S DISSERTATION

Now let us turn to a more systematic description of the work at hand, a dissertation accepted at the University of Utrecht under the supervision of Professors Piet van der Horst (Utrecht) and Peter Schäfer (Berlin), neither of whom can claim to have made a mark on Mishnah-Tosefta studies. Indeed, neither has published so much as a systematic scholarly article on the subject! Impressions and opinions do not suffice to qualify a professor to direct a dissertation on an otherwise-unfamiliar subject. By American standards of doctoral education, therefore, Dr. Houtman must be regarded as an autodidact. That accounts for the formidable flaws in her monograph, chief among them, her utterly naive sense that she is saying what no one before has noticed, when in fact she recapitulates the results given just now. But of these things, van der Horst and Schäfer can have known nothing, and they have not brought themselves honor by promising to guide an education in a subject that neither has studied at a professional level. But Houtman made her choices and bears responsibility for her monograph. Van der Horst and Schäfer merely accepted it for the doctorate — a formality.

Alberdina Houtman's monograph claims to set forth "a new way of dealing with the problematic relationship between the Mishnah and the Tosefta." In prior work she finds the faults that the Mishnah is given "higher religious status," research has focused "on a single relationship in terms of unidirectional dependence," and "most of the comparative research was done on the textus receptus of the texts." That prior research identified multiple relationships she does not concede; had she done so, she would have had no dissertation, no "new methodology." But Houtman insists that she has worked out what she proclaims to be "a new methodology," "a computer-assisted analysis of the texts on the basis of the most important manuscript material, and a computer program was made for the compilation of different synopses. The program can take the Mishnah as a running text to which the Toseftan material is synoptically arranged, but it can also reverse the procedure. This enables an unbiased comparison of the two texts." She then applies this methodology to Mishnah- and Tosefta-tractates Berakhot and Shebiit.

Her thesis is "the texts are interwoven so closely that it is almost possible to consider them as a single literary work." That opaque statement will have pleased our sages of blessed memory, who, after all, did set forth the Mishnah, the Tosefta, and the Yerushalmi, or the Mishnah, the Tosefta, and the Bavli, as single literary works; that is how they wanted us to see the halakhah, and they were absolutely right. My presentations in Chapters Three through Five show how we may read the halakhah from the Mishnah through the Bavli as a seamless, unfolding statement. But Houtman has not set forth to prove our sages to have been right about what they created, namely, the halakhic corpus. She wants the computer to settle some scores of her own, to do so without reference to the contents of the documents. That is something that our sages cannot have approved, because in their view, the halakhah, not the media of the halakhah, is what mattered.

She begins with what she claims to be "a history of research." But her history (12 pp. in all!) shows she has read rather selectively and in a lazy way. She assumes that before her, no one raised the question of complex relationships between materials in the Mishnah and those in the Tosefta. But, as I have just shown, in the decades before Houtman did her work on two of the three score of tractates, a systematic study of the *entirety* of the Mishnah and the Tosefta by myself and my students had shown in detail three relationships now indicated above: the Tosefta cites and glosses the Mishnah and makes no sense except in relationship to the Mishnah; the Tosefta amplifies materials in the Mishnah but can be understood on its own; and the Tosefta makes statements that stand entirely on their own and do not intersect in any way with the Mishnah's. Not only so, but, as I said, the same study has shown the tendency, within the Tosefta, to arrange materials of these three types in distinct groups, first compositions in which Tosefta cites and glosses the Mishnah, then dependent, and finally autonomous compositions, all in a composite situated to match the Mishnah's.

Houtman does not seem to grasp that that study has produced, without computers, a much more systematic and complete analysis of the two documents — not two tractates but all tractates! — than her work on two tractates has yielded, and her results (though not her claims for her results, let alone her interpretation) replicates existing work. Nor does she grasp that others, before her, have concluded that if the Mishnah is a highly crafted document, the Tosefta by the same criteria is not. In her own right, then, she presents the diverse relationships between statements in the two documents, some are called "parallel," some "supplementary," some "additional." But as is obvious, all she is doing is recapitulating published findings of long-available work, which she clearly has not dealt with in a scholarly manner. That is why what is important in the dissertation is not new, and what is new is trivial and mechanical — and in the end, chimerical, for, as I said, she wants us to pretend we do not have the Mishnah, but we do.

The reason that she has not understood and benefited from prior research is that she has not paid much attention to it. She thinks hers is the first synoptic study, ignoring both prior episodic ones and also the complete one in the *History of the Mishnaic Law* series — forty-three volumes! — in print for nearly two decades now, but (predictably) not utilized by her. She knows my summaries (*The Tosefta: Its Structure and its Sources* [Atlanta, 1986] and *Introduction to Rabbinic Literature* [N.Y., 1994]) but not the systematic and complete study. No wonder that she assigns to me a view I find dubious because incomplete: "the authors of the Tosefta cited or glossed the halakhot of the Mishnah or they simply alluded to them. However, Tosefta sometimes reproduced autonomous, obviously older material." That is her rather clumsy formulation of the results summarized above. The "summary" simply is fabricated to suit her purpose, which is to claim to innovate — with the computer, no less — when in fact she replicates results already systematically achieved for the entire Tosefta.

The tripartite division of the materials, the systematic ordering of the several types — these she does not set forth in her account of my reading of matters. That, further, is why she can praise Peter Schäfer's formulation of matters, without recognizing that 1986[3] (without crediting them to me in *Purities* Volume XXI), he merely repeated my conclusions, in print for a decade by then: "Even on the level of the individual tractate, one constant factor determining the relation will not always emerge, but the individual tractate...will contain different material which, within the same tractate, requires different models of the relation between Mishnah and Tosefta." As readers will note, that is precisely the result I set forth from 1974 onward. By identifying the tripartite relationship between pericopes of the Mishnah and the Tosefta, I systematically proved exactly the point Schäfer takes as his own.[4]

---

[3] "Research into Rabbinic Literature: An Attempt to Define the *Status Quaestionis*," *Journal of Jewish Studies* 1986, 37:139-152. I deal at length with this article in *Mopping Up*, cited above.

[4] Still, by showing the tendency to order materials in a consistent manner, I also found reason to reach a conclusion, as to the documentary character of the Tosefta, different from his. In my view, the implication is that the Tosefta is a different sort of compilation from the Mishnah; if the latter is a document, the former is to be classified elsewhere.

Clearly, Houtman writes in haste, wishing to establish that she has something new to say, even at the cost of a shoddy and slipshod reading of the prior literature — not the mark of mature scholarship. Now to what Houtman wishes to do on her own. She wishes to attempt a "two-way intertextual comparison." That sounds mysterious, but all she means by that mantric word, "intertextual," is "comparison between two text corpora." She wants to prepare two sets of textual comparisons ("synopses"), one with the Mishnah as running text and one with the Tosefta: "For the one the arrangement of the Mishnah was accepted and the Tosefta material was arranged to it; for the other, the Tosefta was the point of departure and the Mishnah material was synoptically arranged to it. Only after studying both synopses could it be decided which synopsis illustrated the relationship in the best possible way."

Here the obscurity of her language paralyzes discussion. For I simply cannot understand what she means by the language, "which synopsis illustrated the relationship in the best possible way." What "relationship" does she have in mind, that of the discrete pericopes, that of the whole two documents, or that of something in between? And how are we going to know what is "the best possible way," unless she spells out all of the ways she has in mind and further explains what would indicate "the best" — the clearest, the most economical, or whatever. But, predictably, Houtman never spells out all of the "possible ways" of which the chosen one is the "best." In her defense, I must say, this language is so imprecise as to be unintelligible; we simply cannot know what she means.

Here her ignorance of completed work shows. She notes that the Tosefta is four times larger than the Mishnah. She jumps to the conclusion, "So, even in the hypothetical case that each mishnah [she means, Mishnah-paragraph] had a complete parallel in the Tosefta, three quarters of the Tosefta had no complete parallel in the Mishnah." What can she possibly mean? Here again I find her language incomprehensible. What can she have in mind by "parallel" or "complete parallel"? It is the fact that the Tosefta will present a systematic illustration of a principle stated by the Mishnah, or will instantiate and amplify the implications of a case in the Mishnah. Is this what she means by "a parallel"? But the words are not the same, or not the same throughout. So in such instances the Tosefta clarifies in many words what the Mishnah has stated in a few words. So what's the point of the "four times larger"? All that means is, the Tosefta uses a lot of words to say what the Mishnah says in fewer words. Then when the Tosefta proceeds, it will commonly restate what the Mishnah has said, now through a variety of instances; it may well introduce complications and distinctions, new cases, and the like. This material does not cite the Mishnah, and it can be comprehended in its own terms, but with the Mishnah in hand, we are able to make best sense of it. By "best sense," I mean, we are able to place the Tosefta's statements into the context of the halakhic principles that the Mishnah — and the Mishnah alone — has laid out in a generative formulation.

But to identify those instances of systematic clarification, the Tosefta by the Mishnah, formalities such as a computer identifies hardly suffice. Rather, one has to pay attention to the contents of the Mishnah and to the substantive, not merely formal, relationship of what the Mishnah says to what the Tosefta says. This Houtman does not do, and her monograph never suggests that she could have conducted halakhic analysis had she recognized the need to do so. Her grasp of the halakhah is superficial, seldom transcending the capacity merely to paraphrase the words that are before us and perfectly clear on their own. When, then, I characterize the Tosefta as the Mishnah's first talmud, what I mean is that the Tosefta stands in relationship to the Mishnah as the two Talmuds (sometimes) stand in relationship to the Tosefta, as I shall illustrate in Chapter Two. These are judgments based on the study of the halakhah, the logical relationship of one statement to another.

None of this makes an impact on Houtman's formulation of matters, because, so far as I can see, she has a very limited understanding of the documents she claims to study, being able at best to paraphrase what they say, but not to analyze their contents, the logic of what is said, and how the logic of one document's statement relates to that of the other document's statement. I do not see how one can claim to analyze the relationship between two halakhic documents, if one knows so little of the halakhah. Only if she reduces the whole to a matter of formalities can the computer do any work at all for her, but only if to begin with she brings to the halakhah an infirm grasp of matters could she conceive of doing what she has done, which is simply to ignore the substance of matters and to let the computer dispose of formalities.

She undertakes, then, to compose a "hierarchy, parallels, supplementary, then additional material." Forthwith the computer program emerges: "The material can be treated according to this inherent hierarchy: for a given sentence in the basis [sic! read: basic] corpus, the reference corpus can be searched for a complete parallel. If there is a complete parallel, it is placed in a parallel column at the same level as the sentence of comparison. If there is no complete parallel, the reference corpus is searched for supplementary material. If there is, it is placed in the parallel column one level lower than the sentence of comparison. Subsequently, the reference corpus is searched for additional material. If there is any, it is placed one level below the supplementary material. If there is no supplementary material, the reference corpus is still searched for additional material. If there is additional material, it is placed one level below the sentence of comparison. The same procedure is followed if there is indeed parallel material." There follows "a decision tree," leading to this conclusion: if there is both supplementary and additional material, the supplementary material is given first and then the additional material. if there is only supplementary material, or only additional material, then it is reproduced one level below the sentence of comparison." And so on and so forth.

The computer enters in once she has tagged the materials: "First, the tractates of the two corpora were studied on their own merits in a traditional literary manner. What are the topics of the tractate? Are these topics clustered? If so, how are they clustered? And how are the clusters for their part arranged? Did the compilers use literary means to embellish the texts or to emphasize the structures? If so, what are those means?" Then the computer accomplishes a quantitative analysis, involving word frequencies and indices "to establish which content words were highly frequent and where they occurred." Then she proceeded to the small units of the tractates: "The nature of the halakhic tannaitic material, as found in both Mishnah and Tosefta, meant that these units could be classified as thematic, literary-thematic, or literary. A theme may be discussed without recognizable recurring literary traits, the binding element being purely thematic. Such a unit may be delimited by an inclusion or simply by its contrast with the preceding and following subject matter. The collection of sentences may then be marked as a thematic unit." Again: and so on and so forth.

All of this work was to make possible tests of the arrangement of the material: "the Tosefta text could be used as a basis for comparison, to which the Mishnah material was attached synoptically, the Mishnah text could be used as a basis for comparison, to which the Tosefta material was attached synoptically; material could be selected from both corpora according to thematic or literary criteria, ignoring the original arrangement within the corpora." Why the computer was needed to deal with a mere two tractates I do not grasp; Zahavy and Newman, both of them highly computer literate, never imagined that they would find insight in a computer analysis of what they preferred to take up item by item, in rich, substantive detail.

How then does Houtman interpret the synopsis? "The synopsis enabled us to see at a glance where the texts agreed, and where and how they differed. Both aspects were relevant to the question of the relationship between the corpora...If the Tosefta were composed as a commentary on the Mishnah, one would expect that either every sentence it explained or commented upon would be repeated or none of them. To clarify possible reasons for parallelism, the literal rendering of the texts must be scrutinized and compared with variant readings in a search for minor difference that may throw light upon the question whether perhaps there was disagreement about the wording of the sentences." As I said, for the paltry sample at hand, she has gone to a great deal of trouble to ask machines to do work that can take on weight and meaning only when issues of substance are addressed. She would have done better to spend her intellectual energy on the halakhah, not on epiphenomena of "Are these topics clustered?" and the like. The sloth characteristic of her reading of prior scholarship extends, alas, to her program of research and its methodology.

When she reaches the tractates themselves, she wants to know whether the Tosefta tractate "proves readable and intelligible as it is, without falling back on the Mishnah." Had she asked me, I would have answered, some is, some isn't, some may be. Others who have worked on the problem have produced the same results, though worded differently. Consulting completed research would have told her that some passages are readable and intelligible as is, some are not, and some are intelligible as is but still more consequential in dialogue with the Mishnah. She does not pay attention to content, as I said, and therefore she cannot deal with that third possibility at all, even though, I have shown, fully half of the Tosefta falls into that interstitial category of rhetorical independence, but substantive dependence. In other words, Houtman wants to pretend that the Mishnah does not exist, except when she concedes that it does.

Her discussion from this point deals with the Tosefta. Only in her appendix does she give (in Hebrew) the texts that she discusses. As a result, we have to refer back and forth, and the whole is exceedingly difficult to follow. As to the substance of her presentation of the Tosefta, unit by unit, I state very flatly, there is much less here than meets the eye. The theses announced at the outset are forgotten more often than not. Houtman talks about what she wants to talk about, and there is no predicting what, at any point, that might be. She seems to intend a commentary to the language of the Tosefta, but the program of the commentary is so diffuse and confused that little comes of it all. Then there is a good deal of sheer paraphrase, the necessity of which a translation would have obviated. So we are left with a great deal of "X says this...Y says that...," which is to say, she tells us what the text says, as though we do not know the text. But an absence of intellectual energy leaves her satisfied with quite paltry results. She concludes, "Tosefta Berakhot is for the most part readable without other material. The tractate is well arranged. The sequence of topics is logical..." Indeed so.

But these conclusions, which are incontestable, also beg the question. She wants to know about the relationship between the Mishnah and the Tosefta. No one questions that the Tosefta is for the most part "readable without other material." But by "readable" she seems to me simply, a statement that is comprehensible in its own terms. As I said at the outset, I estimate that a sixth of the Tosefta cites and glosses the Mishnah, so by that estimate, five sixths conform to her conclusion, and I should guess that part of that last sixth could be understood as well (e.g., the Tosefta's citations and glosses of Mishnah-tractate Berakhot Chapter Eight are so fully spelled out that on their own they make perfect sense). In other words, Houtman has proven that the wheel is round. But she has not shown how to use it for transportation.

She has no difficulty in proving that the Mishnah-tractate (in context: Berakhot) also is an "autonomous literary production." I cannot think of anyone who has thought otherwise, not now, and not for the last fifteen centuries, nor does she name her imagined opponent. So here she wants to reinvent the same wheel everyone has been using all along. Having so little to say, she now uses cascades of words to say nothing. The "commentary" is prolix and diffuse, commenting on this, that, and the other thing. One main conclusion is, "There are no instances in Mishnah Berakhot where the formulation of the text suggests that it comments on other texts or refers to them. Nevertheless, there are a few instances where the text is hardly comprehensible without some extra information." Who will be surprised? For the earliest Amoraim noticed a long time ago that their exegetical powers were needed. To deem such a conclusion consequential, one has to have conducted research out of all relationship — personal or intellectual — with any other scholar, let alone anyone who actually believes in and practices the religion that has produced the scholarship. It exquisitely embodies that nihilism to which I referred earlier.

Houtman's "synoptic reading of Tosefta and Mishnah Berakhot," consequent upon her reading of each as autonomous literary productions, concludes, "Both works were indeed independent in that each work could be read and understood without the help of the other. At the same time, however, each work presented some literary difficulties. They were comprehensible at a halakhic level, though there were some scars and irregularities at a literary level." Now comes the issue of relationship: "By considering the synopsis as if the two columns form one compound work — [her footnote: consisting of either a basic text with explanatory additions and supplements or of two parts of an originally larger corpus] — we will try to establish whether this premise [that the two works have relations with each other] is tenable." These results are replicated for Shebi'it.

The synopsis treats "the Mishnah as the running text, with toseftan material arranged to it," then "the Tosefta as running text and the mishnaic material arranged to it." In doing so, Houtman found that it was not necessary to do so: "first, the arrangement of the topics in Tosefta and Mishnah Berakhot was similar. But besides this similarity, each corpus had also its own preferences and peculiarities, the one stressing a certain aspect more than the other. There were also topics discussed in only one of the two corpora. Therefore it was considered prudent occasionally to combine some slightly different units into a larger unit of a more general nature in order to show how the two corpora relate to each other. The original arrangement could be maintained anyway. So a preference for the one or the other was not necessary." (The same results pertain to Shebi'it.) What I take this rather obscure language to mean is more or less the same thing just now set forth, which is, we can indeed read the two documents each on its own. If she wanted to compare the Mishnah and the Tosefta as programmatic statements, all she had to do was outline them — in full, not just in key-words as she does — and set up the outlines side by side, just as I did for the two Talmuds (in fourteen volumes in *The Two Talmuds Compared*. Atlanta, 1995-6: Scholars Press for USF Academic Commentary Series.).

Her other conclusion is more important: "it turned out to be undesirable to choose for one or the other of the synopses. Under the procedure of compiling a synopsis..., taking one of the texts as a starting point automatically causes that text to take the lead in the discourse on a certain topic. If the collation of material within a unit is studied closely in the two synopses, it turns out that the discourse sometimes has a better inner logic with the Tosefta as a starting point and sometimes with the Mishnah. I therefore decided to rearrange the material within the units in a way that renders the most logical discourse. So in some units, the Tosefta takes the lead in the discussion and in other units the Mishnah. This presentation reflects my conclusion that it is not systematically one of the two texts that opens the discussion on a certain topic and the other that always supplements it or comments upon it." This is the heart of her monograph. The key language is, "the most logical discourse."

Much depends, then on which *logically* comes first, the Mishnah or the Tosefta, as Houtman's "logic" dictates. By that statement, I mean, do the premises of a statement of the Tosefta rest upon what is declared by the Mishnah, e.g., the question that is raised, the problem that is solved? Then the Mishnah takes priority. Does the Mishnah take for granted a proposition set forth in the Tosefta? Then the Tosefta takes priority. I systematically pursued these questions in my analysis of *The Rabbinic Traditions about the Pharisees before 70.* Leiden, 1971: Brill. I-III. I. *The Rabbinic Traditions about the Pharisees before 70. The Masters;* II. *The Rabbinic Traditions about the Pharisees before 70. The Houses.*; III. *The Rabbinic Traditions about the Pharisees before 70. Conclusions.* There I wanted to know whether statements attributed to earlier authorities in fact pursued questions, the answers to which are taken for granted by saying attributed to laster authorities. Then, I held, the attribution to the earlier authority indeed is sustained by the logical priority of what is attributed. So this is work that can be and has been done.

But I state flatly, whatever Houtman means does not make much difference, because, so far as the monograph ever undertakes to meet an intellectual and substantive challenge, not just witlessly to compare matters of formality, not much happens. But this is the very point at which the challenge arises. Here, therefore, I looked with special care to identify a passage in which Houtman's own logic dictates that the Tosefta's version "renders the most logical discourse." Her reading of the Tosefta as the baseline, the Mishnah as secondary, yields not a single case. What she alleges she never demonstrates, in so many words, in a coherent argument, start to finish. *Not once!* She apparently thinks that if she says something, it is so. The upshot is disheartening. Houtman promises an exercise in "logic," which will explain why she thinks she will demonstrate that Tosefta takes the lead here, the Mishnah there. I find myself unable to point to the passages in which she does so. Or perhaps she means by the language she uses something other than what she leads us to anticipate.

Still, our sages will have taken pleasure in her results, though not for her reasons. She concludes, "The texts of Mishnah and Tosefta Berakhot are closely interwoven, even to the extent that they might almost be considered one literary work. This close connection reveals itself among other things in the parallel arrangement of the material. Moreover most of the passages marked as problematic in the independent reading of Tosefta and Mishnah Berakhot are elucidated when the two texts are read synoptically [she means: side by side]." I wonder whether the framers of any tractate of either Talmud will want to differ, since that is precisely how they represent matters, citing the Mishnah and the Tosefta out of all documentary context and treating their formulations of a given halakhah, along side formulations not situated in either document ("beraitot") as part of a single, seamless fabric of halakhah. But that has no bearing upon the question at hand, which — by her own word — concerns not how the documents might be read, but how they have been represented, as autonomous and free-standing statements (in the case of the Mishnah) or as partly autonomous, partly contingent and dependent, statements (in the case of the Tosefta). So too, they come to us, each with its own distinctive documentary traits. But Houtman's computer was not programmed to pick up these traits.

If her results produce a rather dubious picture, her conclusion also yields one incontrovertible result. She finds that the Mishnah-Tosefta relationships are complex, yielding these results: Tosefta agrees verbatim with Mishnah or varies only slightly; Tosefta augments Mishnah with glosses and discussions; Tosefta functions like a commentary on unquoted Mishnah material; Tosefta offers additional substance without direct reference to material in common with Mishnah; Tosefta discusses topics that do not occur in Mishnah; Tosefta opens a discussion with a general rule after which both Mishnah and Tosefta treat the subject in more detail, and so on and so forth. As I said, her she assembles much detail that replicates exactly the results I set forth in my *History of the Mishnaic Law.*

The book is a good bit longer than it has to be, because Houtman addresses problems of text-tradition that have no bearing upon her thesis; the chapter on Berakhot (so too the one on Shebiit) is then padded with a sizable portion of irrelevant charts and pointless calculations.

It remains to observe that Houtman simply ignores all problems of textual formulation. Treating the Tosefta's materials as free-standing certainly saved her much work and made it easy to prove the point she wished to demonstrate. But then she asks us to accept a thesis that dismisses a vast amount of relevant evidence. Formulations of rules that occur in the Tosefta find counterparts in other documents, however, and reading the Tosefta out of all relationship with corresponding citations of the same sayings produces no viable thesis at all, but only an empty exercise in vacuous verbiage. Take for instance the fine statement of the facts of the matter by M.D. Herr:

> Very often a baraita quoted in the Talmud in a corrupt form is found in the Tosefta in its original coherent form. Furthermore, very often there is a discussion in the Talmud about the exact meaning of the words of a certain tanna (either in the Mishnah or in the baraita), while the parallel statement as found in the

Tosefta is manifestly clear. It would therefore seem obvious that
the Tosefta in its present form was not edited before the end of
the fourth century c.e. and cannot therefore be identified with
any of the...earlier collections of beraitot. It is certain that the
Tosefta was composed in Erez Israel, since the beraitot which it
contains resemble more those of the Jerusalem Talmud than those
of the Babylonian Talmud.[5]

At no point does Houtman address the question of the relationship between
formulations of rules set forth by the Tosefta and the corresponding formulations
in cognate documents. None of this matters to her. It would have taken a lot of
bother to compare formulations in not only the Mishnah and the Tosefta but the
Tannaite Midrash-compilations, the baraitot of the two Talmuds, and the numerous
other formulations of halakhah on the same issue or principle, that the Mishnah
and the Tosefta set forth. I can state, as a matter of theory, what she will have
found for them all: "The texts [supply:] of the halakhah bearing Tannaite *sigla* are
closely interwoven, even to the extent that they might almost be considered one
literary work." All depends then upon the "almost." That is where rigorous
scholarship begins.

This brings us to the appendix volume, *Synopsis of Tosefta and Mishnah.*
By "synoptic," all Houtman means is, "a research tool that affords a broad view of
the parallel and non-parallel material of different texts" (p. 4). But why call
"parallel...non-parallel" synoptic, when all she means is, a side by side comparison
of documents? When she gives her "synoptic comparison," she does just that.
Houtman's *Synoptic Comparison,* circulated as an appendix, presents the Hebrew
texts, the two documents being laid out in relationship with one another. She
found "the number and character of variant readings did not justify an extended
synopsis." She uses Kaufman for the Mishna, Vienna for the Tosefta. She gives
the Mishnah at the right, the Tosefta at the left: "As the discussion on a certain
topic is usually started by the Mishnah, the Mishnah text was printed in the column
on the right side, and the Tosefta text on the left side."

Houtman cannot be accused of an excess of humility when she predictably
rejects out of hand all emendations of Saul Lieberman, saying, "My reason was
that 'apparent' is not the same as 'obvious.' The emendations suggested by
Lieberman are not always irrefutable. Therefore I have chosen to leave the
assessment of the text to the reader." This is pure fakery — an excuse and not a
reason. For she has not done the work of explaining why she deems Lieberman's
reading "refutable." Here she falls beneath contempt.

---

[5] *Encyclopaedia Judaica* 15:1283-5. In the nearly three decades since the publication of
that article, I have seen no other than has superseded it when it comes to the dating of the
documents and the positioning of the contents in relationship to one another.

The appendix dismisses not only Lieberman but others who have done precisely the work at hand on exactly the same documents. Specifically, while citing their work, she does not give a hint that T. Zahavy, *The Mishnaic Law of Blessings and Prayers: Tractate Berakhot* (Atlanta, 1987: Scholars Press for Brown Judaic Studies) and L. Newman, *The Sanctity of the Seventh Year: A Study of Mishnah-tractate Shebiit* (Chicago, 1983: Scholars Press for Brown Judaic Studies) have already done systematic and detailed comparison of the Mishnah and the Tosefta, unit by unit. The only difference is that they commented upon and explained the relationships between the corresponding statements in the one and the other, and Houtman says absolutely nothing in the context of the presentation of the texts. She discusses the texts in the main book, presents them in her appendix. She should have discussed the texts where she presented them. The upshot is a complete waste: a comparison where nothing is said about similarity and difference.

III

MISHNAH-TOSEFTA RELATIONSHIPS ONCE AGAIN

A huge amount of collecting and arranging has gone into a work that stands or falls not on the information that is gathered, but on the analysis that is conducted. But of analysis there is precious little. What Houtman has produced is a work of enormous confusion. Part of the problem, as readers who have slogged through her heavy and obscure English will have noted, is that she writes in a foreign language, with a devastating consequence for precision and clarity. She would have done better to write in Dutch and have the work translated into English, so that, in her own language, she could have attained that level of grace and effect that in English she is unable to reach. As it is, as I have already noted, I find myself unable to understand much of the theoretical intent of the book.

The upshot is that she has promised a great deal more than she has delivered, and I think the principal reason is her failure to master the scholarship prior to her own. She has not paid attention to work that addressed the same question and produced results that, to say the least, are competitive with the ones that she wished to set forth. The second reason is her halakhic incapacity. Reducing the work to a set of formal relationships solves all problems but the consequential ones. As a result, she misses most of the interesting questions that still require systematic work, as her abysmal failure to carry out her promise to show how logic produces one arrangement, rather than another, of parallel pericopes in the two documents.

That explains why the work is confused, prolix, disorganized, and full of lush verbiage and empty information. Houtman simply does not advance the study of its problem. How to account for this enormous waste of time and energy? As I pointed out earlier, Dr. Houtman did her work with two Doktor-Väter who do not work on Mishnah-Tosefta problems and have published nothing in this area. Nor does either work on the halakhah, to understate matters drastically. Dr. van der Horst is a distinguished Hellenist, working on Hellenistic Judaism; he has not written a line on the Tosefta. In the early stages of his career Dr. Schäfer did some promising work in Talmudic history, mainly producing negative, but useful results. As to halakhah, apart from computer-collations of variant readings of Yerushalmi, he simply has not undertaken original scholarship of any kind. He has yet to show he is capable of reading a line of the Talmud in its own intellectual framework.[6] Though, as here, still passing his opinion on this and that, Schäfer has not contributed a single line of original and constructive scholarship to Rabbinic studies.

Dr. Houtman would have done well to study the Tosefta with specialists in the subject of classical Rabbinics, rather than with people who could teach her nothing about it and would make no demands of her. But she owed it to herself to master the scholarly literature and do her homework. That is why, if Dr. Houtman were to ask me what I consider to be the fundamental cause of her utter failure in this monograph, I should have to say, it is not only intellectual sloth but her incapacity to read the work of others with care and in a systematic way. Matching her superficial knowledge of the sources, her slipshod reading of the prior literature has lead her to believe that she could learn only by looking into the mirror. Her reading of the work of others has persuaded her to suppose that scholarship consists in obscurely, verbosely, and promiscuously alleging what others have said clearly and economically. None of the books she does cite can have taught her such a lesson. In this exercise in scholarly solecism, Houtman has taken the easy way, the lazy way.

---

[6] That is why the scholarly world was astounded when the Chancellor of the Jewish Theological Seminary of America, Dr. Ismar Schorsch, offered Schäfer the Saul Lieberman chair in Talmud. Many thought the move derisive.

2

The Tosefta in Documentary Context: The Mishnah, Tosefta, Yerushalmi, and Bavli

From Houtman's reading of the Tosefta, let us turn to the Tosefta in its documentary context. If we compare the Mishnah, the Tosefta, the Yerushalmi, and the Bavli, in the unfolding of a single chapter.[1] To see how the Tosefta fits into the sweep of the rabbinic literature extending from the Mishnah, ca. 200, through the Tosefta, ca. 200-300, to the Talmud of the Land of Israel or Yerushalmi, ca. 400, and on to the Talmud of Babylonia or Bavli, ca. 600, we follow a single passage. This allows us to place the Tosefta into its larger context, that of a set of documents that reached closure, it is universally assumed, in the stated sequence. What is important, we shall observe, is how the Tosefta receives the Mishnah and transmits it forward; in the passage before us, the two Talmuds address not so much the Mishnah as the Mishnah as transmitted by the Tosefta. Even though this is not necessarily the pattern throughout, still, Saul Lieberman was more right than wrong when he observed that the Tosefta is the hinge on which the door of the Yerushalmi swings. When we see in great detail precisely how for the sample at hand the Tosefta adds its amplification and explanation to the Mishnah, and then how the Yerushalmi and the Bavli in sequence take up the Tosefta's reading of the Mishnah, we shall grasp how profoundly the whole of rabbinic literature in its formative age focuses upon not the Mishnah as the Tosefta, the kind of hub of the whole. Had Houtman understood that fact, she would have understood that reading from the Tosefta to the Mishnah will not have surprised the sages of the Talmuds,

---

[1] I here recapitulate the conclusions set forth in *The Tosefta. An Introduction.* Atlanta, 1992: Scholars Press for South Florida Studies in the History of Judaism.

who did just that: they moved to the Mishnah via the Tosefta, they read the Mishnah through the eyes of the Tosefta.[2]

The following pages present a chapter of the Mishnah, Mishnah-tractate Berakhot Chapter Eight. I then give the Tosefta to that chapter, following the text of Saul Lieberman. I compare (in Houtman's odd language, "synoptically," meaning merely, in parallel columns) the Mishnah and the Tosefta. Had I placed the Tosefta to the left, the governing position, and the Mishnah to the right, the results would have been exactly the same, the relationships fixed. There follows the Yerushalmi's treatment of the same chapter, and, finally, the Bavli's as well. In giving the whole of both Talmuds' chapters, I mean to show how the Tosefta precipitates discourse, which then proceeds in quite unanticipated directions. In this way we get a good sense of proportion and balance: where the Tosefta matters, where it is left behind as the later authorities develop new interests altogether.

I have already presented and carefully explained in detail every line of this passage in my *Invitation to the Talmud. A Teaching Book* (San Francisco, 1987: Harper & Row) Second Edition, completely revised. Readers who wish an explanation of the details of what follows will find it there. The main point I wish to register here is the position of the Tosefta in relationship to the Mishnah before and the two Talmuds afterward. That we see when we follow the words of the Mishnah as these are augmented and revised in the Tosefta, then the words of the Tosefta as these are explained and made the starting point for further discussion in the two Talmuds. Still more important, I want the reader to assess the matter of composition and proportion, with special reference to how the two Talmuds utilize passages of the Tosefta in forming their own discourse. To see the importance, but not the predominance, of the Tosefta in shaping the composition of the two Talmuds, the reader is given a picture of the entire chapter in those Talmuds, even though from a certain point in each case, the exposition of the Mishnah as the Tosefta reads the Mishnah falls away and others interests come to the fore.

Mishnah, Tosefta, Yerushalmi, and Bavli to Berakhot VIII

I. MISHNAH-TRACTATE BERAKHOT CHAPTER EIGHT

I

8:1. A.   These are the things which are between the House of Shammai and the House of Hillel in [regard to] the meal:

 B.   The House of Shammai say, "One blesses over the day, and afterward one blesses over the wine."

 And the House of Hillel say, "One blesses over the wine, and afterward one blesses over the day."

---

[2] Clearly, to understand and value that fact, Houtman would have had to pay attention to the substance, not only the form, of matters. Once again, she has paid a heavy price for whatever benefits she thinks the computer have purchased for her research.

8.2. A. The House of Shammai say, "They wash the hands and afterward mix the cup."

And the House of Hillel say, "They mix the cup and afterward wash the hands."

8:3. A. The House of Shammai say, "He dries his hands on the cloth and lays it on the table."

And the House of Hillel say, "On the pillow."

8:4. A. The House of Shammai say, "They clean the house, and afterward they wash the hands."

And the House of Hillel say, "They wash the hands, and afterward they clean the house."

8:5. A. The House of Shammai say, "Light, and food, and spices, and *Habdalah.*"

And the House of Hillel say, "Light, and spices, and food, and *Habdalah.*"

B. The House of Shammai say, "'Who created the light of the fire.'"

And the House of Hillel say, "'Who creates the lights of the fire.'"

II

8:6. A. They do not bless over the light or the spices of gentiles, nor the light or the spices of the dead, nor the light or the spices which are before an idol.

B. And they do not bless over the light until they make use of its illumination.

III

8:7. A. He who ate and forgot and did not bless [say Grace] —

B. The House of Shammai say, "He should go back to his place and bless."

And the House of Hillel say, "He should bless in the place in which he remembered."

C. Until when does he bless? Until the food has been digested in his bowels.

8:8. A. Wine came to them after the meal, and there is there only that cup —

B. The House of Shammai say, "He blesses the wine, and afterward he blesses the food."

And the House of Hillel say, "He blesses the food, and afterward he blesses the wine."

C. They respond *Amen* after an Israelite who blesses, and they do not respond *Amen* after a Samaritan who blesses, until hearing the entire blessing.

The Mishnah-chapter goes over rules on the conduct of meals, first for Sabbaths and festivals, then in general, with special concern for preserving the cultic purity of the meal. That means the people at the meal keep the laws of cultic cleanness set forth in the book of Leviticus, as these are interpreted by the sages of the Torah. The details are explained in the Tosefta, Yerushalmi, and Bavli, and we do well to allow the course of rabbinic thought and writing to carry us into the matter. Here is how the Tosefta confronts the same themes and also cites some of the passages verbatim.

II. TOSEFTA TO MISHNAH BERAKHOT CHAPTER EIGHT

5:21 (Lieberman, p. 28, ls. 41-2).

>They answer *Amen* after a gentile who says a blessing with the divine name. They do not answer *Amen* after a Samaritan who says a blessing with the divine name until they have heard the entire blessing.

5.25 (Lieberman, p. 29, ls. 53-57).

A.   [The] things which are between the House of Shammai and the House of Hillel in [regard to] the meal:

B.   The House of Shammai say, "One blesses over the day, and afterward he blesses over the wine, for the day causes the wine to come, and the day is already sanctified, but the wine has not yet come."

C.   And the House of Hillel say, "One blesses over the wine, and afterward he blesses over the day, for the wine causes the Sanctification of the day to be said.

"Another explanation: The blessing over the wine is regular [= always required when wine is used], and the blessing over the day is not continual [but is said only on certain days]."

D.   And the law is according to the words of the House of Hillel.

5:26 (Lieberman, pp. 29-30, ls. 57-61).

A.   The House of Shammai say, "They wash the hands and afterward mix the cup, lest the liquids which are on the outer surface of the cup be made unclean on account of the hands, and in turn make the cup unclean."

B.   The House of Hillel say, "The outer surfaces of the cup are always deemed unclean.

"Another explanation: The washing of the hands must always take place immediately before the meal.

C.   "They mix the cup and afterward wash the hands."

5:27 (Lieberman, p. 30, ls. 61-65).

A.   The House of House of Shammai say, "He dries his hand on the napkin and leaves it on the table, lest the liquids which are in the napkin be made unclean on account of the cushion, and then go and make the hands unclean."

B.   And the House of Hillel say, "A doubt in regard to the condition of liquids so far as the hands are concerned is resolved as clean."

C. "Another explanation: Washing the hands does not pertain to unconsecrated food.

D. "But he dries his hands on the napkin and leaves it on the cushion, lest the liquids which are in the napkin be made unclean on account of the table, and they go and render the food unclean."

5:28 (Lieberman, p. 30, ls. 65-68).

A. The House of Shammai say, "They clean the house, on account of the waste of food, and afterward they wash the hands."

B. The House of Hillel say, "If the waiter was a disciple of a sage, he gathers the scraps which contain as much as an olive's bulk.

C. "And they wash the hands and afterward clean the house."

5:29 (Lieberman, p. 30, ls. 68-72).

A. The House of Shammai say, "He holds the cup of wine in his right hand and spiced oil in his left hand."

He blesses over the wine and afterward blesses over the oil.

B. And the House of Hillel say, "He holds the sweet oil in his right hand and the cup of wine in his left hand."

C. He blesses over the oil and smears it on the head of the waiter. If the waiter was a disciple of a sage, he [the diner] smears it on the wall, because it is not praiseworthy for a disciple of a sage to go forth perfumed.

5:30 (Lieberman, pp. 30-31, ls. 72-75).

A. R. Judah said, "The House of Shammai and the House of Hillel did not dispute concerning the blessing of the food, that it is first, or concerning the *Habdalah,* that it is at the end.

"Concerning what did they dispute?

"Concerning the light and the spices, for —

"The House of Shammai say, 'Light and afterward spices.'

"And the House of Hillel say, 'Spices and afterward light.'"

5:30 (Lieberman, p. 31, ls. 75-77).

B. He who enters his home at the end of the Sabbath blesses the wine, the light, the spices, and then says *Habdalah.*

C. And if he has only one cup [of wine] he leaves it for after the meal and then says all [the liturgies] in order after [reciting the blessing for] it.

5:31 (Lieberman, p. 31, ls. 81-85).

A. If a person has a light covered in the folds of his garment or in a lamp, and sees the flame but does not use its light, or uses its light but does not see its flame, he does not bless [that light]. [He says a blessing over the light only] when he both sees the flame and uses its light.

As to a lantern — even though he had not extinguished it (that is, it has been burning throughout the Sabbath), he recites a blessing over it.

B.   They do not bless over the light of gentiles. One may bless over [the flame of] an Israelite kindled from a gentile, or a gentile who kindled from an Israelite.

5:32 (Lieberman, p. 31, Is. 80-81).

In the house of study —

The House of Shammai say, "One [person] blesses for all of them."

And the House of Hillel say,"Each one blesses for himself."

Clearly, the Tosefta has a variety of materials, as I suggested in the Introduction. Some of the materials are free-standing, but some simply cite and gloss the Mishnah. We see in the following comparison just how these things come to the surface. I add in italics the amplificatory language of the Tosefta.

III. THE TOSEFTA AND THE MISHNAH COMPARED

Mishnah	Tosefta
M. 8:1. A. These are the things which are between the House of Shammai and the House of Hillel in [regard to] the meal:	Tos. 5:25. [The] things which are between the House of Shammai and the House of Hillel [as regards] the meal:
B. The House of Shammai say, "One blesses the day, and afterward one blesses over the wine."	The House of Shammai say, "One blesses the day, and afterward one blesses over the wine, *for the day causes the wine to come, and the day is already sanctified, but the wine has not yet come.*"
And the House of Hillel say, "One blesses the wine, and afterward one blesses over the day."	And the House of Hillel say, "One blesses over the wine, and afterward one blesses the day, *for the wine causes the Sanctification of the day to be said.*"
	"Another matter: The blessing of the wine is continual, and the blessing of the day is not continual."
	And the law is according to the words of the House of Hillel.
M. 8:2.A. The House of Shammai say, "They wash the hands and afterward mix the cup."	Tos. 5:26. The House of Shammai say, "They wash the hands and afterward mix the cup, *lest the liquids which are on the outer*

And the House of Hillel say,
"They mix the cup and afterward
wash the hands."

surfaces of the cup may be made
unclean on account of the hands, and
they may go back and make the cup
unclean."

The House of Hillel say, *"The*
outer surfaces of the cup are per-
petually unclean.

"Another matter: The washing
of the hands is only [done] near [at
the outset of] the meal.

"They mix the cup and afterward
wash the hands."

8:3.A. The House of Shammai
say, "He dries his hands on the
napkin and lays it on the table."
And the House of Hillel say,
"On the cushion."

5:27. The House of Shammai
say, "He dries his hand on the
napkin and lays it on the table,
lest the liquids which are in the
napkin may be made unclean on
account of the pillow, and they may
go and make the hands unclean.

The House of Hillel say, *A doubt*
in regard to the condition of liquids
so far as the hands are concerned is
clean.

"Another matter: Washing the
hands does not pertain to
unconsecrated food. But he dries his
hands on the napkin and leaves it on
the cushion lest the liquids which are
in the pillow may be made unclean
on account of the table, and they may
go and render the food unclean."

M. 8:4.A. The House of Shammai say, "They clean the house
and afterward wash the hands."
And the House of Hillel say,
"They wash the hands and afterward clean the house."

Tos. 5:28. The House of Shammai say, "They clean the house
on account of the waste of food
and afterward wash the hands."

The House of Hillel say, *"If the*
waiter was a disciple of a sage, he
gathers the scraps which contain as
much as on olive's bulk.

"They wash the hands and afterward clean the house."

8:5.A. The House of Shammai say, "Light, and food and spices,

and *Habdalah*."
And the House of Hillel say, "Light, and spices, and food, and *Habdalah*."

5:30. R. Judah said, *"The House of Shammai and the House of Hillel did not dispute concerning the blessing of the food, that it is first, and concerning the* Hav-dalah *that it is the end. Concerning what did they dispute? Concerning the light and the spices, for* the House of Shammai say, 'Light and *afterward* spices,' and the House of Hillel say, 'Spices and *afterward* light.'"

B. The House of Shammai say, "'Who created the light of the fire.'"
And the House of Hillel say, "'Who creates the lights of the fire.'"

[No equivalent.]

M. 8:8.A. Wine came to them after the meal, and there is there only that cup —
B. The House of Shammai say, "He blesses over the wine and afterward he blesses over the food."
And the House of Hillel say, "He blesses over the food and afterward he blesses over the wine."
[If wine came to them after the meal and] there is there only that cup House of Shammai say, "He blesses the wine and then the food."
(House of Hillel say, "He blesses the food and then the wine.")

Tos. 5:30 (Lieberman, p. 31, Is. 75-77). A. *He who enters his home at the end of the Sabbath blesses over the wine, the light, the spices, and then says* Hav-dalah.

B. *And if he has only one cup* [of wine], *he leaves it for after the meal and then says them all in order after* [blessing] *it.*
If he has only one cup [of wine] [he leaves if for after the meal and then says them all in order, thus:] Wine, then food.

M. 8:6.A. They do not bless the light or the spices of gentiles, nor the light or the spices of the dead, nor the light or the spices which

Tos. 5:31.B. They do not bless the light of gentiles. *An Israelite who kindled* [a flame] *from a gentile, or a gentile who kindled* are before an idol.

B. And they do not bless the light until they make use of its illumination.

from an Israelite — one may bless [such a flame].

Tos. 5:31 (Lieberman, p. 31, Is. 81-85). A. *If a person has a light covered in the folds of his garment or in a lamp, and he sees the flame but does not use its light, or uses its light but does not see its flame, he does not bless.* [He blesses only] *when he both sees the flame and uses its light.*

M. 8:8.C. They respond *Amen* after an Israelite who blesses, and they do not respond *Amen* after a Samaritan who blesses, until one hears the entire blessing.

Tos. 5:21 (Lieberman, p. 28, Is.41-2). *They answer* "Amen" *after a blessing with the divine name recited by a gentile.*

They do not answer *Amen* after a Samaritan who blesses *with the divine name* until they hear the entire blessing.

The pattern is now clear. We simply cannot understand a line of the Tosefta without turning to the Mishnah. That means that the Tosefta-passage before us must have been composed after the Mishnah was in hand, that is, after 200, and that the authorship of the Tosefta had in mind the clarification of the received document, the Mishnah. So in a very simple sense, the Tosefta is the first talmud, that is to say, it is the first sustained and systematic commentary to the Mishnah. Not only so, but as a talmud, the Tosefta succeeds in ways in which the later Talmuds do not, simply because the Tosefta covers nearly the whole of the Mishnah, nearly all lines of all tractates, while the two Talmuds take up only a selection of the Mishnah-tractates, thirty-nine in the Yerushalmi of the Mishnah's sixty-two tractates (excluding tractate Abot, the fathers, which is post-Mishnaic by about a generation or fifty years), and the Bavli thirty-seven of the Mishnah's tractates.

We come now to the Yerushalmi. To understand what follows we must know that the Yerushalmi will address a chapter of the Mishnah by citing the Mishnah in small blocks, not reading it whole but only in phrases and clauses. Our special interest is in the place of the Tosefta in the Yerushalmi's structure. What we shall see is that the Yerushalmi is consecutive upon not the Mishnah but the Tosefta's reading of the Mishnah.

How do the Yerushalmi's exegetes read the Mishnah and the Tosefta? A few general remarks will prepare us for what is to follow. They brought to the documents no distinctive program of their own. I perceive no hidden agenda. To state matters negatively, the exegetes did not know in advance of their approach to a law of the Mishnah facts about the passage not contained (at least implicitly) within the boundaries of the language of the Mishnah passage itself (except only for facts contained within other units of the same document). Rejecting propositions that were essentially a priori, they proposed to explain and expand precisely the wording and the conceptions supplied by the document under study. I cannot point to a single instance in which the Yerushalmi's exegetes in retrospect appear to twist and turn the language and message of a passage, attempting to make the words mean something other than what they appear to say. Whether the exegetical results remain close to the wording of a passage of the Mishnah, or whether they leap beyond the bounds of the passage, the upshot is the same. There is no exegetical program revealed in the Yerushalmi's reading of the Mishnah other than that defined, to begin with, by the language and conceptions of one Mishnah passage or another.

What then are the sorts of approaches we are apt to find? These are four, of which two are nearly indistinguishable, the third highly distinctive, and the fourth barely consequential.

1. Citation and gloss of the language of the Mishnah (meaning of a phrase or concrete illustration of a rule). A unit of discourse of this type will contain a direct citation of a sentence of the Mishnah. The word choices or phrasing of the Mishnah will be paraphrased or otherwise explained through what is essentially a gloss. Or the rule of the Mishnah will be explained through an example or a restatement of some kind.

2. Specification of the meaning of the law of the Mishnah or the reason for it. Items of this type stand very close to those of the former. What differentiates the one from the other is the absence, in the present set of units of discourse, of direct citation of the Mishnah or close and explicit reading of its language. The discussion then tends to allude to the Mishnah or to generalize, while remaining wholly within its framework. In some units of discourse scriptural proof texts are adduced in evidence of a Mishnah passage. These frequently spill over into discussion of the reason for a rule.

3. Secondary implication or application of the law of the Mishnah. Units of discourse of this catalog generalize beyond the specific rule of the Mishnah. The discussion will commonly restate the principle of the rule at hand or raise a question invited by it. Hence if the Mishnah's law settles one question, participants in this type of discourse will use that as the foundation for raising a second and consequent question. Two or more rules of the Mishnah (or of the Mishnah and Tosefta) will be contrasted with one another and then harmonized, or two or more rulings of a specific authority will be alleged to conflict and then shown not to stand at variance with one another.

4. The matter of authorities and their views: case law. In a handful of items, concrete decisions are attached to specific laws of the Mishnah, or the harmonization or identification of the opinions of Mishnah's authorities forms the center of interest. From this taxonomy it follows that there was a severely

circumscribed repertoire of intellectual initiatives available to the authorities of the Yerushalmi.

Approaching a given rule of the Mishnah, a sage would do one of two things: (1) explain the meaning of the passage, or (2) extend and expand the meaning of the passage. In the former category fall all the items in the first and second approaches, as well as those units of discourse in which either a scriptural proof text is adduced in support of a law or an alleged variant reading of a text is supplied. In the latter category fit all items in the third and fourth approaches, as well as those in which the work is to harmonize laws or principles, on the one side, or to cite and amplify Tosefta's complement to the Mishnah passage, on the other. Within these two categories, which produce, in all, four subdivisions, we may find a place for all units of discourse in which the focus of discussion is a passage of the Mishnah. Of the two sorts, the work of straightforward explanation of the plain meaning of a law of the Mishnah by far predominates. If we may state the outcome very simply: what the framers of the Yerushalmi want to say — whatever else their purpose or aspiration — is what they think the Mishnah means in any given passage.

Then when does the Yerushalmi speak for itself, not for the Mishnah and its close companion, the Tosefta? If we collect all units of discourse, or larger parts of such units, in which exegesis of the Mishnah or expansion upon the law of the Mishnah is absent — about 10% of all the Yerushalmi's units of discourse in my probe — we find at most four types, which in fact are only two.

1. Theoretical questions of law not associated with a particular passage of the Mishnah. Some tendency exists to move beyond the legal boundaries set by the Mishnah's rules themselves. More general inquiries are taken up. These of course remain within the framework of the topic of one tractate or another, although some larger modes of thought are characteristic of more than a single tractate. To explain, I point to the mode of thought in which the scriptural basis of the law of the Mishnah will be investigated, without regard to a given tractate. Along these same lines, I may point to a general inquiry into the count under which one may be liable for a given act, comments on the law governing teaching and judging cases, and the like. But these items tend not to leave the Mishnah far behind.

2. Exegesis of Scripture separate from the Mishnah. It is under this rubric that we find the most important instances in which the Yerushalmi presents materials essentially independent of the Mishnah. They pursue problems or themes through what is said about a biblical figure, expressing ideas and values simply unknown to the Mishnah.

3. Historical statements. The Yerushalmi contains a fair number of statements that something happened or narratives about how something happened. While many of these are replete with biblical quotations, in general they do not provide exegesis of Scripture, which serves merely as illustration or reference point.

4. Stories about, and rules for, sages and disciples, separate from discussion of a passage of the Mishnah. The Mishnah contains a tiny number of tales about rabbis. These serve principally as precedents for, or illustrations of, rules.

The Yerushalmi, by contrast, contains a sizable number of stories about sages and their relationships to other people. Like the items in the second and third lists, these too may be adduced as evidence of the values of the people who stand behind the Yerushalmi, the things they thought important. These tales rarely serve to illustrate a rule or concept of the Mishnah. The main, though not the only, characteristic theme is the power of the rabbi, the honor due to the rabbi, and the tension between the rabbi and others, whether the patriarch, on the one side, the heretic on the second, or the gentile on the third. Units of discourse (or large segments of such units) independent of the interests of the Mishnah are not numerous. Varying in bulk from one tractate to the next, as I said, in my probe of five tractates of the Yerushalmi they added up to not much more than 10% of the whole. Furthermore, among the four types of units of discourse before us, the items on the first do not move far from the principles and concerns of the Mishnah. And this brings us to our task, which is to examine the Yerushalmi's treatment of the Mishnah and therefore also of the Tosefta to Mishnah-tractate Berakhot Chapter Eight. The reader will readily recognize how the Tosefta's materials make their appearance.

IV. YERUSHALMI TO MISHNAH BERAKHOT CHAPTER EIGHT

8:1.   **The House of Shammai say, "One blesses the day and afterward one blesses over the wine."**

And the House of Hillel say, "One blesses over the wine and afterward one blesses the day."

I.   A.   *What is the reason of the House of Shammai?*

The Sanctification of the day causes the wine to be brought, and the man is already liable for the Sanctification of the day before the wine comes.

What is the reason of the House of Hillel?

The wine causes the Sanctification of the day to be said.

Another matter: Wine is perpetual, and the Sanctification is not perpetual. [What is always required takes precedence over what is required only occasionally.]

B.   R. Yosé said, "[It follows] from the opinions of them both that with respect to wine and *Habdalah,* wine comes first."

"It is not the reason of the House of Shammai that the Sanctification of the day causes the wine to be brought, and here, since *Habdalah* does not cause wine to be brought, the wine takes precedence?"

"Is it not the reason of the House of Hillel that the wine is perpetual and the Sanctification is not perpetual, and since the wine is perpetual, and the *Habdalah* is not perpetual, the wine comes first?"

C.   R. Mana said, "From the opinions of both of them [it follows] that with respect to wine and Habdalah, *Habdalah* comes first."

"Is it not the reason of the House of Shammai that one is already obligated [to say] the Sanctification of the day before the wine comes, and here, since he is already obligated for *Habdalah* before the wine comes, *Habdalah* comes first?"

Is it not the reason of the House of Hillel that the wine causes the Sanctification of the Day to be said, and here, since the wine does not cause the *Habdalah* to be said, *Habdalah* comes first?"

D.   R. Zeira said, "From the opinions of both of them [it follows] that they say *Habdalah* without wine, but they say the Sanctification only with wine."

E.   *This is the opinion of R. Zeira, for* R. Zeira said, They may say *Habdalah* over beer, *but they go from place to place* [in search of wine] *for the Sanctification."*

II.   A.   R. Yosé b. Rabbi said, "They are accustomed there [in Babylonia], where there is no wine, for the prayerleader to go before the ark and say one blessing which is a summary of the seven, and complete it with, 'Who sanctifies Israel and the Sabbath Day.'"

B.   *And thus the following poses a difficulty for the opinion of the House of Shammai: How should one act on the evenings of the Sabbath?*

He *who was sitting and eating on the evening of the Sabbath,* and it grew dark and became Sabbath evening, and there was there only that one cup — [The House of Shammai say, "Wine, then food," and the House of Hillel say, "Food, then wine," so Mishnah 8:8].

Do you say he should leave it for the end of the meal and say all of them [the blessings] on it?

What do you prefer?

Should he [first] bless the day? The food takes precedence.

Should he bless the food? The wine takes precedence.

Should he bless the wine? The day takes precedence.

C.   *We may infer* [the answer] *from this:*

If wine came to them after the meal, and there is there only that cup—

R. Ba said, "Because it [the wine's] is a brief blessing, [he says it first, for] perhaps he may forget and drink [the wine]. But here, since he says them all over the cup, he will not forget [to say a blessing over the wine in the cup]."

D.   What, then, should he do according to the opinion of the House of Shammai?

Let him bless the food first, then bless the day, and then bless the wine.

E.   *And this poses difficulty for the opinion of the House of Hillel: How should one act at the end of the Sabbath?*

If he was sitting and eating on the Sabbath and it grew dark and the
Sabbath came to an end, and there is there only that cup —
Do you say he should leave it [the wine] for after the meal and say
them all on it?
What do you prefer?
Should he bless the wine? The food comes first.
Should he bless the food? The light comes first.
Should be bless the light? The *Habdalah* comes first.

F.   *We may infer* [the solution to the impasse] *from this:* R. Judah said,
"The House of Shammai and the House of Hillel did not differ
concerning the blessing of the food, that it comes first, nor concerning
Habdalah, that it comes at the end.
"Concerning what did they differ?
"Concerning the light and the spices, for:
"The House of Shammai say, 'The spices and afterward the light.'
"And the House of Hillel say, 'The light and afterward the spices.'"

G.   R. Ba and R. Judah in the name of Rab (said), "The law is according
to him who says, 'Spices and afterward light.'"]

H.   What should he do according to the opinion of the House of Hillel?
Let him bless the food, afterward bless the wine, and afterward bless
the light.

III. A.   As to [the beginning of the] festival day which coincides with the
end of the Sabbath —
R. Yohanan said, "[The order of prayer is] wine, Sanctification, light,
Habdalah."
Hanin bar Ba said in the name of Rab, "Wine, Sanctification, light,
Habdalah, Sukkah, and season."
And did not Samuel rule according to this teaching of R. Hanina.

B.   R. Aha said in the name of R. Joshua b. Levi, "When a king goes out
and the governor comes in, they accompany the king and afterward
bring in the governor."

C.   Levi said, "Wine, *Habdalah,* light, Sanctification."

IV.   A.   R. Zeira asked before R. Yosé, "How shall we do it in practice?"
He said to him, "According to Rab, and according to R. Yohanan."
And so too did the rule come out in practice — according to Rab and
according to R. Yohanan.

B.   *And when R. Abbahu went south, he would act in accord with R.
Hanina, but when he went down to Tiberias, he would act in accord
with R. Yohanan, for one does not differ from a man*['s ruling] *in his
own place* [out of courtesy].

C.   *According to the opinion of R. Hanina this poses no problem.*

D.   *But it poses a problem to the opinion of R. Yohanan:* In the rest of
the days of the year does he not bless the light, lest it go out [because

of a draft, and he lose the opportunity to say the blessing]? And here too he should bless the light before it goes out!

E. *What did R. Yohanan do in this connection?* [How did he explain this difficulty?]

F. Since he has wine [in hand], his light will not go out [for it is protected].

G. Then let him bless the light at the end?

H. So as not to upset the order [of prayer; lit.: time of the coming Sabbaths, [he does not do so].

8:2. **The House of Shammai say, "They wash the hands and afterward mix the cup." And the House of Hillel say, "They mix the cup first and afterward wash the hands."**

I. A. *What is the reason of the House of Shammai?*
So that the liquids which are on the outer side of the cup may not be made unclean by his hands and go and make the cup unclean.
What is the reason of the House of Hillel?
The outer side of the cup is always unclean [so there is no reason to protect it from the hands' uncleanness].
Another matter: One should wash the hands immediately before saying the blessing.

B. *R. Biban in the name of R. Yohanan* [said], *"The opinion of the House of Shammai is in accord with R. Yosé and that of the House of Hillel with R. Meir, as we have learned there* [Mishnah Kelim 25:7-8]:
"[In all vessels an outer part and an inner part are distinguished, and also a part by which they are held.]"
"R. Meir says, 'For hands which are unclean and clean.'"
"R. Yosé said,'This applies only to clean hands alone.'"

C. R. Yosé in the name of R. Shabbetai, and R. Hiyya in the name of R. Simeon b. Laqish [said], "For *Hallah* [Dough-offering] and for washing the hands, a man goes four miles [to find water]."
R. Abbahu in the name of R. Yosé b. R. Hanina said, "This is what he said, '[If the water is] before him [that is, on his way, in his vicinity, or near at hand, he must proceed to it and wash]. But if it is behind him [that is, not on his way], they do not trouble him [to obtain it and wash].'"

D. Regarding those who guard gardens and orchards [and who cannot leave their posts], what do you do for them as to the insides and the outer sides [of a cup]? [How do we rule in their case? Do we judge them to be in the status of those for whom the water is] on their way, or in the status of those who would have to backtrack?
Let us infer the answer from this [Mishnah Hallah 2:3]:

The woman sits and cuts off her Dough-offering *[Hallah]* **while she is naked, because she can cover herself up, but a man cannot.** Now does not a woman sit in the house, yet you say they do not bother her? So too here they do not bother him.

II.   A.   *It has been taught:*
Washing before the meal is a matter of choice, but afterward it is a matter of obligation.
But in respect to the first washing, he washes and interrupts, and in the case of the second washing, he washes and does not interrupt.

        B.   What is the meaning of "He 'washes and interrupts'?"
R. Jacob b. Aha said, "He washes and then repeats the washing."
R. Samuel bar Isaac said, *"If he is required* to repeat the washing, *how do you claim it is a matter of choice?*
["Or if you want, I may point out you require one to go four miles (in search of water], *so how do you claim* it is a matter of choice!"

        C.   R. Jacob bar Idi said, "On account of the first [washing of hands], a pig's flesh was eaten; on account of the second [washing of hands], a woman left her house.
"And some say, three souls were killed on her account. [It is not a matter of choice at all.]"

III.   A.   *Samuel went up to visit Rab. He saw him eating with* [his hands covered by] *a napkin. He said to him, "How so?* [Did you not wash your hands?]"
He said to him, "I am sensitive."

        B.   *When R. Zeira came up here* [to Palestine], *he saw the priests eating with a napkin. He said to them, "Lo, this is in accord with the story of Rab and Samuel."*

        C.   R. Yosé bar Kahana came [and said] *in the name of Samuel,* "One washes the hands for Heave-offering, not for unconsecrated food."

        D.   R. Yosé says, "For Heave-offering and for unconsecrated food."

        E.   R. Yosah in the name of R. Hiyya bar Ashi, and R. Jonah and R. Hiyya bar Ashi in the name of Rab [said], "They wash the hands for Heave-offering up to the wrist, and for unconsecrated food up to he knuckles."

        F.   *Measha the son of the son of R. Joshua b. Levi said, "If one was eating with my grandfather and did not wash his hands up to the wrist, grandfather would not eat with him."*

        G.   R. Huna said, "Washing the hands applies only for bread."

        H.   R. Hoshia taught, "Whatever is unclean on account of liquid [is protected by washing the hands]."

        I.   R. Zeira said, *"Even for cutting beets, he would wash his hands."*

IV.   A.   Rab said, "He who washed his hands in the morning is not required to do so in the afternoon."

B.	*R. Abina ordered his wine-steward, "Whenever you find sufficient water, wash your hands and rely on this washing all day long."*
C.	*R. Zeira went up to R. Abbahu in Caesarea. He found him saying,* "I shall go to eat."
D.	*He gave him a chunk of bread to cut. He* [Abbahu] *said to him* [Zeira], *"Begin, bless."*
E.	*He* [Zeira] *said to him* [Abbahu], *"The host knows the value of his loaf."* [You should bless.]
F.	*When they had eaten, he* [Abbahu] *said to him* [Zeira], *"Let the elder bless."*
G.	*He said to him, "Rabbi, does the rabbi* [you] *know R. Huna, a great man, who would say, 'He who opens* [blesses first] *must close* [and say Grace after Meals]'?"*
H.	*A Tannaitic teaching differs from R. Huna, as it has been taught:*
I.	The order of washing the hands in this: With up to five people present, they begin with the greatest. [If] more than this [are present], they begin with the least. In the middle of the meal, they begin with the eldest. After the meal they begin with the one who blesses.
J.	Is it not [done] so that he may prepare himself for the blessing? [So he did *not* bless at the beginning!
K.	*If you say* the one who opens is the one who closes, he is already prepared [having opened the meal].
L.	*R. Isaac said, "Explain it in regard to those who come in one by one and did not know which one had blessed* [at the outset]."

8:3.		**The House of Shammai say, "He dries his hands on the napkin and puts it on the table."**
		And the House of Hillel say, "On the cushion."
I.	A.	The Mishnah deals with either a table of marble [which is not susceptible to uncleanness] or a table that can be taken apart and is not susceptible to becoming unclean.
	B.	*What is the reason of the House of Shammai?*
		So that the liquids which are on the napkin may not become unclean from the cushion and go and render his hands unclean.
		And what is the reason of the House of Hillel?
		The condition of doubt[ful uncleanness] with respect to the hands is always regarded as clean.
		Another reason: The [question of the cleanness of] hands does not apply to unconsecrated food [which in any case is not made unclean by unclean hands which are unclean in the second remove].
	C.	*And according to the House of Shammai,* does [the question of the cleanness of] hands [indeed] apply to unconsecrated food?
	D.	*You may interpret* [the tradition] either in accord with R. Simeon b. Eleazar or in accord with R. Eleazar b. R. Saddoq.

      According to R. Simeon b. Eleazar, as it has been taught:

      R. Simeon b. Eleazar says in the name of R. Meir, "Hands unclean in the first remove of uncleanness can affect [even] unconsecrated food, and in the second remove of uncleanness can affect [only] Heave-offering."

E.   *Or according to R. Eleazar b. R. Saddoq, as we have learned there:*

F.   Unconsecrated food which has been prepared along with consecrated [food] is like unconsecrated food [and subject to the same, less strict cleanness rules].

G.   R. Eleazar b. R. Saddoq says, "Lo, it is like Heave-offering, capable of becoming unclean from [something unclean in the] second remove of uncleanness and being rendered unfit from [something unclean in] still a further remove of uncleanness."

H.   *There we have learned:*

I.   He who anoints himself with a clean oil and is made unclean and goes down and bathes [in ritual pool] —

J.   The House of Shammai say, "Even though he drips [with oil], [the oil] is clean."

K.   And the House of Hillel say, "It is unclean [so long as there remains enough to anoint a small member]."

L.   And if the oil was unclean in the first place —

M.   The House of Shammai say, "[It remains unclean, even after he has immersed himself, so long as there remains] sufficient for anointing a small limb."

N.   And the House of Hillel say, "[So long as it remains] a dripping liquid."

O.   R. Judah says in the name of the House of Hillel, "So long as it is dripping so as to moisten something else."

P.   *The principle of the House of Hillel has been turned around.*

Q.   *There* [in the just-cited law] *they say it is* unclean. *And here* [in our Mishnah] *they say it is* clean.

R.   *There* it is present. *But here* it is absorbed in the napkin.

8:4.   **The House of Shammai say, "They clean the house and afterward wash the hands." And the House of Hillel say, "They wash the hands and afterward clean the house."**

I.   A.   *What is the reason of the House of Shammai?*

    B.   Because of the waste of food.

    C.   *And what is the reason of the House of Hillel?*

    D.   If the servant is clever, he removes the crumbs which are less than an olive's bulk, and they wash their hands and afterward they clean the house.

8:5.   **The House of Shammai say, "Light, and food, and spices, and *Habdalah*." And the House of Hillel say, "Light, and spices, and food, and**

> *Habdalah.*" **The House of Shammai say, "'Who created the light of the fire.'" And the House of Hillel say, "'Who creates the lights of the fire.'"**

I. A. It was taught:

B. R. Judah said, "The House of Shammai and the House of Hillel did not differ concerning the [blessing for] the mean, that it comes at the beginning, or concerning *Habdalah,* that it comes at the end. And concerning what did they differ? Concerning the light and spices, for the House of Shammai say, 'Spices and light.' And the House of Hillel say, 'Light and spices.'"

C. R. Ba and R. Judah in the name of Rab [said], "The law is in accord with him who says, 'Spices and afterward light.' [That is, Judah's House of Shammai.]"

D. The House of Shammai say, "The cup [should be] in his right hand, and the sweet oil in his left hand. He says [the blessing for] the cup and afterward says the blessing for the sweet oil."

E. The House of Hillel say, "The sweet oil [should be] in his right hand and the cup in his left hand, and he says [the blessing for] the sweet oil and rubs it in the head of the servant. If the servant is a disciple of a sage, he rubs it on the wall, for it is not fitting for a disciple of a sage to go forth scented in public."

F. *Abba bar bar Hanna and R. Huna were sitting and eating, and R. Zeira was standing and serving them. He went and bore both of them* [oil and cup] *in one hand.*

G. *Abba bar bar Hanna said to him, "Is one of your hands cut off?" And his* [Abba's] *father was angry at him.*

H. *He* [the father] *said to him* [Abba], *"Is it not enough for you that you are sitting and he is standing and serving? And furthermore, he is a priest, and Samuel said,* 'He who makes [secular] use of the priesthood has committed sacrilege.' *You make light of him.*

I. *"I decree for him to sit and you to stand and serve in his place."*

J. How do we know that he who makes use of the priesthood has committed sacrilege?

K. R. Aha in the name of Samuel said, "'And I said to them, You are holy to the Lord and the vessels are holy' [Ezra 8:28]. Just as one who makes use of the vessels commits sacrilege, so he who makes use of the priests commits sacrilege."

L. **[The House of Shammai say, "'Who created ...'"]**

M. According to the opinion of the House of Shammai, [one should say as the blessing for wine], "Who created the fruit of the vine" [instead of "who creates ...," as actually is said].

N. According to the opinion of the House of Hillel, [one should say,] "Who creates the fruit of the vine" [as is indeed the case].

O.   [The Shammaite reply:]

P.   The wine is newly created every year, but the fire is not newly created every hour.

Q.   The fire and the mule, even though they were not created in the six days of creation, were thought of [entered the Creator's mind] in the six days of creation.

R.   Proof of the mule: "These are the sons of Zibeon: Aiah and Anah; he is the Anah who found the hot springs (HYYMYM) in the wilderness [as he pastured the asses of Zibeon his father (Genesis 36:24]."

S.   *What is the meaning of* hot springs (HYYMYM)?

T.   R. Judah b. Simeon says, "Mule." [Greek: *hemiovos.*]

U.   *And the rabbis say,* "Half-a-horse [Greek: *hemi-hippos]*, half was a horse, half an ass."

V.   And what are the marks [to know whether the father was a horse, the mother an ass, or vice versa]?

W.   R. Judah said, "If the ears are small, the mother was a horse and the father an ass. If they are big, the mother was an ass and the father a horse."

X.   *R. Mana instructed the members of the Patriarchate, "If you want to buy a mule, buy those whose ears are small,* for the mother was a horse and the father an ass."

Y.   What did Zibeon and Anah do? They brought a female ass and mated her with a male horse, and they produced a mule.

Z.   The Holy One, blessed be He, said to them, "You have brought into the world something which is destructive. So I too shall bring upon that man [you] something which is destructive."

AA.   What did the Holy One, blessed be He, do?

BB.   He brought a snake and mated it with a lizard and it produced a *habarbar-lizard.*

CC.   A man should never say to you that a *habarbar-lizard* bit him and he lived, or a mad dog nipped him and he lived, or a she-mule butted him and he lived. We speak only of a white she-mule.

DD.   As to the fire:

EE.   R. Levi in the name of R. Nezira [said], "Thirty-six hours that light which was created on the first day served [the world]. Twelve on the eve of the Sabbath [Friday], twelve on the night of the Sabbath, and twelve on the Sabbath.

FF.   "And the First Man [Adam] looked at it from one end of the world to the other. When the light did not cease [from shining], the whole world began to sing, as it is said, 'Under the whole heaven, he lets [his voice] go, and his light to the corners of the earth' [Job 37:3].

GG. "When the Sabbath ended, it began to get dark. Man became frightened, saying, 'This is the one concerning whom it is written,"He will bruise your head, and you shall bruise his heel" [Genesis 3:15].

HH. "'Perhaps this one has come to bite me.' And he said, 'Let only darkness cover me'" [Psalm 139:11].

I I. R. Levi said, "At that moment the Holy One, blessed be He, prepared two flints and struck them against each other, and the light came forth from them. This is the meaning of that which Scripture says, 'And the night around me be light' [Psalm 139:11].

J J. "And he [man] blessed it, 'Who creates the lights of the fire.'"

KK. Samuel said, "Therefore they bless the fire at the end of the Sabbath, for that is when it was first created."

LL. R. Huna in the name of R. Abbahu in the name of R. Yohanan [said], "Also at the end of the Day of Atonement one blesses it, for the light has rested that entire day."

8:6. **They do not bless the light or spices of gentiles, nor the light or spices of the dead, nor the light or spices which are before an idol. They do not bless the light until they make use of its illumination.**

I. A. R. Jacob taught before R. Jeremiah, "They do bless the spices of gentiles."

B. *What is the difference* [between this view and the Mishnah's]?

C. *We explain that the latter refers to the* gentile's deeds before his own store [while the Mishnah refers to a banquet].

D. Even though it has not gone out [but burned the entire Sabbath], they may bless [the light of] a lantern [because no prohibited work has been done by its light].

E. As regards a flame in the folds of one's garment, in a lamp, or in a mirror, if one sees the flame but does not make use of its light, or makes use of its light but not see the flame, one may not bless it. [One may bless] only when one may see the flame and makes use of the light.

F. Five things were said in regard to the burning coal, and five with regard to the flame.

1. A coal of the sanctuary is subject to the law of sacrilege, but a flame is neither used for pleasure nor subject to the law of sacrilege.

2. A burning coal used for idolatry is prohibited, but a flame is permitted.

3. He who vows not to have enjoyment from his fellow may not use his burning coal, but may use his flame.

4. He who brings a coal out to the public way [on the Sabbath] is liable, but if he brings a flame, he is not liable.

5.   They bless the flame, but not the burning coal.

G.   R. Hiyya bar Ashi in the name of Rab said, "If the coals were glowing, they may bless them."

H.   R. Yohanan of Kerasion in the name of R. Nahum bar Simai [said], "On condition that it was cut off." [That is, the flame was shooting up from the coal.]

I.   *It was taught:*

J.   Now the [light of] a gentile who kindled [a light from the flame of] an Israelite, and an Israelite who kindled [a light from the flame of a gentile] — *this poses no problems.*

K.   But [the light of] a gentile who kindled [a light from the flame of] an Israelite [may be blessed]. If so, even [the flame of] a gentile who kindled from a gentile [should be allowed].

L.   *It is indeed taught:* They do *not* bless [a light kindled by] a gentile from a gentile.

M.   R. Abbahu in the name of R. Yohanan [said,] "As to an alleyway which is populated entirely by gentiles with a single Israelite living in its midst — if the light comes from there, they may bless it on account of that one Israelite who lives there."

N.   R. Abbahu in the name of R. Yohanan [said], "They do not bless either the spices on Sabbath evenings in Tiberias or the spices on Saturday nights in Sepphoris, or the light or the spices on Friday mornings in Sepphoris, for these all are prepared only for another purpose [cleaning clothes]."

O.   **Nor over the light or spices of the dead.**

P.   R. Hezekiah and R. Jacob b. Aha in the name of R. Yosé b. R. Hanina [said], "This refers to the following case: 'When they are placed over the bed of the dead. But if they are placed before the bed of the dead, they may be blessed [that is, a blessing may be recited over them].'"

Q.   "[For] I say, they are prepared for the purposes of the living."

R.   **Nor the light nor the spices of idolatry.**

S.   But is not that of gentiles the same as that of idolatry? [Why repeat the same rule?]

T.   Interpret it as applying to an Israelite idol.

They do not bless the light until they make use of its illumination.

I.   A.   R. Zeira, son of R. Abbahu expounded, "'And God saw the light, that it was good' [Genesis 1:4]. And afterward,'And God divided the light from the darkness'" [Genesis 1:5]. [That is, first it was seen and used, then comes the *Habdalah.*]

B.   R. Berekiah said, "Thus the two great men of the world [age], R. Yohanan and R. Simeon b. Laqish, expounded: 'And God divided — a certain division.'" [That is, he did so literally.]

C. R. Judah b. R. Simon said, "They divided for Him."

D. And the rabbis say, "They divided for the righteous who were destined to come into the world.

E. "They drew a parable: To what is the matter to be likened? To a king who has two generals. This one says, 'I shall serve by day,' and this one says, 'I shall serve by night.'

F. "He calls the first and says to him, 'So-and-so, the day will be your division.'

G. "He calls the second and says to him, 'So-and-so, the night will be your division.'

H. "That is the meaning of what is written, 'And God called the light day, and the darkness he called night.'

I. "To the light he said, 'The day will be your province.' And to the darkness he said, 'The night will be your province.'"

J. R. Yohanan said, "This is what the Holy One, blessed be He, said to Job [Job 38:12], 'Have you commanded the morning since your days began, and caused the dawn to know its place?'

K. "What is the place of the light of the six days of creation — where was it hidden?"

L. *R. Tanhuma said, "I give the reason:* 'Who creates light and makes darkness, and makes peace' [Isaiah 45:7]. When he went forth, he made peace between them."

M. **They do not bless the light until they make use of its illumination.**

N. Rab said, "They *use* [spelled with an *'alef]."*

O. And Samuel said, "They *enjoy* [spelled with an *'ayin]."*

P. He who said "they *use"* [may draw support from the following]:

Q. "Only on this condition will we *consent* to you" [Genesis 34:15].

R. He who said *"enjoy"* [may draw support from the following:

S. "How to sustain with a word him that is weary" [Isaiah 50:4].

T. There we have learned: "How do they extend (M'BR) the Sabbath limits of cities?"

U. Rab said, *"Add" ['alef].*

V. And Samuel said, *"Increase" ['ayin].*

W. He who said it is with an *'alef* means they add a limb to it.

X. He who said it with an *'ayin* means it is [increased] like a pregnant woman.

Y. There we learned, "Before the festivals ('YD) of gentiles."

Z. Rab said, *"Testimonies" ['ayin].*

AA. And Samuel said, *"Festivals" ['alef].*

BB. He who said it is with an *'alef* [may cite this verse], "For near is the day of their calamity ['YD]" [Deuteronomy 32:35].

CC. He who said it is with an *'ayin* [may cite], "Their testimonies neither see nor know, they they may be put to shame" [Isaiah 44:9].

DD. How does Samuel deal with the reason of Rab? [He may say,] "And their *testimonies* are destined to *shame* those who keep them on the day of judgment."

EE. **They do not bless the light until they have made use of its illumination.** [How much illumination must there be?]

FF. R. Judah in the name of Samuel said, "So that women may spin by its light."

GG. R. Yohanan said, "So that one's eye can see what is in the cup and what is in the saucer."

HH. R. Hanina said, "So that one may know how to distinguish one coin from another."

II. R. Oshaia taught, "Even [if the flame is in] a hall ten-by-ten, they may say the blessing."

JJ. *R. Zeira drew near the lamp. His disciples said to him, "Rabbi, why do you rule so stringently for us? Lo, R. Oshaia taught,* "One may bless even in a hall ten-by-ten."

8:7 **He who ate and forgot and did not bless —**
The House of Shammai say, "He should go back to his place and bless."
And the House of Hillel say, "He may bless in the place in which he remembered."
"Until when may he say the blessing? Until the food has been digested in his bowels."

I. A. *R. Yusta b. Shunam said, "[There are] two authorities. One gives the reason of the House of Shammai and the other the reason of the House of Hillel."*

B. *"The one who gives the reason of the House of Shammai* [says], 'If he had forgotten a purse of precious stones and pearls there, would he not go back and take his purse? *So too* let him go back to his place and bless.'

C. *"The one who gave the reason of the House of Hillel* [states], 'If he were a worker on the top of the palm or down in a pit, would you trouble him to go back to his place and bless? But he should bless in the place where he remembers [to do so]. *Here too* let him bless in the place where he remembers.'"

D. **Until when does he recite the blessing?**

E. R. Hiyya in the name of Samuel says, "Until the food has been digested in his bowels."

F. And the sages say, "So long as he is thirsty on account of that meal."

G. R. Yohanan says, "Until he becomes hungry again."

8:8. **If wine came to them after the food, and there is there only one cup —**

The House of Shammai say, "He blesses the wine and afterward blesses the food."

And the House of Hillel say, "He blesses the food and afterward blesses the wine."

They answer *Amen* **after an Israelite who blesses, and they do not answer** *Amen* **after a Samaritan who blesses until the entire blessing has been heard.**

I.   A.   R. Ba said, "Because it is a brief blessing, he may forget and drink the wine. But because it is joined to the [blessings for] cup, he will not forget."

      B.   **After an Israelite they answer** *Amen,* even though he has not heard [the Grace]. Has it not been taught, "If he heard [the Grace] and did not answer, he has carried out his obligation [to say Grace]. If he answered *[Amen]* and did not hear [the Grace], he has not carried out his obligation."

      C.   Hiyya the son of Rab said, "The Mishnah speaks of him who] did not eat with them as much as an olive's bulk."

      D.   *So too it has been taught:* If he heard and did not answer, he has carried out his obligation. If he answered and did not hear, he has not carried out his obligation.

      E.   Rab in the name of Abba bar Hanna [said], *and some say Abba bar Hanna in the name of Rab* [said], "And this applies to a case in which he answered at the chapter [paragraph] headings."

      F.   *R. Zeira asked, "What are these chapter headings?"*

      G.   "Praise the Lord, praise the servants of the Lord, praise the name of the Lord" [Psalm 113:1].

      H.   *They asked before R. Hiyya b. Abba, "How do we know that,* if one heard and did not answer [Amen], he has carried out his obligation?"

      I.   *He said, "From what we have seen the great rabbis doing, so they do in public, for they say this:* 'Blessed is he that comes.' *And the others say,* 'In the name of the Lord.' *And both groups thus* complete their obligation."

      J.   R. Oshaia taught, "A man responds *Amen,* even though he has not eaten, and he does not say, 'Let us bless him of whose bounty we have eaten,' unless he actually ate."

      K.   *It has been taught,* They do not respond with an orphaned *Amen,* a cut-off *Amen,* or a hasty *Amen.*

      L.   Ben Azzai says, "If one answers an orphaned *Amen,* his sons will be orphans. A cut-off one — his years will be cut off. A hasty one — his soul will be cut down. A long one — his days and years will be lengthened with goodness."

      M.   What is an orphaned *Amen?*

N.   R. Huna said, *"This refers to a person who sat down to bless,* and he answered, but did not know to what [prayer] he answered *[Amen]."*

O.   It was taught: If a gentile who blessed the divine name, they answer *Amen* after him.

P.   R. Tanhum said, "If a gentile blesses you, answer after him *Amen, as it is written,* 'Blessed will you be by all the peoples'" [Deuteronomy 7:14].

Q.   A gentile met R. Ishmael and blessed him. He said to him, *"You have already been answered."*

R.   *Another met him* and cursed him. He said to him, *"You have already been answered."*

S.   His disciple said to him, *"Rabbi, how could you say the same to both?"* He said to them, "Thus it is written in Scripture: 'Those that curse you will be cursed, and those that bless you will be blessed'" [Genesis 27:29].

We come now to the Bavli and how it receives and reworks the entire antecedent heritage. We see immediately the simple fact that the Bavli's authorship appeals directly to the Tosefta, without addressing the program of the Yerushalmi. While, therefore, both Talmuds are organized as commentaries to the Mishnah, they are entirely autonomous of one another.. The Babylonian Talmud does not expand upon the earlier one but forms its own discussions in accord with its own program. While the Bavli treats the Mishnah in the same way as does the Yerushalmi, in addition, the authorship of the second Talmud moved in a direction all its own, systematically commenting in large and cogent compositions upon not only the Mishnah but also Scripture, that is, on both the oral and the written Torahs. This difference between the two Talmuds may account for the greater acceptance of the later one. In the Land of Israel Mishnah-commentary went into the Talmud of the Land of Israel, Scripture-commentary went into the Midrash-compilations. But in Babylonia both were encompassed within the Talmud of that country, and the one substantial literary-redactional difference between the Bavli and the Yerushalmi is the Bavli framers' inclusion of sizable sequences and proportionately substantial compositions — 30-40% — of Scripture units of discourse. These they inserted whole and complete, not at all in response to the Mishnah's program. The Yerushalmi presents large-composites of scriptural commentary in only limited volume and in significantly modest proportion. Both Talmuds are laid out as a commentary to the Mishnah. These commentaries to the Mishnah are called *gemara*, and the Talmuds are often called simply Gemara.

By extensive resort to units of discourse providing an exegesis of Scripture, the Bavli's framers read their values into the texts of Scripture. In omitting such units of discourse, the Yerushalmi's authors lost the opportunity to spell out in a whole and complete way the larger system of Judaism that both Talmuds portray.

The key to the success of the Bavli lies in the very foundations of its literary structure, in the redactional-literary decision to lay the basis of the main beams of the Bavli's composition upon not only the Mishnah but also upon passages of Scripture. The compositors of the Bavli were encyclopaedists. Their creation turned out to be the encyclopaedia of Judaism, its summa, its point of final reference, its court of last appeal, its definition, it conclusion, its closure. Now let us turn to their final presentation of matters.

v. BAVLI
I
THE HOUSES' DISPUTES

[51b] *Gemara: Our rabbis have taught:*

> **The things which are between the House of Shammai and the House of Hillel in** [regard to] **a meal:**

> **The House of Shammai say, "One blesses over the day and afterward blesses over the wine, for the day causes the wine to come, and the day has already been sanctified, while the wine has not yet come."**

> **And the House of Hillel say, "He blesses over the wine and afterward blesses over the day, for the wine causes the Sanctification to be said.**

> **"Another matter: The blessing over the wine is perpetual, and the blessing over the day is not perpetual. Between that which is perpetual and that which is not perpetual, that which is perpetual takes precedence."**

And the law is in accordance with the words of the House of Hillel.

What is the purpose of "another matter"?

If you should say that there [in regard to the opinion of the House of Shammai] *two* [reasons are given] *and here* [in regard to the opinion of the House of Hillel] *one, here too* [in respect to the House of Hillel], *there are two* [reasons, the second being]: "The blessing of the wine is perpetual and the blessing of the day is not perpetual. That which is perpetual takes precedence over that which is not perpetual."

And the law is in accord with the opinion of the House of Hillel.

This is obvious [that the law is in accord with the House of Hillel], *for the echo has gone forth* [and pronounced from heaven the decision that the law follows the opinion of the House of Hillel].

If you like, I can argue that [this was stated] before the echo.

And if you like, I can argue that it was after the echo, and [the passage is formulated in accord with the [opinion of [52a] R. Joshua, who stated, "They do not pay attention to an echo [from heaven]."

And is it the reasoning of the House of Shammai that the blessing of the day is more important?

But has a Tanna not taught: "He who enters his house at the close of the Sabbath blesses over the wine and the light and the spices and afterward he says *Habdalah.* And if he has only one cup, he leaves it for after the food and then says the other blessings in order after it." *[Habdalah* is the blessing of the day, yet comes last!]

But lo, on what account [do you say] *this is the view of the House of Shammai? Perhaps it is the House of Hillel*['s opinion]?

Let [such a thought] *not enter your mind, for the Tanna teaches:* "Light and afterward spices." *And of whom have you heard who holds this opinion?* The House of Shammai, *as a Tanna has taught:*

R. Judah said, "The House of Shammai and the House of Hillel did not differ concerning the [blessing of the] food, that it is at first, and the *Habdalah,* that it is at the end.

"Concerning what did they dispute? Concerning the light and the spices.

"For the House of Shammai say, 'Light and afterward spices.'

"And the House of Hillel say, 'Spices and afterward the light.'"

And on what account [do you suppose that] *it is the House of Shammai as* [interpreted by] *R. Judah? Perhaps it is [a teaching in accord with] the House of Hillel* [as interpreted by] *R. Meir?*

Do not let such a thing enter your mind, for lo, a Tanna teaches here in our Mishnah: House of Shammai say, "Light and food and spices and *Habdalah."*

And the House of Hillel say, "Light and spices, food and *Habdalah."*

But there, in the "baraita," *lo he has taught:* "If he has only one cup, he leaves it for after the food and then says the other blessings in order after it."

From this it is to be inferred that it is the House of Shammai's teaching, according to the [interpretation] *of R. Judah.*

In any event there is a problem [for the House of Shammai now give precedence to reciting a blessing for the wine over blessing the day].

The House of Shammai suppose that the coming of the holy day is to be distinguished from its leaving. As to the coming of the [holy] *day, the earlier one may bring it in, the better. As to the leaving of the festival day, the later one may take leave of it, the better, so that it should not seem to us as a burden.*

And do the House of Shammai hold the opinion that Grace requires a cup [of wine]? *And lo, we have learned:* [If] wine came to them after the food, and there is there only that cup, the House of Shammai say, "He blesses over the wine and afterward blesses over the food." [So Grace is said *without* the cup.]

Does this not mean that he blesses it and drinks [it]?

No. He blesses it and leaves it.

But has not a master said, "He that blesses must [also] taste [it]."

He does taste it.

And has not a master said, "Tasting it is spoiling it."

He tastes it with his hand [finger].

And has not a master said, "The cup of blessing requires a [fixed] measure." *And lo, he diminishes it from its fixed measure.*

[We speak of a situation in which] *he has more than the fixed measure.*

But lo, has it not been taught: If there is there *only* that cup ... [so he has not more].

There is not enough for two, but more than enough for one.

And has not R. Hiyya taught: House of Shammai say, "He blesses over the wine and drinks it, and afterward he says Grace."

Then we have two Tannaite authorities' [traditions] in respect to the opinion of the House of Shammai.

The House of Shammai say, ["They wash the hands and afterward mix the cup]...

Our Rabbis have taught:

The House of Shammai say, "They wash the hands and afterwards mix the cup, for if you say they mix the cup first, [against this view is] **a** [precautionary] **decree to prevent the liquids on the outer sides of the cup, which are unclean by reason of his hands'** [touching them], **from going back and making the cup unclean."**

But will not the hands make the cup itself unclean [without reference to the liquids]?

The hands are in the second remove of uncleanness, and the [object unclean in] the second remove of uncleanness cannot [then] render [another object unclean] in the third [remove] in respect to profane foods, [but only to Heave-offering]. But [this happens] only by means of liquids [unclean in the first remove].

And the House of Hillel say, "They mix the cup and afterward wash the hands, for if you say they wash the hands first, [against this view is] **a** [precautionary] **decree lest the liquids which are** [already] **on the hands become unclean on account of the cup and go and render the hands unclean."**

But will not the cup [itself] *make the hands unclean?*

A vessel cannot render a man unclean.

But will they [the hands] *not render the liquids which are in it* [the cup] *unclean?*

Here we are dealing with a vessel the outer part of which has been made unclean by liquid. The inner part is clean but the outer part is unclean. *Thus we have learned:*

[If] a vessel is made unclean on the outside by liquid, the outside is unclean, [52b] but its inside and its rim, handle, and haft are clean. If, however, the inside is unclean, the whole [cup] is unclean.

What, then, do they [the Houses] *dispute?*

The House of Shammai hold that it is prohibited to make use of a vessel whose outer parts are unclean by liquids, as a decree on account of the drippings. [There is] *no* [reason] *to decree* lest the liquids on the hands be made unclean by the cup.

And the House of Hillel reckon that it is permitted to make use of a vessel whose outer part is made unclean by liquids, *for drippings are unusual. But there is reason to take care* lest the liquids which are on the hands may be made unclean by the cup.

Another matter: [So that] **immediately upon the washing of the hands** [may come] **the meal** [itself].

What is the reason for this additional explanation?

This is what the House of Hillel said to the House of Shammai: "According to your reasoning, in saying that it is prohibited to make use of a cup whose outer parts are unclean, *we decree on account of the drippings. But even so,* [our opinion] *is better,* for **immediately upon the washing of the hands** [should come] **the meal."**

The House of Shammai say, "He dries his hand on the napkin..."

Our rabbis have taught:

The House of Shammai say, "He wipes his hands with the napkin and lays it on the table, for if you say, 'on the cushion,' [that view is wrong, for it is a precautionary] **decree lest the liquids which are on the napkin become unclean on account of the cushion and go back and render the hands unclean."**

And will not the cushion [itself] *render the napkin unclean?*

A vessel cannot make a vessel unclean.

And will not the cushion [itself] *make the man unclean?*

A vessel cannot make a man unclean.

And the House of Hillel say,"'On the cushion,' for if you say, 'on the table,' [that opinion is wrong, for it is a] **decree lest the liquids become unclean on account of the table and go and render the food unclean."**

But will not the table render the food which is on it unclean?

We here deal with a table which is unclean in the second remove, and something unclean in the second remove does not render something

unclean in the third remove in respect to unconsecrated food, except by
means of liquids [which are always unclean in the first remove].

What [principle] *do they dispute?*

The House of Shammai reckon that it is prohibited to make use of a table
unclean in the second remove, as a decree on account of those who eat
Heave-offering [which is rendered unfit by an object unclean in the
second remove].

And the House of Hillel reckon that it is permitted to make use of table unclean
in the second remove, for those who eat Heave-offering [the priests]
are careful.

Another matter: There is no Scriptural requirement to wash the hands before
eating unconsecrated food.

What is the purpose of "another explanation"?

*This is what the House of Hillel said to the House of Shammai: If you ask
what is the difference in respect to food, concerning which we take
care, and in respect to the hands, concerning which we do not take care
— even in this regard* [our opinion] *is preferable,* for there is no
Scriptural requirement concerning the washing of the hands before
eating unconsecrated food.

It is better that the hands should be made unclean, *for there is no Scriptural
basis for* [washing] *them,* and let not the food be made unclean,
concerning which there is a Scriptural basis [for concern about its
uncleanness].

**The House of Shammai say, "They clean house and afterward wash the
hands ..."**

Our rabbis have taught:

**The House of Shammai say, "They clean the house and afterward wash
the hands, for if you say, 'They wash the hands first,' it turns out
that you spoil the food."**

But the House of Shammai do not reckon that one washes the hands first.

What is the reason?

On account of the crumbs.

And the House of Hillel say, "If the servant is a disciple of a sage, he takes
the crumbs which are as large a an olive [in bulk] and leaves the crumbs
which are not so much as an olive [in bulk]."

(This view supports the opinion of R. Yohanan, for R. Yohanan said, "Crumbs
which are not an olive in bulk may be deliberately destroyed.")

In what do they differ?

The House of Hillel reckon that it is prohibited to employ a servant who is an
ignorant man, *and the House of Shammai reckon that* it is permitted to
employ a servant who is an ignorant man.

R. Yosé bar Hanina said in the name of R. Huna, "In our entire chapter the law is in accord with the House of Hillel, excepting this matter, in which the law is in accord with the House of Shammai."

And R. Oshaia taught the matter contrariwise. And in this matter too the law is in accord with the House of Hillel.

The House of Shammai say, "Light and food ..."

R. Huna bar Judah happened by the house of Raba. He saw that Raba blessed the spices first.

He said to him, "Now the House of Shammai and the House of Hillel did not dispute concerning the light, [it should come first].

"For it was taught: The House of Shammai say, 'Light, and food, spices, and Habdalah,' and the House of Hillel say, 'Light, and spices, and food, and Habdalah.'

Raba answered him, "This is the opinion [=version] of R. Meir, but R. Judah says, 'The House of Shammai and the House of Hillel did not differ concerning the food, that it comes first, and concerning the Habdalah, that it is at the end.

"'Concerning what did they differ?"

"'Concerning the light and the spices.'

"For the House of Shammai say, 'The light and afterward the spices.'

"And the House of Hillel say, 'The spices and afterward the light.'"

And R. Yohanan said, "The people were accustomed to act in accord with the House of Hillel *as presented by* R. Judah."

The House of Shammai say, "Who created ..."

Raba said, *"Concerning the word 'bara' [created] everyone agrees that 'bara' implies [the past tense]. They differ concerning 'boré' [creates]. The House of Shammai reckon that 'boré' means, 'Who will create in the future.' And the House of Hillel reckon that 'boré' also means what was created [in the past]."*

R. Joseph objected, "'Who forms light and creates darkness' [Isaiah 45:7], 'Creates mountains and forms the wind' [Amos 4:13], "Who creates the heavens and spreads them out'" [Isaiah 42:5].

"But," R. Joseph said, *"Concerning 'bara' and 'boré' everyone agrees that [the words] refer to the past. They differ as to whether one should say 'light' or 'lights.'*

"The House of Shammai reckon there is one light in the fire.

"And the House of Hillel reckon that there are many lights in the fire."

We have a Tannaitic teaching along the same lines:

The House of Hillel said to the House of Shammai, "There are many illuminations in the light."

II
THE LIGHT AND THE SPICES

A blessing is not said ...

Certainly, [in the case of] *the light* [of idolators, one should not say a blessing] *because it did not rest on the Sabbath. But what is the reason that for spices* [one may not say the blessing]?

R. Judah said in the name of Rab, *"We here deal with a banquet held by idolators,* because the run-of-the-mill banquet held by idolators is for the sake of idolatry."

But since it has been taught at the end of the clause, "Or over the light or spices of idolatry," *we must infer that the beginning of the clause does not deal with idolatry.*

R. Hanina from Sura said, "What is the reason is what it explains, namely, what is the reason that they do not bless the light or spices of idolators? Because the run-of-the-mill banquet held by idolators is for the sake of idolatry."

Our rabbis have taught:

One may bless a light which has rested on the Sabbath, but one may not bless a light which has not rested on the Sabbath.

And what is the meaning of "which has not rested on the Sabbath"?

[53a] *Shall we say* it has not rested on the Sabbath on account of the work [which has been done with it, including] even work which is permitted?

And has it not been taught: They do bless the light [kindled on the Sabbath for] a woman in confinement or a sick person.

R. Nahman bar Isaac said, *"What is the meaning of* 'which enjoyed Sabbath-rest'? Which enjoyed Sabbath-rest on account of work, the doing of which is a transgression [on the Sabbath]."

We have learned likewise in a baraita:

They may bless a lamp which has been burning throughout the day to the conclusion of the Sabbath.

Our rabbis have taught:

They bless [a light] kindled by a gentile from an Israelite, or by an Israelite from a gentile, but they do not bless [a light] kindled by a gentile from a gentile.

What is the reason one does not do so [from a light kindled by] a gentile from a gentile?

Because it did not enjoy Sabbath-rest.

If so, lo, [a light kindled by] *an Israelite from a gentile also has not enjoyed Sabbath-rest.*

And if you say this prohibited [light] *has vanished, and the one* [in hand] *is another and was born in the hand of the Israelite,* [how will you deal] *with this teaching?*

He who brings out a flame to the public way [on the Sabbath] is liable [for violating the Sabbath rule against carrying from private to public property].

Now why should he be liable? What he raised up he did not put down, and what he put down he did not raise up.

But [we must conclude] *that the prohibited* [flame], *is present, but when he blesses, it is over the additional* [flame], *which is permitted, that he blesses.*

If so, a gentile['s flame kindled] *from a gentile*['s flame] *also* [should be permitted].

That is true, but [it is prohibited by] *decree, on account of the original gentile and the original flame* [of light kindled on the Sabbath by the gentile].

Our rabbis have taught:

[If] one was walking outside of the village and saw a light, if the majority [of the inhabitants of the village] are gentiles, he does not bless it. If the majority are Israelites, he blesses it.

Lo, the statement is self-contradictory. You have said, "If the majority are gentiles, he does not bless it." *Then if they were evenly divided, he may bless it.*

But then it teaches, "If the majority are Israelites, he may bless." *Then if they are evenly divided, he may not bless it.*

Strictly speaking, even if they are evenly divided, he may bless. But since in the opening clause [the language is], "The majority are gentiles," *in the concluding clause,* [the same language is used:] "A majority are Israelites."

Our rabbis have taught:

[If] a man was walking outside of a village and saw a child with a torch in his hand, he makes inquiries about him. If he is an Israelite, he may bless [the light]. If he is a gentile, he may not bless.

Why do we speak of a child? Even an adult also [would be subject to the same rule].

Rab Judah said in the name of Rab, "In this case we are dealing with [a time] *near sunset. As to a gentile, it will be perfectly clear that he certainly is a gentile* [for an Israelite would not use the light immediately after sunset]. *If it is a child, I might say it is an Israelite child who happened to take up* [the torch]."

Our rabbis have taught:

[If] one was walking outside of a village and saw a light, if it was as thick as the opening of a furnace, he may bless it, and if not, he may not bless it.

One Tanna [authority] [says], "They may bless the light of a furnace," *and another Tanna* [says], "They may not bless it."

There is no difficulty. The first speaks at the beginning [of the fire], *the other at the end.*

One authority says, "They may bless the light of an oven or a stove, " *and another authority says,* "They may not bless it."

There is no problem. The former speaks of the beginning, the latter of the end.

One authority says, "They may bless the light of the synagogue and the schoolhouse," *and another authority says,* "They may not bless it."

There is no problem. The former speaks [of a case in which] an important man *is present, the latter* [of a case in which] an important man *is not present.*

And if you want, I shall explain both teachings as applying to a case in which an important man *is present. There still is not difficulty. The former* [teaching speaks of a case in which] *there is a beadle* [who eats in the synagogue], *the latter in which there is none.*

And if you want, I shall explain both teachings as applying to a case in which a beadle is present. There still is no difficulty. The former teaching [speaks of a case in which] *there is moonlight, the latter in which there is no moonlight.*

Our rabbis have taught:

[If] they were sitting in the schoolhouse, and light was brought before them—

The House of Shammai say, "Each one blesses for himself."

And the House of Hillel say, "One blesses for all of them, as it is said, 'In the multitude of people is the King's glory'" [Proverbs 14:28].

Certainly [we can understand the position of the House of Hillel because] *the House of Hillel explain their reason.*

But what is the reason of the House of Shammai?

They reckon [it as they do] *on account of* [avoiding] *interruption in* [Torah study] *in the schoolhouse.*

We have a further Tannaitic tradition to the same effect:

The members of the house of Rabban Gamaliel did not say [the blessing] "Good health" [after a sneeze] in the schoolhouse on account of the interruption [of study] in the schoolhouse.

They say a blessing neither on the light nor on the spices of the dead ...

What is the reason?

The light is made for the honor [of the deceased], *the spices to remove the bad smell.*

Rab Judah in the name of Rab said, ["Light made for] whoever [is of such importance that] they take out [a light] before him both by day and by night is not blessed. [and light made for] whoever [is not important, so that] they take out [a light] before him only by night, is blessed."

R. Huna said, "They do not bless spices of the privy and oil made to remove the grease."

Does this saying imply that wherever [spice] *is not used for smell, they do not bless over it? It may be objected:*

He who enters the stall of a spice dealer and smells the odor, even though he sat there all day long, blesses only one time. He who enters and goes out repeatedly blesses each time.

And lo, here is a case in which it is not used for the scent, and still he blesses.

Yes, but it also is used for the odor — so that people will smell and come and purchase it.

Our rabbis have taught:

If one is walking outside of a village and smelled a scent, if most of the inhabitants are idolators, he does not bless it. If most are Israelites, he blesses it.

R. Yosé says, "Even if most are Israelites, he *still* may not bless, because Israelite women use incense for witchcraft."

But do they "all" burn incense for witchcraft!

A small part is for witchcraft, and a small part is also for scenting garments, which yields a larger part not used for scent, and wherever the majority [of the incense] *is not used for scent, one does not bless it.*

R. Hiyya bar Abba said in the name of R. Yohanan, "He who walks on the eve of the Sabbath in Tiberias and at the end of the Sabbath in Sepphoris and smells an odor does not bless it, because it is presumed to have been made only to perfume garments."

Our rabbis taught: If one was walking in the gentiles' market and was pleased to scent the spices, he is a sinner.

III
USING THE LIGHT

[53b] They do not recite a blessing over the light until it has been used ...

Rab Judah said in the name of Rab, "Not that he has actually used it, but if anyone stood near enough so that he might use the light, even at some distance, [he may say the blessing]."

So too R. Ashi said, "We have learned this teaching even [concerning] those at some distance."

It was objected [on the basis of the following teaching]: If one had a light hidden in the folds of his cloak or in a lamp, or saw the flame but did not make use of its light, or made use of the light but did not [actually] see the flame, he may not say the blessing. [He may say the blessing only when] he [both] sees the flame and uses its light.

Certainly one finds cases in which one may use the light and not see the flame. *This may be when the light is in a corner.*

But where do you find a case in which one may see the flame and not make use of its light? *It is not when he is at a distance?*

No, it is when the flame keeps on flickering.

Our rabbis have taught:

They may say a blessing over glowing coals, but not over dying coals (*'omemot*).

What is meant by glowing coals?

R. Hisda said, "If one puts a chip into them and it kindles on its own, [these are] all [glowing coals]."

It was asked: Is the word 'omemot ['alef] *or* 'omemot ['ayin]?

Come and hear, for R. Hisda b. Abdimi said, "'The cedars in the garden of God could not darken [*'amamuhu*] it'" [Ezekiel 31:8].

And Raba said, "He must make actual use of it."

And how [near must one be]?

Ulla said, "So that he may make out the difference between an *issar* and a *pundion* [two small coins]."

Hezekiah said, "So that he may make out the difference between a *meluzma* [a weight] of Tiberias and one of Sepphoris."

Rab Judah would say the blessing [for the light of the] *house of Adda the waiter* [which as nearby].

Raba would say the blessing [for the light of the] *house of Guria bar Hama.*

Abbaye would say the blessing [for the light of the] *house of Bar Abbahu.*

R. Judah said in the name of Rab, "They do not go looking for the light in the way they go looking for [means to carry out other] commandments."

R. Zera said, "At the outset, I used to go looking [for light]. *Now that I have heard this teaching of R. Judah in the name of Rab, I too will not go searching, but if one comes my way, I shall say the blessing over it."*

IV
FORGETTING GRACE, AMEN.

He who ate [and did not say Grace] ...

R. Zebid, and some say R. Dimi bar Abba, said, "The dispute [between the Houses] applies to a case of forgetfulness, but in a case in which a person deliberately [omitted Grace], all agree that he should return to his place and say the blessing."

This is perfectly obvious. It is [explicitly] *taught,* "And he forgot."

What might you have said? That is the rule even where it was intentional, but the reason that the Tanna taught, "And he forgot," is to tell you how far the House of Shammai were willing to go [in requiring the man to go back to where he ate. They did so even if a man accidentally forgot.] *Thus we are taught* [the contrary. Even if one forgot, unintentionally, he must go back].

It was taught:

The House of Hillel said to the House of Shammai, "According to your opinion, someone who ate on the top of the Temple Mount and forgot and went down without saying Grace should go back to the top of the Mount and say the blessing."

The House of Shammai said to the House of Hillel, "According to your opinion, someone who forgot a purse on the top of the Temple Mount would not go back and retrieve it.

"For his own sake, he [assuredly] will go back. For the sake of Heaven [should he] not all the more so [go back]?"

There were these two disciples. One did it [forgot Grace] *accidentally, and, following the rule of the House of Shammai,* [went back to bless], *and found a purse of gold. And one did it deliberately* [omitted Grace], *and following the rule of the House of Hillel* [did not go back to say it], *and a lion ate him.*

Rabbah bar bar Hanna was traveling in a caravan. He ate and was sated but [forgot and] *did not say Grace.*

He said, "What shall I do? If I tell the men [of the caravan with me] *that I forgot to bless, they will say to me, 'Bless here. Wherever you say the blessing, you are saying the blessing to the Merciful* [God].' *It is better that I tell them I have forgotten a golden dove."*

So he said to them, "Wait for me, for I have forgotten a golden dove."

He went back and blessed and found a golden dove.

And why was a dove so important?

Because the community of Israel is compared to a dove, as it is written, "The wings of the dove are covered with silver, and her pinions with the shimmer of gold" [Psalm 68:14]. Just as the dove is saved only by her wings, so Israel is saved only by the commandments.

Until when can he say the Grace? Until the food is digested in his bowels
...

How long does it take to digest the food?

R. Yohanan said, "As long as one is no longer hungry."

Resh Laqish said, "As long as one [still] is thirsty on account of his meal."

R. Yemar bar Shelamia said to Mar Zutra — and some say, Rab Yemar bar Shizbi said to Mar Zutra — "Did Resh Laqish really say this? And did not R. Ammi say in the name of Resh Laqish, 'How long does it take to digest a meal? The time it takes to go four miles.'"

There is no problem: Here [we speak of] a big meal, there [we speak of] a small meal.

If wine came to them ...

This implies that in the case of an Israelite['s saying Grace], even though one has not heard the entire blessing, he responds *[Amen].*

But if he has not heard [the whole Grace], *how can he have performed his duty by doing so* [assuming he has eaten also? For he has to hear the entire Grace to carry out his obligation to say Grace.]

Hiyya bar Rab said, "[We speak of a case] in which he did not eat with them."

So too did R. Nahman say in the name of Rabbah bar Abbahu, "[We speak of a case] in which he did not eat with them."

Rab said to Hiyya his son, "My son, seize [the cup] *and bless."*

So did R. Huna say to Rabbah his son, "Seize and bless."

This implies that he who says the blessing is better than he who answers Amen. *But has it not been taught:*

R. Yosé says, "The one who answers *Amen* is greater than the one who says the blessing."

R. Nehorai said to him, "By heaven! It is so. You should know it, for behold, common soldiers go ahead and open the battle, but the heroes go in and win it."

It is a matter of dispute between Tannaim, as it has been taught:

Both the one who says the blessing and the one who answers *Amen* are implied [in the Scripture (Nehemiah 9:5)]. But the one who says the blessing is more quickly [answered] than he who answers *Amen.*

Samuel asked Rab, "Should one answer [Amen] after [the blessings of] children in the schoolhouse?"

He said to him, "They answer Amen after everyone except children in the schoolhouse, since they are [saying blessings solely] for the sake of learning."

And this applies when it is not the time for them to say the "Haftarah," *but in the time to say* "Haftarah," *they do respond [Amen].*

Our rabbis have taught:

"The absence of oil holds up the blessing [Grace]," the words of Rabbi Zilai.

R. Zivai says, "It does not hold it up."

R. Aha says, "[The absence of] good oil holds it up."

R. Zuhamai says, "Just as a dirty person *[mezuham]* is unfit for the Temple service, so dirty hands are unfit for the blessing."

R. Nahman Bar Isaac said, "I know neither Zilai nor Zivai nor Zuhamai. But I know a teaching which R. Judah said in the name of Rab, and some say it was taught as a 'baraita':

"'And be you holy' [Leviticus 20:7] — this refers to washing the hands before the meal.

"'And you shall be holy' — this refers to the washing after the meal.

"'For holy' — this refers to the oil.

"'Am I the Lord your God' — this refers to the blessing [Grace]."

This protracted survey of a single chapter of the halakhah as it is set forth by the Mishnah, the Tosefta, the Yerushalmi, and the Bavli, leaves no doubt that the Mishnah has set forth the main beams of the structure of the halakhah, the Tosefta has filled in the ceilings and floors, and the Yerushalmi and the Bavli then have furnished the structure. The Tosefta is subordinated to the Mishnah, and although without the Mishnah we should still know a fair part of the law, in the presence of the Mishnah, with its encompassing program, the Tosefta as a medium of halakhic discourse takes second place. I cannot point to a significant segment of the Tosefta that vastly enriches the discussion of the halakhah already commenced by the Mishnah. More to the point, I cannot identify a single passage of the Tosefta that takes logical priority over its counterpart in the Mishnah. Where we can identify the generative logic, which requires articulation and instantiation, that generative logic animates the Mishnah's statements, to which the Tosefta clearly takes a secondary and derivative position time and again. Houtman's reading of matters would not lead us to anticipate these results. Even though we can read the Tosefta as an autonomous document, for reasons abundantly spelled out in the formal relationships surveyed here, we should not do so. For if we were to do so, we should drastically misinterpret the character of the Tosefta.

3

The Tosefta in Halakhic Context:
Tractate Shebi'it

Now back to Houtman's representation of matters and why it has failed. How do I explain the remarkable failure brought about by Houtman's inattention? What I notice in her monograph is what happens when people do not really grasp the halakhah but work on halakhic documents anyhow. They remark on unremarkable things and miss the important issues altogether. The result is a vast collection of useless and meaningless information. What is crucial is whether we are able to assess the relationships between documents solely on the basis of formal traits, or whether we must pay close attention to the substantive characteristics of those documents: what they say and what they mean. I do not exaggerate the consequence of what Houtman did not notice. She made the choice of resorting to computer analysis of two rather modest pieces of writing, which means she supposed that all she had to do was classify data, not think about them. Houtman seems to imagine that by a computer analysis, which by definition ignores all considerations of the contents of the writings, she can solve any problems at all. She is wrong, and her results leave no doubt that she is wrong. Computer research has merit in collating variant readings and other mechanical tasks. Computers cannot assess on the basis of the classification of formal evidence the logical relationships of documents and their substantive contents.

These are matters of broader erudition and more mature judgment and reflection than Houtman seems to me to possess. She knows a little bit about two modest tractates. That explains why what she did not notice is that the Tosefta and the Mishnah make a great many substantive halakhic statements and set forth a halakhic topic through response to a system therewith that generates the details of the laws. Her computer work did not help her to identify what matters and what does not, with the result that she based her entire project on facts wildly irrelevant to her question concerning documentary autonomy. She shows that the documents are formally autonomous; each *can* be read in its own terms. She admits that is not wholly true for the Tosefta but it is entirely so for the Mishnah. I cannot point to a single scholar in the past hundred and fifty years who has reached any other conclusion.

That is why while my review in Chapter One points to a variety of serious flaws in her preparation and in her results, in the constructive essay that follows in this chapter and in Chapters Four and Five I focus on a single problem, one that I find so weighty as to demand an entire detailed demonstration of how I think the work has to be done, in contrast to how Houtman has done it. As is clear, the burden of my criticism is that Houtman has ignored the contents of the texts that she examines, providing a superficial reprise but no analytical inquiry. As a result, she makes claims as to the relationship of the Tosefta to the Mishnah that appeal solely to formalities, not to matters of substance at all. My response is to show through a systematic repertoire of the halakhic contents of the Mishnah, the Tosefta, the Yerushalmi, and the Bavli, that the Mishnah stands at the head of the halakhic process, not only in form but in logic and in generative problematic. Houtman claims that the Tosefta can be read as if we had no Mishnah, and the Mishnah as if we had no Tosefta. In some part she is right, in some part she is wrong. But her thesis everywhere is monumentally irrelevant to the problem of the relationship of the Mishnah and the Tosefta — it is simply silly and beside the point.

That is, because, as I shall show for one of the two tractates she treats, that *iqqar haser min hassefer:* she misses the very point of the relationship of the Mishnah and the Tosefta. Since both documents undertake a halakhic exercise in exegetics and in hermeneutics, the point of knowing the relationship between the two documents is to determine the relationship of the body of laws set forth by the one in comparison and contrast to the body of laws set forth by the other. What are the traits of the corpus of halakhah expounded by each compilation?

Simply stated, the halakhic exposition of the Mishnah ordinarily finds in a topic a particular point of special interest; sages come with a set of governing principles, which they wish to lay out through the medium of halakhic discourse. The Mishnah is where these governing principles are laid out and exposed in full clarity. The Tosefta takes over the results — the halakhah that has been laid out — and gives numerous instances of the same few principles, or finds secondary and derivative points of clarification to contribute. If we read the Tosefta without the Mishnah, we receive information out of context. Houtman did not notice that, because her computer program paid no attention to the substance of the halakhah, its logic and its problematic.

It is the fact that most, though not all, Mishnah-tractates work out the implications of a generative problematic deemed to inhere in a given topic, a set of problems or questions that sages designate as what matter in the exposition of that topic. And, for the tractates for which we may identify a generative problematic that animates the exposition of the topic, that problematic comes to full exposure in the Mishnah, always in the Mishnah, and only in the Mishnah. The Tosefta for the tractates I have examined simply amplifies what the Mishnah says, and, in its free-standing compositions never contributes a statement that embodies a generative problematic of any sort: information without analysis or the stimulus of analysis. Seeing everything but the main thing, Houtman knows nothing of all this, because her examination of the tractates Berakhot and Shebi'it does not extend to a penetrating account of what imparts to the law its dynamic. Tractate Berakhot would not have signaled to her that the law unfolds in response to a generative problematic, but as I show in Chapter Three, Shebi'it certainly does. That is what I mean when I say that she has paid attention to the form but not the substance of the document.

But that is for a good reason. Alas, in its entirety, her claim that we may read the Tosefta without the Mishnah by its nature requires us to pay no attention to the character of the halakhah that the Mishnah and the Tosefta set forth. When we do, as I show in here and in Chapters Four and Five for most tractates of the halakhah though not all, we may consistently characterize the halakhah of the Mishnah for the large-scale topics as primary and generative, and that of the Tosefta as secondary and derivative. She says that we may read the Mishnah without the Tosefta and the Tosefta without the Mishnah. Indeed so. But what is proved by pretending that we have no Mishnah when we do? So hers is not a comparison, so much as an evasion. And the fact is, we can understand the Mishnah without the Tosefta, meaning, we can identify the generative problematic that defines sages' exposition of a given topic, the problems they find worthy of close attention, the hermeneutics that defines their exegetical program. But we cannot understand the Tosefta without the Mishnah, meaning not make sense of its sentences but rather account for the character of its halakhah.

So while it is the fact that much of the Tosefta can be read on its own, not in relationship to the Mishnah, and all of the Mishnah can be read on its own, not in relationship to the Tosefta, it is also the fact that we do not have the occasion to read the one without the other. That is because we do have both, and gain nothing by pretending we do not. And when we read the two in relationship with one another, we deal with matters of substance, not form alone. And then we see, as I said, that the Mishnah is primary and generative, the Tosefta secondary and derivative.

How do I know and propose to show that fact? It is by laying out the halakhah of a given topic/tractate, first the Mishnah, then clearly differentiated by type face but in exact succession, the Tosefta, then the Yerushalmi, then the Bavli. When we follow the exposition of the halakhah in that way, we see, time and again, that the Mishnah is halakhically the starting point; it defines the principles that require exegesis and amplification. The Tosefta, as I said, never inaugurates an important halakhic initiative in the analysis of a topic. In the three tractates laid out in Chapters Three through Five, readers will test these allegations as to the character of the halakhic contribution of the Mishnah, the Tosefta, the Yerushalmi, and the Bavli. I cannot find a single point in these expositions of the halakhah at which a major analytical initiative occurs later than the Mishnah's statement of the halakhah, though the later documents enrich and amplify the exposition inaugurated by the Mishnah.

I did not undertake this research to demonstrate the logical priority of the Mishnah in the halakhic process — I should say, with little exaggeration, not only priority but *monopoly.* It was a conclusion I did not seek or ever anticipate. But it is one anyone can reach who lays out matters as I have done, that is, a halakhic disquisition as exposed by the documents, read continuously.[1] In any order, the same result will emerge, that is, if we read the Tosefta first, and then the Mishnah, we shall still understand what it is that sages want to expose in their presentation of a topic only when the Mishnah has signalled to us what precipitates attention and attracts concerned analysis.

II.   AN OUTLINE OF THE HALAKHAH OF SHEBI'IT

The key to the logical relationship between the Mishnah and the Tosefta, and among all four halakhic documents, lies in the identification of the generative problematic of the halakhic topic. After I display the halakhah start to finish, I undertake to identify the interiority of the halakhah, by which I mean, the issues or concerns or points of tension that told sages the kinds of information on a given halakhic topic that they ought to investigate. I specify what, if any, elements of a generative problematic I perceive in the halakhic topic at hand. I state in advance that, where I find that starting point in logic for a given halakhic exposition, it is the Mishnah that states what is fundamental; more to the point, I cannot identify a single important and generative conception that first surfaces in the Tosefta and not in the Mishnah. Since, as everyone without exception has known for hundreds of years, the Tosefta came to closure following the Mishnah,

---

[1] This work appears in the following: *The Halakhah of the Oral Torah: A Religious Commentary. Introduction. And* Volume I. *Between Israel and God.* Part One. *Thanksgiving: Tractate Berakhot. Enlandisement: Tractates Kilayim, Shebi'it, and 'Orlah.* Atlanta, 1997: Scholars Press for South Florida Studies in the History of Judaism; *The Halakhah of the Oral Torah: A Religious Commentary.* Volume II. *Within Israel's Social Order.* Part One. *Civil Society. Repairing Damage to, Preserving the Perfection of, the Social Order. Tractates Baba Qamma, Baba Mesia, and Baba Batra.* Atlanta, 1998: Scholars Press for South Florida Studies in the History of Judaism; and *The Halakhah of the Oral Torah: A Religious Commentary.* Volume III. *Inside the Walls of the Israelite Household.* Part One. *At the Meeting of Time and Space. Tractates Shabbat and Erubin.* Atlanta, 1999: Scholars Press for South Florida Studies in the History of Judaism.

there can be no reason to doubt that the Mishnah's formulation of the problematic of a topic indeed defined what the framers of compositions for the later document would explore and further articulate.

This outline identifies the major subunits of the topic of the tractate. It further exposes the way in which the topic is defined and articulated in detail in the four successive documents of the halakhah, **the Mishnah**, the Tosefta, *the Talmud of the Land of Israel,* and THE TALMUD OF BABYLONIA, as signified in the indicated type-faces. I cite from the last three-named documents only the important declarative statements of halakhah, bypassing the secondary clarifications of the Tosefta and the rich analytical discussion of the two Talmuds. In some small measure, I have reorganized the legal declarations to lay out the halakhah in a systematic and logical way, but, in the main, the framers of the Mishnah have already done the work for us, and, with all due respect to the later codifiers, for the theoretical purpose that animated their efforts, that work cannot logically be improved upon.

Tractate Shebi'it elaborates the Torah's commandment, at Lev. 25:1-8: "When you enter the land that I am giving you, the land shall observe a Sabbath of the Lord. Six years you may sow your field and six years you may prune your vineyard and bather in the yield. But in the seventh year the land shall have a Sabbath of complete rest, a Sabbath of the Lord; you shall not sow your field or prune your vineyard. You shall not reap the aftergrowth of your harvest or gather the grapes of your untrimmed vines; it shall ba a year of complete rest for the land. But you may eat whatever the land during its Sabbath will produce — you, your male and female slaves, the hired-hand and bound laborers who live with you, and your cattle and the beasts in your land may eat all its yield." A second, correlative commandment, at Dt. 15:1-3, is treated as well: "Every seventh year you shall practice remission of debts. This shall be the nature of the remission: every creditor shall remit the due that he claims from his neighbor; he shall not dun his neighbor or kinsman, for the remission proclaimed is of the Lord. You may dun the foreigner, but you must remit whatever is due you from your kinsmen."

Throughout I follow the doctoral dissertation, including the Mishnah- and Tosefta-translation, prepared in my seminar, of Louis E. Newman, *The Sanctity of the Seventh Year: A Study of Mishnah Tractate Shebiit* (Chico, 1983: Scholars Press for Brown Judaic Studies); and Alan J. Avery-Peck, *The Talmud of the Land of Israel. A Preliminary Translation and Explanation.* Volume 5. *Shebiit.* Jacob Neusner, General Editor (Chicago, 1991: The University of Chicago Press).

I. ACCORDING SABBATH-REST TO THE LAND: CEASING WORK

A. CEASING IN THE SIXTH YEAR WORK THAT BENEFITS THE CROP IN THE SEVENTH YEAR: ORCHARDS, GRAIN FIELDS

M. 1:1 [The restrictions of the Sabbatical Year begin to apply at the end of the sixth year.] Until what time do they

plough an orchard during the year preceding the Sabbatical year? As long as [the ploughing] continues to benefit the produce [of the Sixth Year.

M. 1:2 Defining an orchard: What is [considered] an orchard? Any [field in which there are at least] three trees within a seah space [within an area large enough to plant a seah of seed]. If [the trees] are capable of producing a loaf of pressed figs weighing sixty maneh according to the Italian [measurement], they plough the entire seah space for their [the trees'] benefit.

M. 1:3 The same law applies both to non-fruit-bearing trees [which do not yield edible produce] and fruit-bearing trees — they view them [in either case] as if they were fig trees. [They compare the size of these trees to that of fig trees].

M. 1:4 [If] one [of three trees planted in a seah space] yields a loaf of pressed figs [weighing sixty maneh according to the Italian measurement], but [the other] two do not [yield anything], or [if] two [of the trees] yield [the required amount] and [the other] one does not — they plough for [each of] them only according to their need.

M. 1:5 Three trees [in a seah space] belonging to three persons, lo, they [the trees] join together [to form a single orchard and [therefore] they [any of the three owners mentioned at A] plough the entire seah space for their [the trees'] benefit. [Farmers plough in this seah space only until they begin to harvest the fruit of the Sixth Year].

M. 1:6 [As regards] ten saplings which are spread out within a seah space — they plough the entire seah space for their [the saplings'] sake until the New Year [of the Sabbatical year]. [But as regards ten saplings which] were formed in a line or in a semicircle — they plough for them only according to their [the saplings'] need, [but they may not plough within the seah space as a whole].

M. 1:7 Saplings and gourds join together [to make up ten plants] within a seah space [which permit one to plough the entire area].

T. 1:3 Three chatemelons, three gourds, and four saplings [planted in a seah's-space] — lo, these join together [to make the requisite ten items which comprise a field of saplings, cf. M. Sheb. 1:7E]. and they plow the entire seah's-space for their sake.

M. 2:1 Until what time do they plough in a field of grain during the year preceding the Sabbatical year? Until the moisture [in the ground] is gone.

B.   CEASING IN THE SIXTH YEAR WORK THAT BENEFITS THE CROP IN THE SEVENTH YEAR, AND LABOR THAT IS PERMITTED BECAUSE THE EFFECTS OF THE WORK PERTAIN MAINLY TO THE SIXTH YEAR

M. 2:2 They (1) manure and (2) hoe in fields of chatemelons and in fields of gourds until the New Year [of the Sabbatical year]. And likewise: they [manure and hoe] in an irrigated field [until the New Year of the Sabbatical year].

T. 1:4 In the year preceding the seventh year, they sell manure to, and bring it out [to the field of,] an Israelite who is suspected [of transgressing the laws] of the seventh year [but they do not do these things after the beginning of the seventh year], and [with regard to selling manure to, or bringing it out to the field of,] a gentile or a Samaritan — even during the seventh year, it is permitted. Until what time is it permitted to manure [a field]? As long as one is permitted to plow, one is permitted to manure [cf. M. Sheb. 2:2].

M. 2:3 They (7) remove stones [from a field] until the New Year [of the Sabbatical year]. They (8) trim [trees], (9) clip [branches] and (10) prune [trees] until the New Year [of the Sabbatical year].

M. 2:4 They (11) smear the saplings [with oil], (12) wrap them, (13) cover them with ash, (14) make shelters for them, and (15) water them until the New Year [of the Sabbatical year].

M. 2:5 They (16) pour oil on unripe figs and (17) pierce them until the New Year [of the Sabbatical year]. Unripe figs [which began growing] during the year preceding the Sabbatical year and which continued growing [and ultimately became ripe] during the Sabbatical year itself, [and unripe figs which began growing] during the Sabbatical year and which continued growing [and ultimately became ripe] during the year following the Sabbatical, they neither pour oil [on them] nor pierce them [during the Sabbatical year].

M. 2:6 They do not (1) plant [a tree], (2) sink [a vine into the ground so that it emerges nearby as an independent plant], or (3) graft [one branch to another] in the year preceding the Sabbatical within thirty days of the New Year. And if one (1) planted [a tree], (2) sank [a vine into the ground], or (3) grafted [one branch to another within thirty days of the beginning of the Sabbatical year], one must uproot [that which was planted, sunk or grafted so as to rectify the transgression which he has committed].

T. 1:12 They plow an irrigated field and irrigate them [i.e., the plants growing in an irrigated field] thirty days before the New Year [of the seventh year; cf. M. Sheb. 2:6].

T. 2:1 They sprinkle a field during the year preceding the seventh year, so that vegetables will sprout during the seventh year. Moreover, even during the seventh year they sprinkle [that is, a field], so that vegetables will sprout in the year following the seventh year. Onions which began growing during the year preceding the seventh year and continued growing during the seventh year — they sprinkle on them, so that they will be easy to uproot.

T. 2:3 One who (1) plants [a tree], (2) sinks [a vine into the ground], or (3) grafts [one branch to another] thirty days before the New Year [of the seventh year, so that the new plants take root before the beginning of that year; cf. M. Sheb. 2:6] — [the plant] is considered to be one year old [at the New Year], and one is permitted to allow it to grow during the seventh year. Less than this [i.e., if the tree is planted or the vine sunk into the ground, or the branch grafted, within the thirty days of the New Year], it is not considered to be one year old [at the New Year]. and one is forbidden to allow it to grow during the seventh year, [rather, one must uproot it].

C. CEASING IN THE SIXTH YEAR WORK THAT BENEFITS THE CROP IN THE SEVENTH YEAR: INTERSTITIAL CASES. THE RESULT OF THE WORK MAY PERTAIN TO EITHER THE SIXTH OR THE SEVENTH YEAR

M. 2:7 (1) Rice, (2) durra, (3) millet, and (4) sesame, that took root before New Year [of any year in the Sabbatical cycle], are tithed according to the [rules which apply to produce of the] previous year, [the year in which they were planted]. And [if they were planted in the Sixth Year], they are permitted during the Sabbatical year [they are not subject to the restrictions which apply to Seventh Year produce].

Y. 2:7 I. Rice, durra, [millet, and sesame: As for fruit: [in determining susceptibility to tithing] they follow [the rules for the year in which it reaches] a third [of its growth]. And as for rice: they follow [the year in which it] takes root. And as for vegetables: they are subject to tithes [according to the rules for the year] in which they are picked.

M. 2:9 (1) Shallots and (2) Egyptian beans, which one deprived of water thirty days before the New Year, are tithed according to the [rule which applies to produce of the] pre-

vious year, and [if they were planted in the Sixth Year] they are permitted during the Sabbatical year. And if not [if one did water them within thirty days of the New Year of the Sabbatical year], they are forbidden during the Sabbatical year, and [if they were planted in any year of the Sabbatical cycle other than the sixth], they are tithed according to the [rule which applies to produce of the] following year.

M. 2:10 Gourds which one stored [in a field] in order [later to break them open and gather their] seeds — if they became hard [and dry] before the New Year of the Sabbatical year [so that the seeds are ready to be gathered], and [if the gourds themselves] became unfit for human food, one is permitted to tend them [to gather the seeds during the Sabbatical year. [Since these seeds are produce of the Sixth Year, the farmer may gather them even after the Sixth Year begins.] And if not [if the gourds do not harden before the New Year so that the seeds are not yet ready to be gathered], one is forbidden during the Sabbatical year to tend them, [Since these vegetables, including the seeds, are produce of the Sabbatical year, the farmer may not gather their seeds for his own use].

II. THE PROHIBITION AGAINST WORKING THE LAND IN THE SEVENTH YEAR

A. APPEARING TO CULTIVATE THE LAND

M. 3:1 <u>Appearing to fertilize the field:</u> From what time [during the Sabbatical year] may they bring manure [out into the field to pile it up] in dung heaps [for use during the following year]?

M. 3:2 [In accordance with the rule of M. 3:1], how much manure [may they bring out to a field during the Sabbatical year]? Up to three dung heaps per seah space [of land], each [dung heap containing no less than] ten baskets [of dung], each [basket containing a volume of no less than] a letek [fifteen seahs o dung].

T. 2:14 [During the seventh year] they do not gather grass [which grows] on dung, but they may gather [loose pieces of] straw [which have been mixed in with the dung]. They add straw or stubble [to a dung-heap] in order to increase [its volume]. They add water [to a dung heap] so that it will decompose. And they hoe it so that it will swell.

M. 3:3 A man constructs within his field three dung heaps per seah space. A person places [all] the manure in his possession in [one large] pile. If one had a small amount [of manure already piled up in the field], he continually adds to it.

M. 3:4 One who uses his field as a fold [for his flock during the Sabbatical year, which results in the spreading of manure throughout his field], makes an enclosure [that measures] two seah spaces in area. [After the enclosed area is filled with manure he creates a second fold adjacent to the first]. He removes three sides [of the original enclosure] and leaves the middle side [that is, the fourth side, in place. With the other three sides of the original fold he creates a second enclosure of the same size]. The result is that he creates a fold [with an area] of four seah spaces.

T. 2:19 They construct enclosures using all [types of materials]: with (1) stones, (2) matting, (3) straw, (4) reeds, and (5) stalks. They may make an enclosure] even with three ropes, one on top of another, so long as there is not a space of [more than] three handbreadths between [one] rope and another, [that is, sufficient space] for a young goat to enter.

M. 3:5 <u>Appearing to clear the field for planting:</u> [During the Sabbatical year] a man may not begin to open a stone quarry in his field, unless it contains [enough stones to construct] three piles [of hewn blocks], each [pile] three [cubits long] by three [cubits wide] by three [cubits] high, [so that] their measure is [equivalent to] twenty-seven stones. [That is, each pile must contain no less than twenty-seven blocks, each measuring one cubic cubit].

T. 3:3 A rock which lies [partly buried] in the ground, and [its] tip juts out from it [that is, through the earth] — if it [viz., the tip, considered by itself] is of this measure [viz, one cubic cubit; cf. M. Sheb. 3:5], it is permitted [to remove it]. And if not [that is, if the tip of the rock is smaller than this], it is forbidden [to remove it].

M. 3:6 A wall consisting of ten stones, [each of which is so large that it is capable of being] carried [only] by two men — lo, these [stones] may be removed [from the field] during the Sabbatical year. [The preceding rule applies only if] the height of the wall is ten handbreadths. Less than this [if the wall is less than ten handbreadths high], he may chisel [stones from the wall], but he may level it [the wall] only until it is

one handbreadth from ground level. [This indicates that he
is not clearing the land for cultivation].

**M. 3:7 Stones which a plough moved, or that were covered
[in the ground] and were uncovered [after ploughing] — if
there are among them two [stones so large that they are] capable of being carried [only] by two men, lo, these [stones]
may be removed. One who removed stones from his field,
removes the topmost ones and leaves those which are touching the ground. And so [in the case] of a heap of pebbles or
a pile of stones — one removes the topmost ones and leaves
those which are touching the ground. If there is beneath
them [the pebbles or stones] a [large] rock or straw, lo, these
[stones also] may be removed.**

T. 3 :7 Olives [that began growing during the] year preceding
the seventh year and continued [growing] during the seventh
year — they (1) clear stones [from the ground surrounding the
olive tree], (2) remove thorns, (3) fill holes that are under them
[the trees' roots] with dirt, (4) dig trenches from one [tree] to
another. Moreover, even in the case of olives [that began growing during the] seventh year and continued [growing] during the
year following the seventh year, it is permitted to do so [that is,
to perform the types of labor listed at B] [cf. M. Sheb. 3:7-9].

T. 3:21 [As regards] unripe figs [which began growing] during
the year preceding the seventh year they do not boil them during
the seventh year. [As regards] late-ripening figs [which are hard
and remain inedible unless they are processed] — it is permitted
to boil them during the seventh year, because that is the normal
manner [of preparing them]. [As regards] hearts of palms [so E]
and the inflorescence of palms — it is permitted [to boil them
during the seventh year] [cf. M. Sheb. 3:7-9].

**M. 3:8 During the year preceding the Sabbatical, after the
rains have ceased, they do not build terraces on the sides of
ravines, for this prepares them [the ravines, for cultivation]
during the Sabbatical year. However, during the Sabbatical
year, after the rains have ceased, one may build them [ter-
races,] for this prepares them [the ravines, for cultivation]
during the year following the Sabbatical [when cultivation
is permitted.] And [when building a retaining wall for a ter-
race,] he may not support [it] with dirt, [for this appears to
be an act of cultivation,] but he constructs a rough embank-
ment [using only stones.]**

M. 3:9 Stones [so large that they can be carried only on one's] shoulder may come from anywhere [for use in construction. That is, large stones, which clearly will be used for construction, may be brought from a distance.] But a contractor brings [stones of any size] from anywhere. [Since he obviously has been hired to build a wall, he is not suspected of preparing this land for cultivation.]

M. 3:10 One who builds a fence [during the Sabbatical year] between his [property] and the public domain is permitted to dig down to rock level [in order to supply a firm foundation for the fence.]

B.   ACTUALLY CULTIVATING THE LAND

M. 4:1 Forbidden labor: At first they held: [During the Sabbatical year] a man may gather wood, stones and grass from his own [field] in the same manner as he gathers [them] from [the field] of his neighbor [in other years of the Sabbatical cycle,] [that is to say, he gathers only] the large ones. [Since he leaves the small pieces of wood, he does not appear to be clearing the field for cultivation.] When transgressors [of the laws of the Sabbatical year, by using the fallow year to prepare the fields for future cultivation] increased in number, they ordained that: one man should gather [stones] from the field of another and the other should gather [stones] from his [the first man's field,] [so long as they do] not [do so] as a [mutual] favor. And, needless to say, one may [not] stipulate [to provide] the other [with meals [as payment for his labor]. [That unreciprocated act of grace was permitted.]

M. 4:2 A field which was cleared of thorns [during the Sabbatical year] may be sown during the year following the Sabbatical, [for removing thorns is not a forbidden act of cultivation]. [But a field] which was improved [by the removal of stones during the Sabbatical year] or which was used as a fold [for animals during the Sabbatical year, such that it was fertilized by the dung which the animals left on the ground, cf. M. 3:4,] may not be sown during the year following the Sabbatical, [since these activities have effect of preparing land for cultivation].

M. 4:3 During the Sabbatical year they lease from gentiles fields newly ploughed [during that year for the purpose of cultivating them during the following year,] but [they do] not [lease] from an Israelite [a field which he has ploughed during the Sabbatical year, in violation of the law]. And they

assist gentiles [in their agricultural labors] during the Sabbatical year, but [they do] not [assist] an Israelite [who engages in such activities during the Sabbatical year, in violation of the law].

T. 3:11 [During the year following the seventh year] they do not lease a newly-plowed field from an Israelite suspected of transgressing the laws of the seventh year [cf. M. Sheb. 4:3; since this field clearly was plowed during the seventh year, one may not lease it and so become an accessory to this transgression]. But [during the year following the seventh year] they may buy from him [that is, one who violates the law] a field sown [during that year, since in this case it is unclear whether the field was plowed during the seventh year, in violation of the law, or during the eighth year, when plowing is permitted].

M. 4:4 <u>Permitted labor</u> **[even with a secondary affect upon the crop of the seventh year]: [As regards] one who thins out olive trees [during the Sabbatical year] — he may uproot [them].**

M. 4:5 One who truncates an olive tree [during the Sabbatical year in order to obtain wood for building] should not cover [the stump] with dirt. [This would be the usual way of sealing the surface of the stump when one cuts back a tree in order to cultivate new branches]. Rather, he covers it with stones or with stubble. [Since this is not the usual manner of sealing the tree's stump, it indicates that the farmer is not engaged in cultivating the growth of new branches]. One who cuts down the branches of a sycamore [during the Sabbatical year in order to obtain wood for building] should not cover [the stump] with dirt. Rather, he covers it with stones or with stubble.

T. 3:17 [As regards] one who uproots a carob tree or the trunk of a sycamore [and thereby overturns a large amount of soil] — [if he does so] for the [use of the] wood, it is permitted. But [if he does so] for the [benefit of the] field, it is forbidden.

M. 4:6 One who (1) snips off the ends of vines or (2) cuts reeds [during the Sabbatical year, in order to obtain materials for weaving or for use as wood] should cut at a distance of one handbreadth [from the usual place where vines or reeds are trimmed for the purpose of cultivating them. In this way one avoids the appearance of engaging in forbidden labor]. A tree that was split — they may bind it during the Sabbatical year, not so that [the tree] will grow together [again] but

so that [the tree] will not [split] further.

M. 4:7 After what time during the Sabbatical year do they eat the fruit of trees? As regards] (1) unripe figs: From the time they begin to glisten [when they begin to mature and become shiny,] [the farmer] may eat them with his bread in the field. [And when] they have ripened, he may gather them into his house [and eat them]. And similarly, [when the figs have ripened] during the other years of the Sabbatical cycle, they become liable to tithes.

4:8 [As regards] (2) unripe grapes: From the time they produce liquid [the farmer] may eat them with his bread in the field. [And when] they have ripened he may gather them into his house [and eat them]. And similarly, [when the grapes have ripened] during the other years of the Sabbatical cycle, they become liable to tithes.

4:9 [As regards] (3) olives: From the time a seah [of olives] will yield a quarter [-log of oil,] [the farmer] may crush them and eat [them] in the field. [When a seah of olives] yields a half [-log of oil,] he may press [them] and anoint [himself] in the field. When a seah of olives] yields a third [of its total eventual output, a full log of oil,] he may press [the olives] in the field and gather them into his house. **4:10 After what time during the Sabbatical year may they not cut down a [fruit-bearing] tree** [because, in doing so, one will prevent the fruit already growing on the branch from ripening]? (1) [Regarding] carob trees — after their [branches] begin to droop, (2) [regarding] vines — after they produce berries, (3) [regarding] olive trees — after they blossom, (4) and [regarding] all other trees after they produce [fruit]. And [concerning] every [fruit-bearing] tree — after it has reached the point [when, in other years of the Sabbatical cycle, its fruit is subject to the separation] of tithes, it [again] is permitted to cut it down, [for, at this point, the fruit is ready for harvest and so will not be lost when the tree is cut down].

III. SPECIAL PROBLEMS IN CONNECTION WITH THE PROHIBITION AGAINST WORKING THE LAND IN THE SEVENTH YEAR

A. PRODUCE THAT GROWS OVER TWO OR MORE CALENDAR YEARS

M. 5:1 White figs [which appear in the Seventh Year — the restrictions of the] Sabbatical year [apply] to them [in the]

second [year of the new Sabbatical cycle, rather than in the Seventh Year itself], because they [white figs] take three years to ripen fully.

M. 5:2 One who stores arum [for preservation, by covering it with earth] during the Sabbatical year — [must] not [store] less than four qab, [he must not make a pile less] than a handbreadth high, and [he must put no less than] a handbreadth of dirt above it, and he [must] store it in a thoroughfare.

M. 5:3 An arum [tuber which began to grow before the Sabbatical year and remained in the ground] after the Sabbatical year had passed — if the poor gathered its leaves [which sprouted during the Sabbatical year], it is well. But if [the poor did] not [gather its leaves during the Sabbatical year], the poor have no account with him [the owner of the arum owes them nothing after the Sabbatical year is over].

M. 5:4 Arum [which finished growing] during the Sixth Year [but] which remained

[in the ground] in the Seventh Year, and also summer onions, and madder from good soil — [farmers] uproot them with metal spades.

M. 5:5 When is one permitted to buy arum in the year following the Sabbatical [in the first year of the new Sabbatical cycle]? When the new [produce] becomes plentiful in the marketplace.

B. ASSISTING OTHERS IN HARVESTING CROPS OR PROCESSING PRODUCE DURING THE SEVENTH YEAR

M. 5:6 These are tools which the artisan is not permitted to sell during the Sabbatical year: (1) a plough and all its accessories, (2) a yoke, (3) a pitchfork, (4) and a mattock. But he [the artisan] may sell: (1) a hand sickle, (2) a reaping sickle, (3) and a wagon and all its accessories. This is the general rule: As regards any [tool] the use of which [during the Sabbatical year] is limited to a transgression — it is forbidden [to sell such a tool during the Sabbatical year]. [But as for any tool which may be used both for work which is] forbidden and [for work which is] permitted [according to the laws of the Sabbatical year it is permissible [to sell such a tool during the Sabbatical year].

M. 5:7 [During the Sabbatical year] a potter may sell [to one person] five oil containers and fifteen wine containers, because it is usual [for a person] to process [this amount of oil and wine during the Sabbatical year] from ownerless produce. And if [during the Sabbatical year a person] processed more than this amount [of oil and wine], it is permissible [to sell that person more than this number of containers].

M. 5:8 [During the Sabbatical year] a person may sell to another fruit [the seeds of which are used for planting], even in the planting season. And a person may lend to another a seah measure [used for measuring harvested produce], even if one knows that he has a threshing floor. And a person may make change for another, even if one knows that he employs laborers. And regarding all of these [transactions — if he] explicitly [stated his intention to violate the law], they are forbidden.

M. 5:9 A woman may lend to a neighbor who is suspected [of not observing the law] of the Sabbatical year: (1) a sifter, (2) a sieve, (3) a millstone, (4) or an oven. But she may not sift or grind [flour] with her [since the grain was gathered in violation of the law].

C. APPLICATION OF THE SEVENTH YEAR LAWS TO DIVERSE REGIONS WITHIN THE LAND OF ISRAEL

M. 6:1 Three provinces [are delineated] with regard to [the laws of] the Sabbatical year: (1) All [of the land] which was occupied by those who returned from Babylonia [the area] from the Land of Israel [in the south] to Kezib [in the north]: [That which grows of itself in this region] may not be eaten, and [the land of this region] may not be cultivated. (2) All [of the land] which was occupied by those who came out of Egypt, [the area] from Kezib to the river [the brook of Egypt, in the south], and [from Kezib] to Amana [in the north]: [That which grows of itself in these regions] may be eaten, but [the land of these regions] may not be cultivated. (3) [The land] from the river and from Amana and beyond: [That which grows of itself in these regions] may be eaten, and [the land of these regions] may be cultivated.

M. 6:2 In Syria, [farmers] may do work [during the Sabbatical year] involving harvested [produce], but [they] may not [do work] involving unharvested [produce]. (1) They may thresh, winnow, trample, and bind [wheat into sheaves], but they may not reap, harvest grapes, or cut olives.

T. 4:11 For any agricultural activity of a type which is permitted [during the seventh year] in the Land of Israel — they may do such work] in Syria [M. Sheb. 6:2D-E]. In Syria, one may not engage in [an agricultural activity] involving produce which is unharvested. But [if gentiles] uproot [produce, the Israelites] may bind [the produce] for them, provided that it is not he [the Israelite] who reaps [the produce] and they [the gentiles] who bind it for him. [If gentiles] harvest grapes, [an Israelite] may trample [the grapes] for them. [If gentiles] harvest olives, [an Israelite] may pack [the olives into the press for processing] for them [E-H = T. Hal. 2:5 L-M]. Under what circumstances does the ruling [that one may not process produce harvested by an Israelite] apply? When one takes produce out of [an Israelite's] home [for he assumes that the Israelite harvested this produce]. Or, when one's friend [who is an Israelite] sent him produce [for he assumes that his friend harvested the produce]. But [as for] one who buys [produce] in the marketplace — lo, this one the gentile seller] harvests [the produce] with his own hand, so [the buyer] need not scruple [viz, he may process this produce since he assumes that the gentile who sold it to him likewise harvested it].

M. 6:3 Onions [which remained in the ground from the Sixth Year into the Sabbatical year] upon which rain has fallen and which sprouted leaves — if the leaves are dark [green, in the Sabbatical year], they [the onions] are forbidden [they may not be harvested and eaten] [but] if [the leaves] become light green, lo, these [onions] are permitted.

M. 6:4 When in the year following the Sabbatical is one permitted to buy a [given type of] vegetable? Once [the new crop of] that same vegetable has become ripe. Once the [portion of the crop which] ripens early [in the year, in one location] has become ripe, the [portion of the crop which] ripens later [in the year, in another location] is [also] permitted [may be purchased].

T. 4:14 One may eat a vegetable which ripens late on [the basis of the permitted status of] that which ripens early. [One may eat a vegetable] from far away on [the basis of the permitted status of] that which grows nearby. [When produce] is permitted in one place, [that produce] is permitted in all places. [As regards] garlic, arum and onions — once the dry produce is permitted, the fresh produce is permitted. [However, once the] fresh produce [is permitted], the dry produce is not permitted, until the time of threshing.

Y. 6:4 I At first [they ruled that it is] forbidden [to purchase] vegetables [immediately after the Sabbatical year] in the bor-

der areas of the land of Israel. This was forbidden since the produce may have grown during the Sabbatical year in the land of Israel itself. They ordained that it would be permitted [to purchase] vegetables [immediately after the Sabbatical year] in the border areas of the land of Israel. Even so, it remained forbidden [during the Sabbatical year] to import vegetables from outside of the land [of Israel] to the land [of Israel]. They ordained that it would be permitted to import vegetables from outside of the land [of Israel] to the land [of Israel]. Even so, it remained forbidden to buy vegetables immediately at the end of the Sabbatical year.

M. 6:5 They may not export oil [in the status of heave offering which has become unclean and is fit] for burning, or produce of the Sabbatical year, from the Land of Israel to another country.

M. 6:6 They may not import heave offering from another country to the Land of Israel.

T. 4:18 [As regards] produce of the seventh year which comes from abroad into the Land [of Israel] — they may not sell it by volume or by weight or by number. Rather, it is [handled] like the produce of the Land [of Israel].

T. 4:19 [During the seventh year] one may import plants or *karmulin* [a kind of gourd the leaves of which are edible] from another country into the Land [of Israel], but not from another country into the Land [of Israel in order] to eat their leaves in the Land [of Israel]. One may not import grapes from another country into the Land [of Israel] and trample them in the Land [of Israel]. [And [one may] not [import] olives from another country into the Land [of Israel] and pack them in the Land [of Israel]. And [one may] not [import] stalks of flax from another country into the Land [of Israel] and soak them in the Land [of Israel]. But one may import dried figs and raisins and stalks of flax [which have been processed] from another country into the Land [of Israel], but not from another country into the Land [of Israel] in order to process them in the Land [of Israel].

IV. RESTRICTIONS ON THE USE OF PRODUCE THAT GROWS IN THE SEVENTH YEAR

A. SPECIES OF PRODUCE THAT ARE DEEMED SANCTIFIED, THEREFORE PROHIBITED FOR COMMON USE, DURING THE SEVENTH YEAR

M. 7:1 They stated an important general rule concerning [the laws of the Sabbatical year: All [produce] which is (1) fit for human consumption, animal consumption, or is a species [of plant used for] dyeing, (2) and which does not continue to grow in the ground [for longer than one season, i.e., plants which are not perennials] is subject to [the laws of] the Sabbatical year, and the money [received when the produce is sold] is subject to [the laws of] the Sabbatical year, [This produce also] is subject to removal [the produce must be removed from one's possession when similar produce is no longer available in the fields,] and the money [received when the produce is sold] is subject to removal. [This produce must be treated with the dignity owing to produce that has been consecrated, thus not weighed or measured like common commodities; and it must be used for food and not for some lesser purpose than nourishing man.]

T. 5:3 Pepperwort, 2) endive, 3) rose petals, and 4) oak-tree leaves, are subject to [the laws of] the seventh year, and the money received when the produce is sold is subject to [the laws of] the seventh year,and they are subject to removal, and the money [received when the produce is sold] is subject to removal [M. Sheb. 7:1C-F]. Lesbian-fig root, (2) rose root, and (3) oak-tree root, are not subject to [the laws of~ the seventh year, and the money [received when the produce is sold] is not subject to [the laws of] the seventh year, and they are exempt from removal, and the money [received when the produce is sold] is exempt from removal.

M. 7:2 And they stated yet another general rule [concerning the laws of the Sabbatical year]: All [produce] which is (1) fit for human consumption, animal consumption, or is a species [of plant used for] dyeing, (2) and which continues to grow in the ground [from one season to the next, i.e. , plants which are perennials] is subject to [the laws of] the Sabbatical year, and the money [received when the produce is sold] is subject to [the laws of] the Sabbatical year. [But such produce] is exempt from removal, and the money [received from the sale of the produce] is exempt from removal.

M. 7:3 The husk and blossom of pomegranates, walnut shells, and fruit kernels are subject to [the laws of] the Sabbatical year, and the money [received from the sale of this produce] is subject to [the laws of] the Sabbatical year. The dyer may dye [with produce of the Sabbatical year only] for himself, but [the dyer] may not dye for a fee, For they may not do

business with: (1) produce of the Sabbatical year, (2) firstfruits, (3) heave offering, 4) carrion, (5) meat from an animal which has not been properly slaughtered (6) animals the eating of which is forbidden, or (7) creeping things. And one may not buy vegetables which grow wild and sell [them] in the market. But [if] one gathers [vegetables], his son may sell [them] for him. [If] one buys [produce] for his own use, and left [some of the produce unused], it is permissible to sell [the produce which remained].

M. 7:4 One who buys a firstling [which is blemished and so, unfit for consumption by priests, cf. M. Bekhorot. 5:2] for his son's wedding feast or for a festival, and does not need it, is permitted to sell [the firstling]. Hunters of wild animals, fowl or fish who accidentally caught unclean animals [cf. Lev. ll:1ff..] are permitted to sell [such unclean animals].

M. 7:5 Branches of the sorb tree and of the carob tree are subject to [the laws of] the Sabbatical year and the money [received from the sale of this produce] is subject to [the laws of] the Sabbatical year. They are subject to removal and the money [received from the sale of this produce] is subject to removal. Branches of the terebinth, the pistachio tree and the white thorn are subject to [the laws of] the Sabbatical year and the money [received from the sale of such produce] is subject to [the laws of] the Sabbatical year.

T. 5:12 Olive leaves, leaves of reed, and carob leaves are exempt from removal, because they do not disappear from the field [even though they may fall off of the stem; cf. M. Sheb. 7:5K-L].

M. 7:6 Rose, henna, balsam, and lotus are subject to [the laws of] the Sabbatical year and the money [received from the sale of this produce] is subject to [the laws of] the Sabbatical year.

M. 7:7 A fresh rose [of the Sabbatical year] which has been preserved in old oil [of the Sixth Year] — one removes the rose [from the oil, and the oil is then exempt from removal]. But an old [rose, of the Sabbatical year which has been preserved] in new [oil, of the year following the Sabbatical] — [the oil] is subject to removal. Fresh carobs [of the Sabbatical year] which have been preserved in old wine [of the Sixth Year], and old [carobs of the Sabbatical year which have been preserved] in new [wine, of the year following the Sabbatical year] — [in both cases, the wine together with the carobs] are subject to removal. This is the general rule: [In the case of] any [produce which is subject to removal] which imparts its flavor [to produce with which it is mixed] — one must remove [the resulting mixture, even if it consists of]two separate species [only one of which is subject to removal]. But [if all produce is] of the same species [and only one is subject to removal], [one must remove the resulting mixture] however [small the amount of produce, i.e. , even if it is not enough to impart its flavor to the mixture as a whole]. [Produce of the] Sabbatical year renders forbidden [subject to the laws of the Sabbatical year] all other [permitted produce] of the same species [with which it has been mixed]. But [if the two lots of produce are] not of the same species, [only if the produce of the Sabbatical year] imparts its flavor [does it render the other produce forbidden].

B. RESTRICTIONS UPON USING SEVENTH YEAR PRODUCE

M. 8:1 An important general rule they stated concerning [produce of] the Sabbatical year: All [produce] which is designated particularly as food for human beings — they may not make of it [such produce] an emollient for human beings, and, it goes without saying, [they may not do so] for cattle. But any [type of produce] which is not exclusively food for human beings [which is generally eaten by animals] — they may make of it [such produce] an emollient for human beings, but [they may] not [do so] for cattle. And any [type of produce] which is neither exclusively food for human beings nor for cattle [which may be eaten by either] — [if the one who gathers it] intends [to use] it as food for human beings and as food for cattle, they impose upon it the stringencies [which apply to food for] human beings, and the stringencies [which apply to food for] cattle [one may not use such produce as an emollient either for human beings or for cattle]. [If the one who gathers such produce] intends [to use] it [only] for wood, lo, it [this produce is deemed to be] like wood.

T. 5:19 A. An oven that was fired with straw or with stubble of the seventh year must be cooled down [i.e., one may not cook with it]. They sell food for human beings and animal feed [in order] to buy [with the money received from the sale] food for human beings. But they may not sell animal feed [in order] to buy other animal feed. And it goes without saying that food for human beings [may not be sold in order] to buy animal feed.

T. 5:20 Produce of the seventh year [which is fit for human consumption] — they do not feed it to cattle, to wild animals, or to fowl. If an animal walked on its own under a fig tree and ate figs, or under a carob tree and ate carobs, they do not require him [i.e., the owner or the farmer] to chase the animal away, as it is written, "And your cattle and the beasts in your land may eat all its yield" (Lev. 25:7).

M. 8:2 [Produce of the] Sabbatical year is permitted for [purposes of] eating, drinking and anointing [as a salve]. [One may eat that which is customarily eaten, and one may anoint [with] that which is customarily [used] for anointing. One may not anoint [with] wine or vinegar, but one may anoint with oil. And such [is the law] with respect to heave offering and second tithe. [The ruling regarding produce of the] Sabbatical year is more lenient than [the ruling regarding] them [heave offering and second tithe], for [produce of the Sabbatical year] is permitted for [purposes of] kindling a lamp.

T. 6:7. One who ties up [in a bundle] spices [of the seventh year] and places them in a dish [which is cooking] — if they lose their flavor [in the mixture], they are permitted [i.e., exempt from the restrictions of the seventh year]. But if [they do] not [lose their flavor], they are forbidden, [i.e., subject to the restrictions of the law].

T. 6:12 A man may anoint himself with oil of the seventh year and [then] roll around on a new leather-spread and need not scruple [since, one produce of the seventh year has been used, it is no longer subject to the restrictions of the law].

M. 8:3 They may not sell produce of the Sabbatical year by volume, weight or quantity [number of pieces]. And [they may] not [sell] figs by number, and [they may] not [sell] vegetables by weight.

T. 6:17 And one may not fill a jug [with wine or oil of the seventh year] and sell it as is [for it appears that he is selling produce by a fixed measure], nor [fill] a basket [with produce of the seventh year] and sell it as is. Rather [one who wishes to sell produce of the seventh year] says [E lacks: to him; i.e., to the prospective buyer], "This jug I sell to you for a *dinar,*" or "This basket I sell to you for a *tressit.*"

T. 6:18 One may not fill a basket [with produce of the seventh year] and go and sell it in the marketplace [for he thereby sells a fixed quantity of produce]. Even in the other years of the Sabbatical cycle this is prohibited, for this is a method of deception [since the seller alone knows the quantity of produce in the basket].

M. 8:4 One who says to his worker, "Here is an issar for you and gather vegetables [of the Sabbatical year] for me today" — his payment is permitted. [If, however, he said], "For this [issar,] gather vegetables for me today" — his payment is forbidden [since the payment is specified as wages for services rendered].

T. 5:21 They feed boarders with produce of the seventh year, but they do not feed either a gentile or a hired [day-] laborer with produce of the seventh year. But if he was a worker hired for the week, the month, the year, or for seven years, or [if the employer] has obligated himself [to provide the laborer's board] — they feed him with produce of the seventh year [cf. M. Sheb. 8:4].

M. 8:5 They may not give [money received from the sale of produce of the Sabbatical year as payment of wages] to a well-digger, a bathhouse attendant, a barber or a sailor. But one may give [money received from the sale of this produce] to a well-digger [in exchange for water] to drink. [Since drawing water is not the well-digger's job, this is not a payment of wages.] And to any of those [persons one may give money received from the sale of this produce] as a free gift.

T. 6 :26 [As regards] ass-drivers, camel-drivers, and sailors, who performed their trade with produce of the seventh year [that is, who transported such produce] — their wages are [subject to the restrictions of] produce of the seventh year.

M. 8:6 Figs of the Sabbatical year — they may not harvest them with a fig knife, but one may harvest them with an ordinary knife. They may not trample grapes in a vat, but one may trample [them] in a trough. And they may not prepare olives in an olive press or with an olive crusher, but he may crush them and place [them] in a small press.

M. 8:7 They may not cook vegetables of the Sabbatical year in oil in the status of heave offering, so that one will not cause [the vegetables] to become invalid [so that the produce of the Sabbatical year will not be wasted in the event that the oil becomes unclean and must be burned].

M. 8:8 They may not buy slaves, real estate or an unclean animal with money [received from the sale of produce] of the Sabbatical year. But if one [used money received in this

way and] purchased [one of the things listed,] he must [purchase and] eat produce of equal value [to replace the produce of the Sabbatical year which he sold]. They may not buy (lit.: bring) bird offerings required of men who have suffered a flux, women who have suffered a flux, or women after childbirth with money [received from the sale of produce] of the Sabbatical year. But if one brought [such an offering], he must [purchase and] eat produce of equal value [to replace that which he sold]. They may not anoint [leather] garments with oil of the Sabbatical year. But if one anointed [a garment with such oil], he must [purchase and] eat produce of equal value [to replace that which he sold].

T. 7:1 They may not deconsecrate [coins in the status of second tithe [by exchanging it in Jerusalem] for produce of the seventh year [viz., one may not restrict the opportunities for consuming produce of the seventh year by subjecting it to the restrictions governing second tithe]. But if one deconsecrated [coins] in the status of second tithe in this manner], he must eat it, [i.e., the produce of the seventh year for which the coins were exchanged] in accordance with the restrictions [which apply] to both of them [i.e., both those restrictions which apply to produce in the status of second tithe and those which apply to produce of the seventh year]. [As regards] produce of the seventh year and produce in the status of second tithe which were mixed together — one must eat it [i.e., the mixture] in accordance with the restrictions which apply to both of them. [As regards] produce of the seventh year in exchange for which one purchased other [consecrated] foods — one must eat it [the other consecrated produce] in accordance with the restrictions [which apply] to both kinds of produce. [As regards] produce in the status of second tithe in exchange for which one purchased other [consecrated] foods — one must eat it [the other consecrated produce] in accordance with the restrictions [which apply] to both [kinds of produce].

M. 8:11 A bath which was heated by straw or stubble of the Sabbatical year — it is permissible to bathe in it.

M. 9:1 Rue, goose-foot, wild coriander, water parsley, and eruca of the field are exempt from [separation of] tithes and may be bought from anyone during the Sabbatical year, because produce of their type is not cultivated [but grows wild].

C. NOT HOARDING SEVENTH YEAR PRODUCE: THE LAW OF REMOVAL

9:2-3 Three regions [are delineated] with respect to [the laws of] removal: Judah, Transjordan, and Galilee. And each of these [is divided] into three regions. [The Galilee is divided into]: the upper Galilee, the lower Galilee and the valley. From Kfar Hananiah and northward, all [places] in which sycamores do not grow] are regarded as] upper Galilee. And from Kfar Hananiah and southward, all [places] in which sycamores do grow [are regarded as] lower Galilee. And why have they stated [that the three main areas are each divided into] three regions? That they may eat [produce of the Sabbatical year] in each region only until the last [produce] of that region is gone [without regard to whether or not such produce remains in the other regions]. [At that point people may not hoard the produce but must remove it from their homes, affording all Israelites equal access to the limited food supply (Avery-Peck, p. 305).]

M. 9:4 They may eat [produce of the Sabbatical year which they have gathered into their homes only] by virtue of the fact that ownerless produce [is available in the fields], but [they may] not [eat such produce] by virtue of the fact that [it is found] in protected [places, where it is inaccessible to the animals of the field].

T. 7:14 They may [continue to] eat figs [of the seventh year which they have brought into their homes] until the undeveloped figs disappear [from the fields of] Beth Oni [cf. M. Sheb. 9:4].

M. 9:6 One who gathers fresh herbs [of the Sabbatical year may eat that which he gathered] until the [ground] moisture (lit: "sweetness") dries up. One who gathers dried plants [of the Sabbatical year may eat that which he gathered] until the second rainfall. [One who gathers fresh] leaves of reeds or leaves of vines [during the Sabbatical year may eat that which he gathered] until they fall off their stems. And one who gathers dried [leaves of reeds or vines during the Sabbatical year may eat that which he gathered] until the second rainfall.

M. 9:7 And likewise [the time of the second rainfall is determinative in the following cases]: One who leases a house to his fellow, "Until the rains," — [The renter retains possession of the house] until the second rainfall. One who has vowed [not to] benefit from his fellow, "Until the rains," — [the vow remains in force] until the second rainfall. Until when may the poor enter the orchards [to glean the corner

**of the field]? Until the second rainfall. After what time may
they derive benefit from or burn straw and stubble [of the
Sabbatical year]? After the second rainfall.**

**M. 9:8 One who has [in his possession] produce of the Sab-
batical year when the time for removal [of that produce]
arrives, allots food [enough for] three meals for each [mem-
ber of his household and then removes any remaining pro-
duce].**

T. 8:1 A. In the past, agents of the court would sit near the gates
of the cities. [From] each person [who harvested produce of the
seventh year and] who carried it [to them, these agents] would
take it from him and return to that person [enough] food for
three meals [cf. M. Sheb. 9:8A-B], and the remainder they would
deposit in the city's storehouse. When the time for [harvesting]
figs arrived, the agents of the court would hire workers [to harvest them], harvest [the figs], press them into cakes of pressed
figs, place them in jars and deposit [these jars] in the city's
storehouse. When the time for [harvesting] grapes arrived, the
agents of the court would hire workers [to harvest them], harvest the grapes, press them in presses, place the wine in jars
and deposit [these jars] in the city's storehouse. When the time
for [harvesting] olives arrived, the agents of the court would
hire workers [to harvest them], harvest the olives, pack them in
a vat, place them in jars and deposit [these jars] in the city's
storehouse. And they would distribute [portions] of this [stored-
up produce] on the eve of the Sabbath [and] each person [would
receive an amount of produce] in accordance with [the size of
his household.

The law of removal, which prevents hoarding, is part of the larger account
of who may eat the produce of the ownerless fields that the Land comprises in
the Sabbatical year, and how people are to obtain food during the Sabbatical
year. The following passage of Sifra expands on the same theme:

Sifra CCXLVI:I.10. A. "[The Sabbath of the land shall provide food] for you":

B.   not for others.

11.   A.   "...food":

B.   not for presenting meal-offerings from that produce, nor for
presenting drink-offerings from it.

12.   A.   "...for yourself and for your male and female slaves":

B.   What is the point of Scripture here?

C.   Since it is said, "[For six years you shall sow your land and gather
in its yield, but the seventh year you shall let it rest and lie fallow,]

that the poor of your people may eat; and what they leave the wild beasts may eat. You shall do likewise with your vineyard and with your olive orchard]" (Ex. 23:10-11),

D. I might have supposed that produce of the seventh year may be eaten only by the poor alone.

E. How do I know that even the rich may eat it?

F. Scripture says, "for yourself and for your male and female slaves."

G. Lo, wealthy landowners are covered, bondmen and bondwomen are covered.

H. Then why is it written, "that the poor of your people may eat"?

I. "The poor, but not the rich, may consume the available crop after the removal of stored crops from the household," the words of R. Judah.

J. R. Yosé says, "All the same are the poor and the rich: all of them may consume the crop after the time for the removal of stored crops from the household has come."

What follows once more stresses that the food grown not through cultivate in the Sabbatical year must be treated as sanctified, in that it may not be wasted or used for any purpose other than nourishing life:

13. A. Another matter concerning the statement, "that the poor of your people may eat; [and what they leave the wild beasts may eat]":

B. What is suitable for human consumption is given to human beings.

C. What is suitable for animals is given to animals.

14. A. "...and for your hired servant and the sojourner":

B. from among gentiles.

15. A. "...who lives with you":

B. this serves to encompass guests.

16. A. "...for your cattle also and for the domesticated beasts":

B. What is the point of Scripture here [for the point can be made without specifying both categories of beasts]?

C. If a wild beast, which is not within your domain, lo, it may eat [produce of the seventh year],

D. a domesticated cattle, which is within your domain, surely should eat produce of the seventh year!

E. If that were the case, then I should say, let the farmer collect produce for his domesticated beast and let the beast consume that fodder without limit of time,

F. in which case how am I to carry out the requirement of removing stored produce of the seventh year along with the produce that serves for human consumption?

G. Then is the domesticated beast truly going to eat produce without limit [ignoring the limit imposed by the requirement of removal]?

H.   When Scripture says, therefore, "for your cattle also and for the domesticated beasts,"

I.   it draws an analogy between the domesticated beast and the wild beast, indicating,

J.   so long as a wild beast finds produce of a given sort growing wild in the field, a domesticated beast may eat produce of that same sort in the born. But when the produce of that sort has disappeared from the field, then the produce of the same species is no longer to be made available to the domesticated beast in the barn. [The law requires people to remove produce of the sabbatical year from their homes when edibles of the same species are no longer available for people to gather from the field; once all vegetables of a certain type have been gathered or have dried up, people may not longer retain in storage similar vegetables in their homes (Newman, *op. cit.*, p. 179). This same rule extends to fodder.]

20.   A.   "...for food":

B.   and not to use it for aromatic sprinkling,

C.   not to make ointment with it,

D.   not to make poultices with it,

E.   and not to make an emetic with it.

These points prove coherent with the exposition of the halakhah of Shebi'it set forth in the Mishnah and the continuator-documents.

V. REMISSION OF DEBTS BY THE ADVENT OF THE SEVENTH YEAR

A.   WHAT TYPES OF DEBTS ARE CANCELLED

M. 10:1 **The Sabbatical year cancels a loan [which is secured] by a bond and [a loan which is] not [secured] by a bond. A debt [owed to a] shopkeeper is not cancelled [by the Sabbatical year]. But if [the debt] was made into a loan, lo, this [loan] is cancelled [by the Sabbatical year]. The [unpaid] wage of a hired laborer is not cancelled [by the Sabbatical year]. But if [the amount of the wage] was made into a loan, lo, this [loan] is cancelled [by the Sabbatical year].**

T. 8:4 A.woman's marriage contract [which stipulates the amount of money which her husband owes her if he either divorces her or dies] — [if] she accepted partial payment [of this sum of money from her husband before the seventh year] and converted to a loan [to him the remaining amount], lo, the seventh year cancels [this loan]. [But if] she accepted partial payment and did not loan [the remaining amount to her husband, or if] she loaned [to her husband the full amount specified in her marriage document] and did not accept partial payment [of this sum], lo, the seventh year does not cancel [this loan].

M. 10:2 One who slaughters a heifer and divides it [among purchasers] on the New Year [of the year following the Sabbatical] — if the month was intercalated [if the last month of the Sabbatical year was given an extra day, so that the transaction occurred during the Sabbatical year], [the money owed to the butcher] is cancelled [by the Sabbatical year]. But if [the month was] not [intercalated], [the money owed to the slaughterer of the heifer] is not cancelled [because the slaughtering did not take place during the Sabbatical year].

B. THE PROSBUL

M. 10:3 [A loan against which] a Prosbul [has been written] is not cancelled [by the Sabbatical year].

M. 10:5 An antedated prosbul is valid, but a postdated [Prosbul] is invalid. Antedated bonds are invalid, but postdated bonds are valid. If one [person] borrows [money] from five [persons], they write a Prosbul for each [of the creditors individually]. [But if] five [persons] borrow [money] from one person, he writes only one Prosbul for all [of the debtors].

M. 10:6 They write a Prosbul only against real estate [in cases in which the debtor owns real estate] — If the [debtor] has none, he [the creditor] transfers [to the debtor] some [trivial] amount [of property] from his field [and then a Prosbul is written]. If [the debtor] had a field in the region [which he had already] used as security [against another loan], they write a Prosbul against [such property].

C. REPAYING DEBTS REMITTED BY THE ADVENT OF THE SEVENTH YEAR

M. 10:8 One who repays a debt [cancelled] by the Sabbatical year — [the creditor] must [nevertheless] say to him, "I cancel [the debt]." [If the debtor then] said to him, "Even so [I will repay it],"

M. 10:9 One who repays a debt [cancelled] by the Sabbatical year — the sages are pleased with him. One who borrows [money] from a convert whose children converted with him, need not repay [the debt] to his children. But if [the debtor] repaid [the children, for the debt owed to their father]— the sages are pleased with him.

The remission of debts is tied to the Land, but it is practiced outside of the Land as well. Here is how the matter is worked out in Sifré to Deuteronomy:

Sifré to Deuteronomy CXI:II **1.** A.   "[Every seventh year] you shall practice remission of debts":

B.   so long as you have a release of land, you have a remission of debts.

But the cycle is tied to the Land, the counting beginning, as we shall note presently, from the point at which Israel has taken up possession of the Land:

Sifré to Deuteronomy CXI:II **2.** A.   "...Every seventh year":

B.   Might one claim that there is a distinct cycle of seven years applicable to each individual person?

C.   You may reason to the contrary in the following manner:

D.   One is liable to observe seven years in the cycle of release, and one is liable to observe seven years in the matter of loans. Just as the seven years observed in the release of land involves seven years for the entire world, so the seven years in the matter of loans involves seven years for the entire world [and is not measured by the length of an individual loan].

E.   But you might take this route:

F.   A span of seven years covers the obligation of the Hebrew slave, and a span of seven years covers the obligation of a loan.

G.   Just as in the case of the Hebrew slave, there is a distinct cycle of seven years applicable to each individual person, so in the case of the loan, there is a distinct cycle of seven years applicable to each individual person.

H.   Let us then establish the appropriate analogy, comparing a matter that is not dependent on the jubilee year to another matter that is not dependent on the jubilee year, and let the matter of the Hebrew slave not apply, since it does depend on the jubilee year.

I.   Or take this route:

J.   We compare a matter which applies both in the land and abroad to another matter that applies in the land and abroad, but let the matter of the release of lands pertain, which applies only in the land.

K.   [To resolve this impasse,] Scripture states, "seven years," and repeats the same clause.

L.   This establishes grounds for an analogy. Just as "seven years" states with reference to the release of real estate involves seven years for everyone, so "seven years" stated with reference to the release of loans involves seven years for everyone.

III.   ANALYSIS: THE PROBLEMATICS OF THE TOPIC, SHEBI'IT

The Torah represents God as the sole master of creation, the Sabbath as testimony to God's pleasure with, and therefore sanctification of, creation. Tractate

Shebi'it sets forth the law that in relationship to the Land of Israel embodies that conviction. The law systematically works through Scripture's rules, treating [1] the prohibition of farming the land during the seventh year; [2] the use of the produce in the seventh year solely for eating, and [3] the remission of debts. During the Sabbatical year, Israel relinquishes its ownership of the Land of Israel. At that time Israelites in farming may do nothing that in secular years effects the assertion of ownership over the land (Avery-Peck, p. 2). Just as one may not utilize land he does not own, in the Sabbatical year, the farmer gives up ownership of the land that he does own.

So much for the topic. What defines the particular problems that attract sages attention? The problematic of the tractate is the interplay between the Land of Israel, the People of Israel dwelling on the Land of Israel, and God's Sabbath, and what imparts energy to the analysis of the law is the particular role accorded to man's — Israelite man's — intentionality and attitude. These form the variable, to be shown able to determine what is, or is not, permitted in the holy time of the seventh year. Specifically, the focus of the law of Shebi'it as set forth in the Mishnah centers upon the role of the human will in bringing about the reordering of the world (of which we shall hear more in the next section). By laying emphasis upon the power of the human will, sages express the conviction that the Israelite has the power by an act of will to restore creation to its perfection. That is why the details of the law time and again spin out the implications of the conviction at hand, that all things depend upon man's intentionality in a given action or man's likely perception of an action. I state very simply that section ii demonstrates the logical priority of the Mishnah's component of the halakhah. That is because the entire problematics of the halakhah is set forth in the Mishnah, none of it first surfacing in the Tosefta. That is why, while we can read the Tosefta as a free-standing document, when we do so we err.

In setting forth the focus and critical tension of the halakhah, Newman states, "The cornerstone of the Mishnah's theory of the Sabbatical year is that ordinary Israelites, through their actions and perceptions, play a role in determining how the agricultural restrictions of the Sabbatical year apply...they have the power within specified limits to decide when, how, and where the laws of the Sabbatical year take effect" (Newman, p. 17). Newman amplifies in the following way (Newman, p. 19):

> The sanctity of the seventh year depends in the last analysis upon the actions and will of the people of Israel They are the instruments of sanctification. The Israelite farmer when he cultivates his field during the sixth year helps to determine when the restrictions of the seventh year first take effect. The perceptions of Israelites when they see others who appear to be violating the law play a role in defining what, in fact, is permitted behavior. Finally, Israelites, merely by dwelling in their Land, increase its holiness...The Mishnah affirms that what Israelites do to their land is decisive, the way in which they perceive the world is definitive. The message of tractate Shebiit

then is that the sanctity of the seventh year is activated and regulated by the thoughts and deeds of the community of Israel.

Developing the same point, Avery-Peck (pp. 4-5) states the matter in this language:

The authorities of Mishnah Shebiit question the role of human intention and perception in defining what labor is forbidden or permitted under the Sabbatical law. The tractate answers this question along lines familiar from the legal ideology expressed throughout Mishnaic law. [They] insist that observance of the Sabbatical restrictions does not simply require cessation during the Sabbatical year of all field labors that promote the growth of crops. While they recognize that what is permitted or forbidden must be judged on the basis of its effect upon the crops, their understanding is significantly colored by two caveats, first, that this judgment applies no matter when the labor is performed, and, second, that in judging the labor's permissibility, we must examine the intentions of the individual who performs it. In light of these premises, tractate Shebiit pointedly expresses the idea that ordinary Israelites play a central role in determining how, when, and where the agricultural restrictions apply. Israelites determine how these restrictions apply insofar as the Mishnah views an action to be permitted so long as the individual who performs it does not intend to break the rules of the seventh year. For example, during the Sabbatical year an individual may gather stones from a field or trim trees, even though these labors comprise acts of cultivation. This is the case so long as the person does not intend to cultivate the land but only wants to gather material for building. Israelites determine when the Sabbatical restrictions apply...In the Mishnah's view, the Sabbatical restrictions operate as a response to Israelites' actions in tilling and planting the soil. They are not confined to the divinely ordained seven year cycle described by Scripture. And Israelites determine where the Sabbatical restrictions apply insofar as...these restrictions apply to varying degrees in different areas of the land of Israel, depending upon the length of time that Israelites have dwelled in the particular area. ...The Mishnah develops Scripture's rules on the basis of the rabbis' unique theory of the centrality of the Israelites' intentions and desires in defining what does or does not conform to God's will...they do so by focusing upon the power of individual Israelites. They thus recognize no order in the world other than that imposed by Israelites who, through their own intentions and perceptions, give meaning to their activities in planting, tilling, and harvesting produce on the land of Israel. In the Mishnaic authors' view, there is no absolute right or wrong, holy or profane. The character of an individual's actions is determined...on the basis of his particular intentions and perspectives.

Both concur, then, that the legal problems to be resolved derive from the uncertainties involved in assessing where, when, and why man's will intervenes in the realization of the Written Torah's laws of the Sabbatical year.

Our rapid review of the state of the halakhah in the formative age impresses us with the urgency of the issues as sages define them. The topic therefore appears fully exposed, the requisite laws entirely laid out — in the Mishnah, there alone. Everything else is a matter of detail. The success of the founders of the Mishnah in persuading us that their program takes up the self-evidently paramount issues of the law should not be missed. That is why we may ask, what other questions might have been addressed? Were we dealing with aggadic expositions of the theme, rather than halakhic ones, the answer is clear. The results of *The Theology of the Oral Torah*[2] leave little doubt that one critical issue deemed to inhere in the topic of the Sabbatical year ought to compare the Land of Israel in the seventh year to the Garden of Eden before the fall; another would take up how the Sabbatical year compares to the World to come, within the restorationist theology at hand. But the metaphor of Eden, and the theology of restoration of Israel to the Land in consequence, so far as I can see in no way influence the questions that are raised in the halakhic exposition.

To imagine a halakhic problematics other than the one before us with its stress on the variable introduced by man's perceptions nonetheless is simple. Let us dismiss the notion that, within broad limits, human attitudes govern. Then, losing a large portion of the tractate, we find left a perfectly plausible model, which is Mishnah-tractate Shebi'it Chapter Ten, that is to say, an account of factual clarification, a merely-informative, standard legal exposition. For example: what sort of loans qualify for remission, what not? Here the problems concern secondary and tertiary questions of an interstitial character. Provoked by the primary categories that are introduced, e.g., debt, they are such as these:What constitutes a loan and what a debt of a secured character? What about debts imposed by Heaven, e.g., the marriage settlement, and the diverse conditions pertaining thereto? In other words, once we remove the variable of the human attitude, a quite different set of questions, provoked by other considerations altogether, arises. That fact makes all the more striking the paramount position accorded to the chosen problematics: the role and power of man's attitude and intention and perception. Sages can have, and in some measure did, define as their task the solution to a different set of problems from the ones that the halakhah has chosen to address.

How, in concrete terms, do we locate the legal expressions of the problematics at hand? When we consider the rules for the sixth year, we find close attention to work that, performed prior to the Sabbatical year, is intended to benefit the crops in the Sabbatical year itself. Since, manifestly, the action itself, viewed in isolation from its effects, does not take place in, and therefore has no bearing upon, the Sabbatical year, the priority of the farmer's intentionality in assessing his action becomes blatant. Through their own actions, manifestly

---

[2] *The Theology of the Oral Torah. Revealing the Justice of God.* Kingston and Montreal, 1998: McGill-Queens University Press.

intended to affect the crop in the Sabbatical year itself, Israelite farmers inaugurate the prohibitions of the Sabbatical year. The rules for working the land during the Sabbatical year make the further point that, so long as the farmer intends to carry out a permitted purpose, his labor is permitted, even though his labor has the secondary effect of cultivating the land (Avery-Peck, p. 8). The intention of the farmer has to be signaled, so that he does not appear to plan to violate the prohibitions of the Seventh year. When farmers remove stones from their fields to build with them, they may look as though they are clearing the land, and that appearance of violating the law must be avoided; they may stockpile manure but must not appear to fertilize the field. How people see the action dictates whether or not it may be done (Newman, p. 18). The importance of the union of the Israelite with the Land of Israel, a further point of continuing interest, comes to expression in the law that the Sabbatical year applies in varying degrees, depending upon how long Israelites have dwelled in a particular area (Avery-Peck, p. 9).

The rules on using the produce of the Sabbatical year likewise respond to the perceptions of Israelites and their intention with respect to food. Specifically, foods are subject to, or exempt from Sabbatical year prohibitions in accord with Israelites' view of the food as edible or inedible. A further point of some interest is that produce that ordinarily is used exclusively for food for human beings must serve that purpose and no other in the Sabbatical year; nothing may be treated in a wasteful manner. The food may also not be treated in a secular way, but, just as Holy Things and gifts to the priests may not be weighed out as in the market, e.g., sold by volume, weight, or fixed quantity, so produce of the Sabbatical year must be treated in the same way, that is, disposed of not in a calculated pattern. In all, as Avery-Peck concludes, "Through their actions and intentions, ordinary Israelites determine what conforms to or breaks the law of the Sabbatical year."

It suffices to state that the problematics of the halakhah emerges wholly in the formulation of the Mishnah, and not a single component makes its initial appearance in the Tosefta. To read the Tosefta out of phase with the Mishnah is indeed quite feasible, as Houtman alleges. But it is to miss the point of the halakhah — and to misconstrue the character of the Tosefta. Here is my answer to Houtman: it is what she did not notice.

So much for the tractate she treats that does take shape around a generative problematics. What about others of the same classification? Does the Mishnah's statement of the law take logical priority in those tractates as well? To answer that question we turn to two large and important corpora of halakhah, Baba Qamma and Shabbat.

4

The Tosefta in Halakhic Context: Tractate Baba Qamma

I. AN OUTLINE OF THE HALAKHAH OF BABA QAMMA

The goal of the system of civil law is the recovery of the just order that characterized Israel upon entry into the Land. The law aims at the preservation of the established wholeness, balance, proportion, and stability of the social economy realized at that moment. This idea is powerfully expressed in the organization of the three tractates that comprise the civil law, which treat first abnormal and then normal transactions. The framers deal with damages done by chattels and by human beings, thefts and other sorts of malfeasance against the persons and the property of others. The civil law in both aspects pays closest attention to how the property and person of the injured party so far as possible are restored to their prior condition, that is, the state of normality disrupted by the damage done to property or injury done to a person. So attention to torts focuses upon penalties paid by the malefactor to the victim, rather than upon penalties inflicted by the court on the malefactor for what he has done.

When speaking of damages, the halakhah, initially stated by the Mishnah in the terms of injury and misappropriation, takes as its principal concern the restoration of the fortune of victims of assault or robbery. In its account of damages inflicted by chattel and persons, the native category defined by tractate Baba Qamma incorporates facts supplied by Scripture but frames the topic in its own way. That way makes itself manifest only when we consider the three Babas together as a single coherent statement, an approach postponed until Chapter Three. To state the character of the halakhah of the Oral Torah in the present category, it suffices simply to note that what Scripture presents episodically, the halakhah portrays systematically.

I. DAMAGE BY CHATTELS

A. THE FUNDAMENTAL RULES OF ASSESSING DAMAGES WHEN THE CAUSE IS ONE'S PROPERTY, ANIMATE OR INANIMATE

M. 1:1 [There are] four generative causes of damages: (1) ox [Ex. 21:35-36], (2) pit [Ex. 21:33], (3) crop-destroying beast [Ex. 22:4], and (4) conflagration [Ex. 22:5]. What they have in common is that they customarily do damage and taking care of them is your responsibility. And when one [of them] has caused damage, the [owner] of that which causes the damage is liable to pay compensation for damage out of the best of his land [Ex. 22:4].

M. 1:1 IV.2/5B: FOR WHAT DEFINITIVE PURPOSE DID SCRIPTURE FIND IT NECESSARY TO MAKE EXPLICIT REFERENCE TO EACH SUCH CLASSIFICATION? [1] HORN: TO MAKE THE DISTINCTION BETWEEN THE BEAST DEEMED HARMLESS AND THAT ONE THAT IS AN ATTESTED DANGER. [2] TOOTH AND FOOT: TO EXEMPT THE OWNER FROM DAMAGE THAT WAS DONE WITHIN THESE CLASSIFICATIONS IN PUBLIC DOMAIN. [3] PIT: TO EXEMPT THE OWNER FROM DAMAGE DONE TO INANIMATE OBJECTS; [4] MAN: TO IMPOSE UPON HIM THE FOUR ADDITIONAL CLASSIFICATIONS OF COMPENSATION TO BE PAID FOR DAMAGE DONE BY A HUMAN BEING TO ANOTHER HUMAN BEING. [5] FIRE: TO MAKE ONE IMMUNE FOR DAMAGE DONE TO OBJECTS THAT WERE HIDDEN AWAY [AND NOT KNOWN BY THE PERSON WHO KINDLED THE FIRE] BY A FIRE ONE HAS KINDLED.

T. 6:29 A strict rule applies to an ox which does not apply to a pit, and a strict rule applies to a pit which does not apply to an ox. For [the owner of] an ox is liable to pay ransom and liable for the thirty *selas* to be paid in the case of killing a slave. And when [the ox's] court-process has been completed, it is prohibited for the owner to gain benefit from it. And it is assumed usually to walk along and to do damage which is not the case with a pit. A more strict aspect of the pit is that the pit is always deemed to be an attested danger, which is not the case with an ox.

T. 6:30 A more strict rule applies to an ox which does not apply to fire and a strict rule applies to fire which does not apply to an ox. For [the owner of] an ox is liable to pay ransom and liable for the thirty *selas* to be paid in the case of killing a slave. And when [the ox's] court-process has been completed, it is prohibited for the owner to gain benefit from it. And if one has handed it over [to the guardianship of] a deaf-mute, idiot, or minor, he remains liable, which is not the case with fire A more strict aspect of fire is that fire is always deemed to be an attested danger, which is not the case with an ox.

T. 6:31 A strict rule applies to a pit which does not apply to fire, and to fire which does not apply to a pit. For in the case of a pit, [if] one has handed it over [to the guardianship] of a deaf-mute, idiot, or minor, he remains liable, which is not the case with fire. A more strict aspect of fire is that fire is assumed to go along and to do damage."

M. 1:2 In the case of anything of which I am liable to take care, I am deemed to render possible whatever damage it may do. [If] l am deemed to have rendered possible part of the damage it may do, I am liable for compensation as if [I have] made possible all of the damage it may do. (1) Property which is not subject to the law of Sacrilege, (2) property belonging to members of the covenant [Israelites], (3) property that is held in ownership, and that is located in any place other than in the domain which is in the ownership of the one who has caused the damage, or in the domain which is shared by the one who suffers injury and the one who causes injury — when one has caused damage [under any of the aforelisted circumstances] [the owner of] that one which has caused the damage is liable to pay compensation for damage out of the best of his land

B. 1:2 I:1/9B: IN THE CASE OF ANYTHING OF WHICH I AM LIABLE TO TAKE CARE, I AM DEEMED TO RENDER POSSIBLE WHATEVER DAMAGE IT MAY DO. HOW SO? IN THE CASE OF AN OX OR A PIT THAT ONE HAS HANDED OVER TO A DEAF-MUTE, AN INSANE PERSON, OR A MINOR, WHICH DID DAMAGE, ONE IS LIABLE TO PAY COMPENSATION, WHICH IS NOT THE CASE WITH FIRE.

M. 1:2 II.1/10A: [IF] I AM DEEMED TO HAVE RENDERED POSSIBLE PART OF THE DAMAGE IT MAY DO, I AM LIABLE FOR COMPENSATION AS IF [I HAVE] MADE POSSIBLE ALL OF THE DAMAGE IT MAY DO: HOW SO? HE WHO DIGS A PIT NINE CUBITS DEEP, AND SOMEONE ELSE COMES ALONG AND FINISHES IT TO TEN — THE LATTER IS LIABLE [HAVING COMPLETED THE PIT SO THAT IT CAN KILL SOMEONE].

M. 1:3 Assessment [of the compensation for an injury to be paid] is in terms of ready cash [but is paid in kind — that is,] in what is worth money, before a court, on the basis of evidence given by witnesses who are freemen and members of the covenant. Women fall into the category of [parties to suits concerning] damages. And the one who suffers damages

and the one who causes damages [may share] in the compensation.

M. 1:4 1:4 [There are] five [deemed] harmless, and five [deemed] attested dangers. A domesticated beast is not regarded as an attested danger in regard to butting, (2) pushing, (3) biting, (4) lying down, or (5) kicking. (1) A tooth is deemed an attested danger in regard to eating what is suitable for [eating]. (2) The leg is deemed an attested danger in regard to breaking something as it walks along. (3) And an ox which is an attested danger [so far as goring is concerned]; (4) and an ox which causes damage in the domain of the one who is injured; and (5) man. If that which is deemed harmless [causes damage], [the owner] pays half of the value of the damage which has been caused, [with liability limited to the value of the] carcass [of the beast which has caused the damage]. But [if that which is] an attested danger [causes damage], [the owner] pays the whole of the value of the damage which has been caused from the best property [he may own, and his liability is by no means limited to the value of the animal which has done the damage].

B. 1:4A-J I.1/16A: [THERE ARE] FIVE [DEEMED] HARMLESS, BUT IF THEY ARE SUBJECTED TO A WARNING, THEN ALL FIVE OF THEM ARE THEN CLASSIFIED AS ATTESTED DANGERS. AND THE TOOTH AND FOOT ARE HELD TO BE ATTESTED DANGERS TO BEGIN WITH. AND THIS IS THE WAY IN WHICH THE OX IS AN ATTESTED DANGER. THERE ARE, MOREOVER, OTHER CLASSIFICATIONS OF THOSE THAT ARE ATTESTED DANGER IN THE SAME CATEGORY AS THESE: (1) A WOLF, (2) LION, (3) BEAR, (4) LEOPARD, (5) PANTHER, AND (6) A SERPENT — LO, THESE ARE ATTESTED DANGERS.

M. 2:1 A beast is an attested danger to go along in the normal way and to break [something]. [But if] it was kicking, or if pebbles were scattered from under its feet and it [thereby] broke utensils — [the owner] pays half of the value of the damages [caused by his ox]. [If] it stepped on a utensil and broke it, and [the utensil] fell on another utensil and broke it, for the first [the owner] pays the full value of the damage. But for the second he pays half of the value of the damage. Fowl are an attested danger to go along in the normal way and to break [something].

T. 2:1 Fowl which were scratching at dough or at pieces of fruit, or which pecked — [the owner] pays half-damages. [If] they scratched dirt onto dough or onto pieces of fruit, [the owner] pays full damages. [If] they were pecking at the rope of a well-bucket, and [in consequence it was weakened and] fell and broke, [the owner] pays full damages. [If] it fell and broke and furthermore broke another utensil [alongside], for the first, [the owner] pays full damages, and for the second, [he pays] half-damages. Fowl which went down into a vegetable patch and broke the young shoots and chopped off the leaves [of the plants] — [the owner] pays full damages.

M. 2:2 An ox is an attested danger to eat fruit and vegetables. [If, however,] it ate [a piece of] clothing or utensils, [the owner] pays half of the value of the damage it has caused. Under what circumstances? [When this takes place] in the domain of the injured party. But [if it takes place] in the public domain, he is exempt. But if it [the ox] derived benefit [from damage done in public domain], [the owner] pays for the value of what [his ox] has enjoyed. How does he pay for the benefit of what [his ox] has enjoyed? [If] it ate something in the midst of the marketplace, he pays for the value of what it has enjoyed. [If it ate] from the sides of the marketplace, he pays for the value of the damage that [the ox] has caused. [If he ate] from [what is located at] the doorway of a store, the owner pays for the value of what it has enjoyed. [If it ate] from [what is located] inside the store, the owner pays for the value of the damages that it has caused.

T. 1:6 A beast which on its own entered private domain and did damage with its foreleg, hind-leg, or horn, with the yoke which is on it, the saddlebag which is on it, the pack which is on its back, or with the wagon which it is pulling — [the owner] pays the full value of the damage which has been done. He who causes damage in neutral domain [neither public nor private] pays the full value of the damage which has been done.

T. 1:7 A beast which was going along in its usual way in public domain and fell into a garden and derived benefit [by eating the vegetables there] pays for the value of the benefit it has derived [If it has eaten things growing] on the sides of the road or located in a store, it pays the value of the damage which it has caused How [do we assess damages in a case in which] it pays the value of what it has eaten? They make an estimate of how much a man is willing to pay to feed his beast in the amount of what it has eaten, in food he does not regularly feed to the beast. Therefore if it ate grain which is suitable [for feeding] to it, lo, this one is exempt. [If it] chewed and ate, one pays the value of the damage which it has caused.

T. 1:8 A beast which ate food which is not suitable for it, or drank liquid which is not suitable for it , and so too, a wild beast which ate food which is not suitable for it, [which] tore [meat] off of a beast and ate the flesh — an ass which ate lupines — a cow which ate barley — a pig which ate pieces of meat — a dog which licked up oil — [the owners of these animals] pay the full value of the damages [their beasts have caused].

M. 2:3 The dog or the goat which jumped from the top of the roof and broke utensils — [the owner] pays the full value of the damage [they have caused], because they are attested dangers. The dog which took a cake [to which a cinder adhered] and went to standing grain, ate the cake, and set the stack on fire — for the cake the owner pays full damages, but for the standing grain he pays only for half of the damages [his dog has caused].

T. 2:1 A dog or a goat which fell and did damage — lo [their owners] are exempt. [But if] they jumped down and did damage, lo, [their owners] are liable [M. B.Q. 2:3A]. But a man who jumped, whether from above or from below, and did damage, lo, this one is liable. [If] he fell onto his fellow and did damage — [if] the one below [did damage] to the one above, the one above is liable. [If] the one above [did damage] to the one below, the one below is exempt from liability. If he said to him, "Catch me!" then both of them are responsible for the safety of one another [and share liability for damages].

B. 2:3 I.2/21B: A DOG OR A GOAT THAT JUMPED — IF IT WAS FROM BELOW TO ABOVE, THE OWNER IS EXEMPT. IF IT WAS FROM ABOVE TO BELOW, THE OWNER IS LIABLE. [IN THE FORMER CASE, THIS WOULD BE UNUSUAL, AND THE OWNER DOES NOT HAVE TO PAY FULL DAMAGES, BUT ONLY HALF-DAMAGES IN THE CLASSIFICATION OF HORN.] IN THE CASE OF MEN OR CHICKENS, WHETHER THEY JUMPED FROM BELOW TO ABOVE OR ABOVE TO BELOW, THEY ARE LIABLE [SINCE MEN AND CHICKENS JUMP A LOT].

M. 2:4 How does he pay for the benefit of what [his ox] has enjoyed? [If] it ate something in the midst of the marketplace, he pays for the value of what it has enjoyed. [If it ate] from the sides of the marketplace, he pays for the value of the damage that [the ox] has caused. [If he ate] from [what is located at] the doorway of a store, the owner pays for the

value of what it has enjoyed. [If it ate] from [what is located] inside the store, the owner pays for the value of the damages that it has caused.

M. 2:5 An ox which causes damage in the domain of the one who is injured — how so? [If] it gored, pushed, bit, lay down, or kicked, in the public domain, [the owner] pays half of the value of the damages [the ox has caused]. [If it did so] in the domain of the injured party, the owner pays half of the value.

M. 2:6 Man is perpetually an attested danger whether [what is done is done] inadvertently or deliberately, whether man is awake or asleep. [If] he blinded the eye of his fellow or broke his utensils, he pays the full value of the damage he has caused.

T. 2:2 Under no circumstances is an ox declared an attested danger unless people give testimony in the presence of the owner and of the court. [If] they gave testimony in the presence of the owner but not in the presence of the court, in the presence of the court but not in the presence of the owner, it is not declared to be an attested danger — unless people gave testimony in the presence of the owner and the court. If] they gave testimony before two on the first occasion, before two on the second occasion, and before two on the third occasion, lo, these constitute three distinct acts of giving testimony. But they constitute a single act of testimony so far as an accusation of conspiracy [against the witnesses] is concerned. [If] the first set [of witnesses] turns out to be perjured, lo, [the witnesses as to] the other two occasions [on which the ox allegedly misbehaved] are exempt from paying compensation [along with the conspirators].

2:3 [If] the second set of witnesses turns out to be perjured, lo, [the witnesses as to] one occasion [namely, the third] are exempt from paying compensation [along with the conspirators]. [If] all three sets of witnesses turn out to be perjured, [the owner] is exempt [from paying compensation for damage done by his ox], but they are liable.

B. 2:4 I.4/24A: AN OX IS NOT DECLARED AN ATTESTED DANGER UNLESS THE WITNESSES GIVE TESTIMONY AGAINST HIM BEFORE THE OWNER AND BEFORE THE COURT. IF THEY GAVE THEIR TESTIMONY AGAINST THE OX BEFORE THE COURT BUT NOT BEFORE THE OWNER, OR BEFORE THE OWNER BUT NOT BEFORE THE COURT, THE OX IS NOT DECLARED AN ATTESTED DANGER. THAT CAN ONLY BE IF THE TESTIMONY IS GIVEN AGAINST THE OX BOTH BEFORE THE COURT AND BEFORE THE OWNER. IF TESTIMONY

WAS GIVEN AGAINST IT BY TWO ON THE FIRST DAY, TWO ON THE SECOND, AND TWO ON THE THIRD, LO, THERE ARE IN HAND THREE ACTS OF TESTIMONY, WHICH FORM A SINGLE ACT OF TESTIMONY FOR THE PURPOSES OF DECLARING THE WITNESSES A CONSPIRACY [SHOULD THAT BE THE FACT]. IF, THEREFORE, THE FIRST OF THE THREE PAIRS OF WITNESSES IS FOUND TO FORM A CONSPIRACY, LO, ONLY TWO ACTS OF TESTIMONY THAT ARE VALID REMAIN, WITH THE RESULT THAT THE OX IS EXEMPT FROM THE STATUS OF AN ATTESTED DANGER, AND THE WITNESSES ARE EXEMPT FROM PENALTY. IF THE SECOND GROUP IS LIKEWISE FOUND TO BE A CONSPIRACY, LO, ONLY A SINGLE ACT OF TESTIMONY IS IN HAND [OF THE REQUIRED THREE], WITH THE RESULT THAT THE OX IS EXEMPT FROM THE DEFINED STATUS AND THEY ARE EXEMPT FROM PENALTY. IF THE THIRD OF THE THREE SETS IS FOUND A CONSPIRACY, THEN ALL THREE SETS OF WITNESSES ARE LIABLE TO THE PENALTY, AND IN THIS CASE SCRIPTURE DECLARES, "THEN YOU SHALL TO DO HIM AS HE HAD THOUGHT TO HAVE DONE TO HIS BROTHER" (DEUT. 19:19).

B.   DAMAGES DONE BY CHATTELS IN THE PUBLIC DOMAIN

M. 3:1 He who leaves a jug in the public domain, and someone else came along and stumbled on it and broke it — [the one who broke it] is exempt. And if [the one who broke it] was injured by it, the owner of the jug is liable [to pay damages for] his injury. [If] his jug was broken in the public domain, and someone slipped on the water, or was hurt by the sherds, he is liable.

Y. 3:1 I.2 An ox which mounted its fellow, and the owner of the one beneath came along and pulled his beast out from underneath: if before it had mounted, he pulled it out, and the ox fell down and died, the one who did so [and saved his property] is exempt. If he pushed it off and it fell and died, he is liable. [That is, the owner pulled his ox away before the other ox mounted up; he in no way bears responsibility for the death of the other ox, nor can he be accused of saving his own capital at the expense of the other party's. Clearly, then, there is a distinction to be drawn between saving one's property at the expense of someone else when the damage already has been done, and doing so when it has not yet been done. If the damage has been done, one may not necessarily injure one's fellow.. If the damage has not been done, one may save himself at the cost of his fellow so that he will not suffer any damage at all.]

M. 3:2 He who pours water out into the public domain, and someone else was injured on it, is liable [to pay compensation for] his injury. He who put away thorns or glass, and he

who makes his fence out of thorns, and a fence which fell into the public way — and others were injured by them — he is liable [to pay compensation for] their injury.

T, 2:5 He who places thorns and pebbles on his wall, [which extends] into the public domain, and someone else came along and was injured by them, lo, this one is exempt. [If the walls] fell down, and someone else came along and was injured by them, lo, this person is liable [M. B.Q. 3:2D-H]. [If] he built them in the normal way, he is exempt, unless they gave him time [to clear them out]. [If] they gave him time, and they fell down during that time, he is exempt. [If they fell] after that time, he is liable. How much is the time [they must give the man]? J. No less than thirty days.

T. 2:6 He who stored away thorns and glass in the wall of his fellow, and the owner of the wall came along and tore it down, and someone else came along and was injured by them, lo, this one [nonetheless] is liable.

M. 3:3 He who brings out his straw and stubble into the public domain to turn them into manure and someone else was injured on them — he is liable [to pay compensation for] his injury. But whoever grabs them first effects possession of them.

T. 2 :4 If] one's jug or jar broke in public domain, and someone else came along and was injured by them, lo, this person is liable. [If he left his stone or burden in the public way, [and] they said to him, "Clear them out," [and] he said to them, "I don't want them," whoever grabs them first acquires possession of them. [If] someone else came along and was injured by them, lo, this person [nonetheless] is liable. [If] his walls fell into the public domain, and they said to him, "Clean them out," and he said to them, "I don't want them," — whoever grabs [the stones of the walls] first acquires possession of them. [If] someone else came along and was injured by them, lo, this person is liable [cf. M. B.Q. 3:3A-F].

T. 2 :8 He who heaps up cattle dung to acquire possession of it in the public domain, and someone else came along and was injured by it — lo, this person is liable. And [to others the dung] is prohibited under the laws of robbery [vs. M. B.Q. 3:3].

M. 3:4 Two pot sellers who were going along, one after another, and the first of them stumbled and fell down, and the second stumbled over the first — the first one is liable [to pay compensation for] the injuries of the second.

T. 2:9 Ass-drivers going after one another — the first of them stumbled and fell down, and his fellow came along and stumbled on him and fell down — even if they are a hundred — all of them are exempt [from having to pay damages]. An ox which pushed its fellow, and its fellow pushed its fellow — the first pays [compensation] to the second, and the second to the third. But if it was on account of the first one that they all fell down, the first one pays for all of them. Five people who sat down on a bench, which broke — all of them are liable to pay [compensation for the bench]. But if it was on account of the last one [alone] that it broke, the last one must pay damages for all of them.

T. 2:10 Asses, the legs of one of which were infirm — they are not permitted [e.g., in a narrow passage] to set him aside [and pass him]. [If] one of [the asses] was loaded and one of them was mounted, they set aside the one which was loaded in favor of the one which was mounted. [If] one of them was mounted and one of them was unburdened, they set aside the one which is unburdened in favor of the one which is mounted. [If] both of them were carrying burdens, both of them were mounted, or both of them were unburdened, they make a compromise-agreement among themselves. And so is the rule governing two boats which were coming toward one another, one of them unloaded, and one of them loaded — they set aside the one which is unloaded in favor of the one which is bearing a burden. [If] both of them were unloaded or both of them were carrying cargo, they make a compromise between themselves.

B. 3:4 I.1/31A: POTTERS OR GLASS CARRIERS WHO WERE WALKING INDIAN FILE, THE FIRST OF THEM STUMBLED AND FELL, AND THE SECOND STUMBLED ON THE FIRST, THE THIRD ON THE SECOND — THE FIRST IS LIABLE FOR THE DAMAGES SUFFERED BY THE SECOND, THE SECOND IS LIABLE FOR THE DAMAGES SUFFERED BY THE THIRD, BUT IF IT WAS ON ACCOUNT ONLY OF THE FIRST ONE THAT THEY FELL DOWN, THEN THE FIRST ONE IS LIABLE FOR THE DAMAGES SUFFERED BY ALL OF THEM. BUT IF EACH OF THEM GAVE A WARNING TO THE OTHERS, THEN ALL OF THEM ARE EXEMPT FROM HAVING TO PAY COMPENSATION.

M. 3:5 This one comes along with his jar, and that one comes along with his beam — [if] the jar of this one was broken by the beam of that one, [the owner of the beam] is exempt, for this one has every right to walk along [in the street], and that one has every right to walk along [in the same street]

M. 3:6 Two who were going along in the public domain, one

was running, the other ambling, or both of them running, and they injured one another, both of them are exempt. M. 3:7 He who chops wood in private property, and [the chips] injured someone in public domain, in public domain, and [the chips] injured someone in private property, in private property, and [the chips] injured someone in someone else's private property — he is liable.

B. 3:7 I.7/33A: A WORKER WHO HAS COME TO COLLECT HIS WAGES FROM THE HOUSEHOLD, AND THE OX OF THE HOUSEHOLDER GORED HIM, OR THE DOG OF THE HOUSEHOLDER BIT HIM, AND HE DIED — THE HOUSEHOLDER IS EXEMPT [FROM HAVING TO PAY RANSOM].

C.   DAMAGES DONE BY THE OX

M. 3:8 Two oxen [generally deemed] harmless which injured one another — [the owner] pays half-damages for the excess [of the value of the injury done by the less injured to the more injured ox]. [If] both of them were attested dangers, [the owner] pays full damages for the excess [of the injury done by the less injured to the more injured ox]. [If] one was deemed harmless and one an attested danger, [if] it was an ox which was an attested danger [which injured] an ox deemed harmless, [the owner] pays full damages for the excess. [If] it was the ox deemed harmless [which injured] the one which was an attested danger, [the owner] pays half — damages for the excess. [If it was a case of] a man who injured an ox which was an attested danger, or an ox which was an attested danger which injured a man, one pays full damages for the excess [of the injury done by the one to the other].

3:1 An ox, which was an attested danger as to use of its horn [e.g., in goring] but harmless as to use of its tooth, which inflicted injury both with this and with that — [as to the injury inflicted by that on account of which it was deemed] harmless, [the owner] pays half-damages, limited to the value of its own carcass. [And as to the injury inflicted by that on account of which it was deemed] an attested danger, [the owner] pays full damages, out of the best of his real property. [If] there is no real property of suitable quality, [as to the injury caused by that on account of which it was deemed] harmless, [the owner] pays half-damages limited to the value of its own carcass. [And as to the injury inflicted by that on account of which it was deemed] an attested danger, let [the owner] lay out funds and seek property of suitable quality.

T. 3 :2 A governing principle did they state in connection with damages: [if] one has killed another's ox, torn his garment, or cut down his shoots, [the injured party] may not say to him, "Take the carcass and give me a cow, ". . . the rags and give me a cloak," "Take the broken shoots and give me whole plants." But they make an estimate of the value [of the damaged] items as to their worth before they were damaged and as to their worth now that they have been damaged. And in accord with that calculation do they pay compensation.

M. 3:9 Two oxen [generally deemed] harmless which injured one another — [the owner] pays half-damages for the excess [of the value of the injury done by the less injured to the more injured ox].[If] both of them were attested dangers, [the owner] pays full damages for the excess [of the injury done by the less injured to the more injured ox]. [If] one was deemed harmless and one an attested danger, [if] it was an ox which was an attested danger [which injured] an ox deemed harmless, [the owner] pays full damages for the excess. [If] it was the ox deemed harmless [which injured] the one which was an attested danger, [the owner] pays half-damages for the excess. And so is the rule for two men who injured one another: they pay full damages for the excess [of the injury done by the less injured to the more injured man]. [If it was a case of] a man who injured an ox which was an attested danger, or an ox which was an attested danger which injured a man, one pays full damages for the excess [of the injury done by the one to the other]. [If it was] a man [who injured] an ox deemed harmless, or an ox deemed harmless [which injured] a man — [if it was] the man [who injured] the ox deemed harmless, he pays full damages for the excess. [If it was] the ox deemed harmless [which injured] the man, one pays half-damages for the excess. An ox [deemed harmless] worth a maneh [a hundred zuz] which gored an ox worth two hundred [zuz], and the carcass [of the latter] is worth nothing — [the owner of the ox which is gored and worthless] takes the ox [worth a maneh, which did the goring].

T. 3:5 How does one pay half damages for the excess [of the value of the injury done by the less injured to the more injured one]. An ox which is worth a maneh [a hundred zuz] which gored an ox worth two hundred zuz — they both lost fifty zuz in value — [but] the latter [of the two oxen which gored one another] lost [better: gained] in value another three golden denars [in addition} [the owner of] the latter pays [the owner of] the former a half a golden denar. An ox worth two hundred zuz which gored an ox worth two hundred zuz and did fifty zuz damage — the animal which had been gored gained in value, so that it was worth four hundred zuz — but if [the former ox] had not done injury to it, it would have been worth eight hundred zuz — now, if before the case came to court, the gored ox gained in value, the owner has a claim only for the value of the ox as it stood at the time of its being injured. And if it was after the case came to court that it diminished in value, the owner has a claim only for the value of the ox as it stood at the time the case came to court.

B. 3:9A-C I.9/34A: AN OX WORTH TWO HUNDRED ZUZ THAT GORED AN OX WORTH TWO HUNDRED ZUZ, AND DID TO THE BEAST DAMAGES WORTH FIFTY ZUZ, BUT THEN THE INJURED OX INCREASED IN VALUE AND WAS WORTH FOR HUNDRED ZUZ, SINCE ONE MAY CLAIM THAT, IF IT HAD NOT BEEN INJURED, IT WOULD HAVE BEEN WORTH EIGHT HUNDRED ZUZ, THE RESPONSIBLE PARTY HAS TO PAY DAMAGES IN ACCORD WITH THE STATE OF AFFAIRS AT THE TIME OF THE INJURY. IF THE VALUE OF THE INJURED BEAST DEPRECIATED, THE ASSESSMENT IS MADE IN ACCORD WITH THE STATE OF AFFAIRS AT THE TIME OF THE VALUATION IN COURT. IF THE OX THAT DID THE DAMAGE GAINED IN VALUE, COMPENSATION IS STILL ASSESSED IN ACCORD WITH THE STATE OF AFFAIRS AT THE TIME OF THE INJURY. IF IT LOST IN VALUE, THE ASSESSMENT IS MADE IN ACCORD WITH THE STATE OF AFFAIRS AT THE TIME OF THE VALUATION IN COURT.

M. 3:10 There is (1) he who is liable for the deed of his ox and exempt on account of his own deed, exempt for the deed of his ox and liable on account of his own deed. His ox which inflicted embarrassment — [the owner] is exempt. But he who inflicted embarrassment is liable. His ox which blinded the eye of his slave or knocked out his tooth — [the owner] is exempt. But he who blinded the eye of his slave or knocked out his tooth is liable. His ox which injured his father or his mother — [the owner] is liable. But he who injured his father and his mother is exempt. His ox which set fire to a shock of grain on the Sabbath — [the owner] is liable. But he who set fire to a shock of grain on the Sabbath is exempt because he is subject to liability for his life.

T. 3:4 There is one who is liable for damages caused by himself and for damages caused by his ox or his ass, exempt both for damages caused by himself and for damages caused by his ox or his ass [cf. M. B.Q. 3:10A]. How is one liable for damages caused by himself and for damages caused by his ox or his ass? [If] he is responsible for causing damage in private domain, he is liable, [and] his ox or his ass is liable. [If] he caused injury unintentionally, he is liable, [and] his ox or his ass is liable. [If] he set fire to the standing grain of his fellow on the Day of Atonement, he is liable, and his ox or his ass is liable. How is he exempt for damages caused by himself and for damages caused by his ox or his ass? [If] he is responsible for causing damage in public domain [through the normal manner of walking of his ox or his ass, he is exempt, [and] his ox or his ass is exempt. [If] he [through his beast] killed someone inadvertently, he is exempt, [and] his ox or his ass is exempt. [If] he did damage to property belonging to the sanctuary, to a proselyte, or a freed slave, he is exempt, and his ox or his ass is exempt. And he is exempt for injuries caused by his boy-slave or his girl-slave.

M. 3:11 An ox which was running after another ox, and [that latter ox] was injured — this one claims, "Your ox did the injury," and that one claims, "Not so, but it was hit by a stone" — he who wants to exact [compensation] from his fellow bears the burden of proof. If two [oxen] were running after one [ox] — this one says, "Your ox did the damage," and that one says, "Your ox did the damage" — both of them are exempt. [But] if both of them belonged to the same man, both of them [oxen] are liable [to pay compensation]. [If] one of them was big and one little — the one whose ox has suffered an injury says, "The big one did the damage," but the one who is responsible for the damage says, "Not so, but the little one did the damage" — one of them was deemed harmless, and one was an attested danger — the one whose ox has suffered an injury says, "The one which was the attested danger has done the damage," but the one who is responsible for the damage says, "Not so, but the one which had been deemed harmless did the damage, — he who wants to exact [compensation] from his fellow bears the burden of proof.

T. 3 :6 An ox which was running after its fellow, [and] the one which was being pursued turned around and clobbered [the partner] — [if] others clobbered the pursuer — lo, these are liable. [If] the pursuing ox was injured by the one which was being pursued, [the latter] is exempt. [If] the one which was being pursued was injured by the pursuer, [the owner of the latter] is liable. An ox which mounted its fellow, and the owner of the one beneath came along and pulled [his beast] out [from underneath] — or if [the ox] pulled itself off, and fell and died — [the owner of the ox underneath] is exempt. [If] he pushed him and he fell and died, [the owner of the ox underneath] is liable. An ox which was grazing, and another ox went out after it, and the one which was grazing was found dead — even if this one has been gored, and that one is an attested danger as to goring, or this one died of a bite, and that one was an attested danger as to biting, [the owner of the surviving ox] is exempt. T. 3:7 Two oxen who were grazing, and two other oxen went out after them, and these which were known [to be grazing] were found dead — it is a matter of doubt whether these killed them, or whether death came from some other source and they died — lo, [the owners of] these are exempt. If it is a matter of certainty that they killed them, lo, [the owners of] these [oxen] pay compensation, in accord with the value of the smaller of the two, not in accord with the value of the larger of the two; in the assumption that the one which was deemed harmless did the killing, not in the assumption that the one which was an attested danger did the killing. If it is a matter of certainty that the black [oxen] did the killing of the white ones, [if] there was there one large one and one small one, one which was deemed harmless and one which was an attested danger, lo, these pay compensation for the large ox and for the small one — for the large ox from the carcass of the small one, and for the small ox from the carcass of the large one; for the large ox from the value of the one which had been deemed harmless, and for the small ox from the value of the one which had been an attested danger. [If] the oxen which had been injured belonged to two people, and the oxen which had done the damages belonged to one person, [if it is then] a matter of doubt that those oxen had killed them, or that death had come from some other source and they died, lo, these [owners of the accused oxen] are exempt. If it is a matter of certainty that they had killed them, lo, these pay compensation — in accord with the value of the small one, and not in accord with the value of the large one; in accord with the rules governing the one which had been deemed harmless, and not in accord with the rules governing an attested danger. If it is a matter of certainty that the black ones had killed the white ones, if there were there one which was large and one which was small, one which was deemed harmless and one which was an attested danger, lo, these pay compensation for the large one and for the small one — for the large one from the [value of the] smaller [of the two oxen which had done the killing], and for the smaller one from the larger one; for the large ox from the value of the one which had been deemed harmless, and for the small ox from the value of the one which had been an attested danger. And the owners of those oxen which had been injured divide the compensation between them — this one takes a sum in accord with the value of his ox, and that one takes a sum in accord with the value of his ox.

M. 4:2 An ox which is an attested danger as to its own species, but not an attested danger as to what is not its own species — [or] an attested danger as to man, and not an attested danger as to beast, [or] an attested danger to small [beasts] but not an attested danger as to large ones — for that for which it is an attested danger, [the owner] pays full damages, and for that for which it is not an attested danger, he pays half — damages.

B. 4:2 I.2-3/37A: IF THE OX SEES ANOTHER OX AND GORES IT, ANOTHER AND DOES NOT GORE IT, ANOTHER AND GORES IT, ANOTHER AND DOES NOT GORE IT, ANOTHER AND GORES IT, ANOTHER AND DOES NOT GORE IT, IT IS DEEMED AN OX THAT IS AN ATTESTED DANGER ALTERNATELY TO GORE OTHER OXEN. IF THE OX SEES ANOTHER OX AND GORES IT, AN ASS AND DOES NOT GORE IT, A HORSE AND GORES IT, A CAMEL AND DOES NOT GORE IT, A MULE AND GORES IT, A WILD ASS AND DOES NOT GORE IT, IT IS DEEMED AN OX THAT IS AN ATTESTED DANGER ALTERNATELY TO GORE OTHER SPECIES.

M. 4:3 An ox of an Israelite which gored an ox belonging to the sanctuary or an ox belonging to the sanctuary which gored an ox belonging to an Israelite [M. 1:21 — [the owner] is exempt, since it is said, "The ox belonging to his neighbor" (Ex. 21:35) — and not an ox belonging to the sanctuary. An ox belonging to an Israelite which gored an ox belonging to a gentile — [the Israelite owner] is exempt. And one of a gentile which gored one of an Israelite — whether it is harmless or an attested danger, [the gentile owner] pays full damages.

T. 4:1 An ox, half of which belongs to an Israelite and half of which belongs to the sanctuary, which inflicted injury upon an ox which belongs to an Israelite — [if it is] an attested danger, [the owner] pays full damages. [And if it is] deemed harmless, [the owner] pays half-damages. [An ox] belonging to the sanctuary, whether it is deemed harmless or whether it is an attested danger, is exempt. [If] it is injured by another [ox], belonging to an Israelite, [the owner] is liable. [And if it is injured by one] belonging to the sanctuary, it is exempt. An ox which belongs to the sanctuary [by reason of dedication on the part of the original owner] — [the original] owner is liable to replace it if it is lost. And the owner receives damages paid if it is injured. And the owner pays damages owing if it injures [another ox]. An ox, half of which belongs to an Israelite and half of which belongs to a gentile which injured one belonging to an Israelite — [if it is] an attested danger, [the owners] pay full damages. [If it is] deemed harmless, [the owners] pay half-damages. But one belonging to a gentile, whether it is deemed harmless or whether it is an attested danger — [the owner] pays full damages.

T. 4:2 An ox belonging to a gentile which injured an ox belonging to another gentile, his fellow, even though they accepted upon themselves the authority of the laws of Israel — [the owner] pays full damages. For the distinction between an ox deemed harmless and one which is an attested danger does not apply in the case of damages done in regard to a gentile.

T. 4:3 An ox belonging to an Israelite which gored an ox belonging to a Samaritan, and an ox belonging to a Samaritan which gored an ox belonging to an Israelite — [the owner of] one which is an attested danger pays full damages, and [the owner of] one which is deemed harmless pays half-damages.

M. 4:4 An ox of a person of sound senses which gored an ox belonging to a deaf-mute, an idiot, or a minor — [the owner] is liable. But one of a deaf-mute, idiot, or minor which gored an ox belonging to a person of sound senses — [the owner] is exempt. [As to] the ox of a deaf-mute, idiot, or minor, the court appoints a guardian for them, and they bring testimony against [the ox, to have it declared an attested danger] to the guardian.

B. 4:4 I:9/40A: IF SOMEONE BORROWED AN OX ASSUMING THAT IT WAS HARMLESS BUT IT TURNED OUT AN ATTESTED DANGER, THE OWNER WOULD HAVE TO PAY HALF-DAMAGES, AND THE ONE WHO BORROWED IT WOULD PAY HALF-DAMAGES. IF THE BEAST WAS DECLARED AN ATTESTED DANGER WHILE IN THE HOUSEHOLD OF THE BORROWER AND HE RETURNED IT TO THE OWNER, THE OWNER WOULD THEN HAVE TO PAY HALF-DAMAGE AND THE OWNER WOULD BE EXEMPT FROM ANY PAYMENT WHATSOEVER.

M. 4:5 An ox which gored a man, who died — [if it was] an attested danger, [the owner] pays a ransom price [of the value of the deceased]. But [if it was deemed] harmless, he is exempt from paying the ransom price. And in this case and in that case, [the oxen] are liable to the death penalty. And so is the rule [if it killed] a little boy or girl [son, daughter: Ex. 21:31]. [If] it gored a boy slave or a girl slave, [the owner] pays thirty selas [Ex. 21:32], whether [the slave] was worth a maneh or a single denar.

T.4:6 There is [the beast] which is liable to a ransom-payment and liable to death, liable to the death penalty but exempt from the ransom-payment, liable to the ransom-payment but exempt from the death-penalty, exempt from the death-penalty and exempt from the ransom-payment [delete: and exempt from the death-penalty]. An ox deemed an attested danger which killed someone — [the owner] is liable to the ransom-payment, and [the ox] is liable to be put to death. An ox deemed harmless which killed somebody, an ox belonging to a deaf-mute or an idiot which killed, and [an ox which] killed a proselyte or a freed slave — [the ox] is liable to the death penalty but [the owner] is exempt from the ransom-payment [which is omitted, since there are no heirs].

T. 4:7 How does one estimate the compensation to be paid? They estimate the value of the one who has been injured [and is now deceased]: how much he is worth. In accord with that [estimate] the owner pays compensation.

T. 4:8 In any case in which one is liable for damages done to a free man, he is liable for damages done to a slave, whether this is in regard to the ransom-payment or the death-penalty. In any case in which one is exempt from liability to damages done to a free man, he is exempt from liability for damages done to a slave, whether this is in regard to the ransom-payment or the death penalty. [If an ox] killed a Hebrew slave, [the owner] pays all his ransom money. [If an ox killed] a slave belonging to two partners, [the owner] pays it to both of them. [If half of the man] was slave, and half free, [the owner] pays it proportionately: half of the ransom goes to the estate, and half of thirty *selas* goes to the owner.

M. 4:6 An ox which was rubbing itself against a wall, and [the wall] fell on a man, [if] it had intended to kill (1) another beast, but killed a man, (2) a gentile but killed an Israelite, (3) an untimely birth but killed a viable infant — [the ox] is exempt [from death by stoning.

B. 4:6 I.2/44B: THERE IS THE BEAST THAT IS LIABLE TO A RANSOM PAYMENT AND LIABLE TO DEATH, LIABLE TO THE DEATH PENALTY BUT EXEMPT FROM THE RANSOM PAYMENT, LIABLE TO THE RANSOM PAYMENT BUT EXEMPT FROM THE DEATH PENALTY, EXEMPT FROM THE DEATH PENALTY AND EXEMPT FROM THE RANSOM PAYMENT. HOW SO? AN OX DEEMED AN ATTESTED DANGER THAT INTENTIONALLY KILLED SOMEONE — THE OWNER IS LIABLE TO THE RANSOM PAYMENT AND THE OX IS LIABLE TO BE PUT TO DEATH. AN OX DEEMED AN ATTESTED DANGER THAT UNINTENTIONALLY KILLED SOMEBODY — THE OWNER IS LIABLE TO THE RANSOM, BUT THE OX IS NOT LIABLE TO THE DEATH PENALTY. AN OX DEEMED HARMLESS THAT UNINTENTIONALLY KILLED SOMEBODY, THE OWNER IS EXEMPT, AND THE OX IS EXEMPT, FROM ANY PENALTY. [TOSEFTA'S VERSION: AN OX BELONGING TO A DEAF-MUTE OR AN IDIOT THAT KILLED, AND AN OX THAT KILLED A PROSELYTE OR A FREED SLAVE — THE OX IS LIABLE TO THE DEATH PENALTY, BUT THE OWNER IS EXEMPT FROM THE RANSOM PAYMENT, THERE BEING NO HEIRS. AN OX THAT WAS RUBBING ITSELF AGAINST A WALL AND THE WALL FELL ON A MAN, IF IT HAD INTENDED TO KILL ANOTHER BEAST BUT KILLED A MAN, A GENTILE BUT KILLED AN ISRAELITE, AN UNTIMELY BIRTH BUT KILLED A VIABLE INFANT, THE OWNER IS LIABLE TO THE RANSOM PAYMENT, BUT THE BEAST IS EXEMPT FROM THE DEATH PENALTY.

M. 4:7 (1) An ox belonging to a woman, (2) an ox belonging to orphans, (3) an ox belonging to a guardian, (4) an ox of the wilderness, (5) an ox belonging to the sanctuary, (6) an ox belonging to a proselyte who died lacking heirs — lo, these [oxen] are liable to the death penalty.

M. 4:8 An ox which goes forth to be stoned, and which the owner [then] declared to be sanctified is not deemed to have been sanctified. [If] one has slaughtered it, its meat is prohibited [Ex. 21:28]. But if before the court process had been completed the owner declared it sanctified, it is deemed sanctified. And [if] one had slaughtered it, its meat is permitted.

T. 4:9 That ox which is accused of manslaughter at the testimony of a single witness, or which is accused of having committed bestiality or having been a victim of bestiality on the evidence of a single witness is invalid for use on the altar. And is exempt from the death-penalty. And it is available for the benefit [of the owner]. And an ox which is accused of manslaughter at the testimony of two witnesses, or of having committed bestiality or having been a victim of bestiality on the evidence of two witnesses is invalid for use on the altar. It is liable to the death-penalty. And it is prohibited from use for the benefit [of the owner]. And [that ox which has] committed manslaughter, whether it belongs to him [who has been killed] or to someone else, whether the manslaughter takes place before it has been consecrated or after it has been consecrated [M. B.Q. 4:8], whether [the manslaughter was] inadvertent, deliberate, under constraint, or by choice, is prohibited for use on the altar. An animal which commits bestiality or upon which bestiality is committed, whether it belongs to him [who has done the deed] or to someone else, whether this takes place before it has been consecrated or after it has been consecrated, [whether the act of bestiality] was inadvertent or deliberate — is invalid for use on the altar. [If the act] was done under constraint, it is valid [for use on the altar]. [If it was done] willingly, it is invalid [for use on the altar].

T. 5:1 An ox which had been deemed harmless which inflicted injury — [if] before it came to court, the owner declared it consecrated, it is consecrated. [If] he slaughtered it, sold it, or gave it away as a gift, what he has done is valid. [If] after it came to court, the owner declared it consecrated, it is not deemed consecrated. [If] he slaughtered it or sold it or gave it away as a gift, what he has done is not valid. For he has to pay compensation from the corpus of the animal itself [which therefore must be kept available, once the court has made its decision, for use for compensation].

5:2 An ox which had been deemed an attested danger which inflicted injury, whether before or after it has come to court — [if] the owner declared it consecrated, it is deemed consecrated. [If] the owner slaughtered it, sold it, or gave it away, what he had done is deemed valid. For [the owner] pays damages from the choicest real estate [no matter the condition of the corpus of the beast].

B. 4:8, 4:9A-F I.1/44B-45A: AN OX THAT KILLED SOMEONE — IF THE OWNER SOLD IT BEFORE THE COURT DECREE WAS ISSUED, IT IS DEEMED TO HAVE BEEN VALIDLY SOLD. IF THE OWNER SANCTIFIED IT TO THE TEMPLE, IT IS VALIDLY SANCTIFIED. IF HE SLAUGHTERED IT, ITS MEAT IS PERMITTED. IF THE BAILEE RETURNED IT TO THE HOUSEHOLD OF THE OWNER, IT IS VALIDLY RETURNED [AND THE BAILEE HAS NO FURTHER OBLIGATION]. IF AFTER THE COURT DECREE WAS ISSUED, THE OWNER SOLD IT, IT IS DEEMED NOT TO HAVE BEEN VALIDLY SOLD. IF THE OWNER SANCTIFIED IT TO THE TEMPLE, IT IS NOT VALIDLY SANCTIFIED. IF HE SLAUGHTERED IT, ITS MEAT IS NOT PERMITTED. IF THE BAILEE

RETURNED IT TO THE HOUSEHOLD OF THE OWNER, IT IS NOT VALIDLY
RETURNED.

**M. 4:9 [If] one had handed it over to an unpaid bailee, or to
a borrower, to a paid bailee, or to a renter, they take the
place [and assume the liabilities] of the owner. [For an ox
deemed an] attested danger [one of these] pays full damages,
and [for one] deemed harmless [he] pays half-damages.**

T. 5:3 An ox which had been deemed harmless which inflicted
injury, and afterward it killed someone, [or] it killed someone,
and afterward it inflicted injury — [the owner] is exempt. An
ox which was an attested danger which inflicted injury and
afterward killed [someone] — [the owner] bears liability. [If] it
killed someone and afterward inflicted injury, [if] this was before
its court-process was completed, [the owner] is liable. [If this
was] after its court-process was completed, [the owner] is
exempt.

T. 5:4 An unpaid bailee, a borrower, a paid bailee, or a renter
[of an ox], in the domain of any of whom the ox has inflicted
injury — [any of the afore-named, responsible for] an ox deemed
an attested danger pays full damages, and one deemed harmless
pays half-damages [M. B.Q. 4:9A-F]. [If] one had borrowed it
in the assumption that it was harmless and it turned out to be an
attested danger, [however], the owner pays half-damages, and
the borrower is exempt. [If a] warning [attesting the animal as
dangerous] was made in the presence of the borrower, and
afterward [the borrower] gave it back to the owner, the owner
pays half-damages, and the borrower pays half-damages. [If] it
committed manslaughter in his domain, and afterward he handed
it back to the owner, if before the court-process concerning it
was complete, he had handed it back to the owner, he is exempt.
[If] after the court-process concerning it was complete, he had
handed it back to the owner, he is liable.

T. 5:5 A cow which committed manslaughter and afterward
gave birth, [if] before its court-process was completed, it gave
birth, its offspring are permitted. [If] after its court-process was
completed, it gave birth, its offspring are prohibited. [If] they
were confused with others, and the others yet with others, all
of them are prohibited from being so used as to derive benefit.
What should they do with them? They keep them in a stockade
until they perish.

**M. 5:1 An ox [deemed harmless] which gored a cow [which
died] and her newly born calf was found [dead] beside her**

— and it is not known whether, before it gored her, she gave birth, or after it gored her, she gave birth — [the owner of the ox] pays half — damages for the cow, and quarter — damages for the offspring. And so too, a cow [deemed harmless] which gored an ox, and her newly born young was found beside her, and it is not known whether before she gored, she gave birth, or after she gored, she gave birth — [the owner of the cow] pays half-damages from the corpus of the cow, and a quarter-damages from the corpus of the offspring.

M. 5:2 (1) The potter who brought his pots into the courtyard of the householder without permission, and the beast of the householder broke them — [the householder] is exempt. (2) And if [the beast] was injured on them, the owner of the pots is liable. (3) If [however], he brought them in with permission, the owner of the courtyard is liable, (1) [If] he brought his produce into the courtyard of the householder without permission, and the beast of the householder ate them up, [the householder] is exempt. (2) And if [the beast] was injured by them, the owner of the produce is liable. (3) But if he brought them in with permission, the owner of the courtyard is liable.

M. 5:3 (1) [If] he brought his ox into the courtyard of a householder without permission, and the ox of the householder gored it, or the dog of the householder bit it, [the householder] is exempt. (2) [If] that [ox] gored the ox of the householder, [the owner] is liable. [If] it fell into his well and polluted its water, [the owner of the ox] is liable. [If] his father or son was in [the well and was killed], [the owner of the ox] pays ransom money. (3) But if he brought it in with permission, the owner of the courtyard is liable.

T. 5:13 There is that [owner] who pays the ransom, and [the ox] is not stoned, there is that ox which is stoned, and the [owner] does not pay ransom. He who digs a pit with permission and an ox fell in on him and killed him — [the owner of the ox] pays the ransom, but [the ox] is not stoned. [If] he went into the courtyard of a householder without permission, and the ox of the householder gored him, or the dog of the householder bit him, and he died — [the animal] is stoned, but [the owner] does not pay the ransom.

T. 6 :2 He who digs a pit in his own domain, and an ox fell on him and killed him — [the owner of the ox] is liable to pay the ransom-money. And if the ox was injured [in the pit], the owner of the pit is exempt.

T. 6.3 He who digs a pit in public domain and an ox fell on him and killed him — [the owner of the ox] is exempt from having to pay the ransom money. And [if] the ox is injured in the pit, the owner of the pit is liable.

M. 5:4 An ox which was intending [to gore] its fellow, but hit a woman, and her offspring came forth [as a miscarriage] — [the owner of the ox] is exempt from paying compensation for the offspring. And a man who was intending [to hit] his fellow but hit a woman, and her offspring came forth, pays compensation for the offspring.

D. DAMAGES DONE BY THE PIT

M. 5:5 He who digs a pit in private domain and opens it into public domain, or in public domain and opens it into private domain, or in private domain and opens it into private domain belonging to someone else, is liable [for damage done by the pit]. He who digs a pit in public domain, and an ox or an ass fell into it and died, is liable. It is all the same whether one digs a pit, a trench, cavern, ditches, or channels: he is liable.

T. 6:4 [If] he dug a pit in public domain with its opening into private domain, even if it belonged to the public, he is liable, until he gives over [the pit] to the public. What is the sort of pit concerning which the Torah spoke? [If] one dug a pit in private property and opened it into private property. [If] he has the right to open [a pit] in public domain, and he opened it in public domain, [if] he has no right to dig and no right to open [a pit] in private domain, and he opened it in public domain, [if] he has the right to dig it but has no right to open it, but he has the right to do so in public domain, [if he has the right] to enter there in public domain, and he opened it in private domain — even if it is public property, he is exempt.

T. 6:5. [If] he dug a pit [cistern] and opened it up and handed it over to the public, he is exempt.

T. 6:6 [If] one has dug a hole in the proper way and covered it up in the proper way, and made a fence around it in the proper way, ten handbreadths high, and handed it over to a sick person or to an old person who is intelligent, he is exempt [having done his duty for the protection of the well].

T. 6:7 [If] he has dug [a hole] not in the proper way, and covered it up not in the proper way, or [if] he handed it over to a deaf-mute, idiot, or minor, who lack intelligence, he is liable.

T. 6 :9 If one has dug ten handbreadths, and someone else came along and put in plaster and cemented it, the one who came along at the end is liable. [If] one person has dug ten handbreadths, another dug twenty, another dug a hundred, and another dug two hundred, all of them are liable.

T. 6 :12 And what is the measure of a pit so as to cause injury? Any depth at all. And to cause death? Ten handbreadths.

M. 5:6 A pit belonging to two partners — one of them passed by it and did not cover it, and the second one also did not cover it, the second one is liable. [If] the first one covered it up, and the second one came along and found it uncovered and did not cover it up. the second one is liable. [If] he covered it up in a proper way, and an ox or an ass fell into it and died, he is exempt. [If] he did not cover it up in the proper way and an ox or an ass fell into it and died, he is liable. [If] it fell forward [not into the pit] because of the sound of the digging, [the owner of the pit] is liable. [If] it fell backward [not into the pit] because of the sound of the digging, [the owner of the pit] is exempt. [If] an ox carrying its trappings fell into it and they were broken, an ass and its trappings and they were split, [the owner of the pit] is liable for the beast but exempt for the trappings. [If] an ox belonging to a deaf-mute, an idiot, or a minor fell into it, [the owner] is liable. [If] a little boy or girl, a slave boy or a slave girl [fell into it], he is exempt [from paying a ransom].

T. 6:10 A pit belonging to two people, one covers it, and one uncovers it — the one who uncovers it is liable. [If] he covered it up and it became uncovered, while he was standing there and saw it uncovered but did not cover it up, lo, this one is liable. [If] he covered it up and went along, even though it became uncovered later on, he is exempt.

M. 5:7 All the same are an ox and all other beasts so far as (1) falling into a pit, (2) keeping apart from Mount Sinai [Ex. 19:12], (3) a double indemnity [Ex. 22:7], (4) the returning of that which is lost [Dt. 22:3, Ex. 23:4] (5), unloading [Ex. 23:51, (6) muzzling [Dt. 25:4], (7) hybridization [Lev. 19:19, Dt. 22:10], and the (8) Sabbath [Ex. 20:10, Dt. 5:14]. And so too are wild beasts and fowl subject to the same laws. If so, why is an ox or an ass specified? But Scripture spoken in terms of prevailing conditions.

T. 6:18 All the same are an ox, an ass, and all other beasts, wild animals, and fowl, as to the payment of damages: the owner of an attested danger pays full damages, and of one deemed harmless pays half-damages. All the same are an ox, an ass, and all other domesticated beasts, wild beasts, and fowl, as to bestiality and as to hybridization.

E.   DAMAGES DONE BY THE CROP-DESTROYING BEAST

M. 6:1 He who brings a flock into a fold and shut the gate before it as required, but [the flock] got out and did damage, is exempt. [If] he did not shut the gate before it as required, and [the flock] got out and did damage, he is liable. [If the fence] was broken down by night, or thugs broke it down, and [the flock] got out and did damage, he is exempt. [If] the thugs took [the flock] out, [and the flock did damage], the thugs are liable.

T. 6 :19 [If] he shut the gate as is required [M . B.Q. 6:1 A], tied up [the beasts] as is required, made for [the flock] a fence ten handbreadths high, or handed it over to a sick person or an old person of sound senses, [the owner of the flock] is exempt [from liability to damages done by the flock]. [If] he shut the gate not as is required, tied up the gate not as is required, made for [the flock] a fence less than ten handbreadths high, or handed it over to a deaf-mute, an idiot, or a minor, he is liable [to pay compensation for damages done by the flock]. What is the definition of doing so in a way not such as is required? Any situation in which [the corral-fence] cannot stand up to the wind.

M. 6:2 [If] he left it in the sun, [or if] he handed it over to a deaf-mute, idiot, or minor, and [the flock] got out and did damage, he is liable. [If] he handed it over to a shepherd, the shepherd takes the place of the owner [as to liability]. [If the flock] [accidentally] fell into a vegetable patch and derived benefit [from the produce], [the owner must] pay compensation [only] for the value of the benefit [derived by the flock]. [If the flock] went down in the normal way and did damage, [the owner must] pay compensation for the [actual] damage which [the flock] inflicted.

T. 6:20 A shepherd who hands over his flock to another shepherd — the first is liable, and the second is exempt. He who hands over his flock to a shepherd, even if it is one who is lame, or even sick, or even if there are under his oversight as many as three hundred sheep, is exempt [cf. M. Q.B. 6:2E]. [If] he handed it over to a deaf-mute, an idiot, or a minor, he is liable. [If he handed it over to] a slave or a woman, he is exempt. And they pay compensation after an interval. How [does a woman or a slave pay compensation after an interval]? They call a court into session to deal with their case. They write a writ of debt against them. [If] the woman is divorced or the slave freed, they are then liable to pay compensation.

M. 6:3 He who stacks sheaves in the field of his fellow without permission, and the beast of the owner of the field ate them up, [the owner of the field] is exempt. And [if] it was injured by them, the owner of the sheaves is liable. But if he had put his sheaves there with permission, the owner of the field is liable.

T. 6:25 [If one] went into the shop of a carpenter without permission [and] a chip flew and hit him in the face, [the carpenter] is exempt [from liability for damages]. If he went in with permission, the owner of the shop is liable [cf. M. B.Q. 6:3]

T. 6:26 [If] one went into the shop of a smith without permission, [and] sparks flew and did damage to him, [the smith] is exempt. If he went in with permission, the owner of the shop is liable [cf. M. B.Q. 6:3].

6:27 A worker who went into the courtyard of a householder without permission, even though he has the right to go in and to collect their [the workers'] salary, if the ox of the householder gored him, or if his dog bit him, [the householder] is exempt. But if [the householder] said to him, "Come in," the householder is liable [cf. M. B.Q. 6:3].

F.   DAMAGES DONE BY FIRE

M. 6:4 He who causes a fire to break out through the action of a deaf-mute, idiot, or minor, is exempt from punishment under the laws of man, but liable to punishment under the laws of heaven. [If] he did so through the action of a person of sound senses, the person of sound senses is liable. [If] one person brought the flame, then another person brought the wood, the one who brings the wood is liable. [If] one person brought the wood and the other person then brought the flame, the one who brought the flame is liable. [If] a third party came along and fanned the fire, the one who fanned the flame is liable. [If] the wind fanned the flame, all of them are exempt. He who causes a fire to break out, which consumed wood, stones, or dirt, is liable.

T. 6:23 [If the fire] crossed a stream, a fence, or rivulet, any of which is eight cubits wide, he is exempt [cf. M. B.Q. 6:4].

T. 6:16 He who frightens his fellow to death is exempt from punishment by the laws of man, and his case is handed to Heaven. [If] he shouted into his ear and deafened him, he is exempt. [If] he seized him and shouted into his ear and deafened him, he is liable. He who frightens the ox of his fellow to death is exempt from punishment by the laws of man, and his case is handed over to Heaven.

T. 6:17 [If] one force-fed [the ox of his fellow] with asafoetida, creeper-berries, a poisonous ointment, or chicken shit, he is exempt from punishment under the laws of man, and his case is handed over to Heaven. He who performs an extraneous act of labor while preparing purification-water or a cow for purification belonging to his fellow [thus spoiling what has been done] is exempt from punishment by the laws of man, and his case is handed over to Heaven. A court-official who administered a blow by the decision of a court and did injury is exempt from punishment by the laws of man, and his case is handed over to Heaven. He who chops up the foetus in the belly of a woman by the decision of a court and did damage is exempt from punishment by the laws of man, and his case is handed over to Heaven. A seasoned physician who administered a remedy by a decision of a court and did damage is exempt from punishment by the laws of man, and his case is handed over to Heaven.

6:6 A spark which flew out from under the hammer and did damage — [the smith] is liable. A camel which was carrying flax and passed by in the public way, and the flax it was carrying got poked into a store and caught fire from the lamp of the storekeeper and set fire to the building — the owner of the camel is liable.

II. DAMAGES DONE BY PERSONS

A. PENALTIES FOR THE THEFT OF AN OX OR A SHEEP

M. 7:1 More encompassing is the rule covering payment of twofold restitution than the rule covering payment of fourfold or fivefold restitution. For the rule covering twofold restitution applies to something whether animate or inanimate. But the rule covering fourfold or fivefold restitution applies only to an ox or a sheep alone, since it says, "If a man shall steal an ox or a sheep and kill it, or sell it, he shall pay five oxen for an ox and four sheep for a sheep" (Ex. 22:1 [21:37]). The one who steals from a thief does not

pay twofold restitution. And the one who slaughters or sells what is stolen does not pay fourfold or fivefold restitution.

T. 7:14 If one stole and gave the ox and sheep to someone else, who slaughtered it, or stole and gave it to someone else, who sold it, or stole and traded an ox, or stole and consecrated the ox or sheep, or stole and gave the ox or sheep to someone else as a gift, or stole and gave the ox or sheep to someone as a loan, or stole and paid with the ox or sheep a debt that he owed, or stole and sent the ox or sheep to his father-in-law's house as a gift, he must pay the fourfold or fivefold indemnity.

T. 7:15 He who steals [an ox or a sheep which was] mutilated, lame, or blind, he who steals [an ox or a sheep] belonging to partners pays fourfold or fivefold restitution. Partners who stole [an ox or a sheep] pay twofold restitution, but are exempt from having to pay threefold restitution in addition].

T. 7:17 He who steals a pregnant cow and slaughtered or sold it pays fourfold or fivefold restitution. [If he stole] a pregnant cow, which then gave birth, and afterward he slaughtered its offspring, he pays twofold restitution, but is exempt from having to pay an additional threefold restitution. He who steals a pregnant cow, which gave birth, and afterward which he slaughtered, or a goat and which he milked and afterward slaughtered — or a fat cow and it lost weight — he pays twofold restitution of the value of the beast as at the time it was stolen, and fourfold or fivefold restitution for the beast as at the time it was slaughtered or sold. [If] it was scrawny and it got fat, he pays twofold restitution and fourfold or fivefold restitution of the beast [assessed] as at the time it was stolen.

M. 7:2 [If] one stole [an ox or a sheep] on the evidence of two witnesses, and [was convicted of having] slaughtered or sold on the basis of their testimony, or on the basis of the testimony of two other witnesses, he pays fourfold or fivefold restitution. (1) [If] he stole or sold [an ox or a sheep] on the Sabbath, (2) stole and sold [an ox or a sheep] for idolatrous purposes, (3) stole and slaughtered [an ox or a sheep] on the Day of Atonement, (4) stole [an ox or a sheep] belonging to his father and slaughtered or sold it, and afterward his father died, (5) stole and slaughtered, and afterward consecrated [an ox or a sheep], he pays fourfold or fivefold restitution. (1) [If] he stole and slaughtered [an ox or a sheep] for use in healing or for food for dogs, (2) he who [steals and] slaughters [an ox or a sheep] which turns out to be terefah, (3) he who

slaughters unconsecrated beasts in the Temple courtyard — he pays fourfold or fivefold restitution.

M. 7:3 [If] one stole [an ox or a sheep] on the evidence of two witnesses, and [was convicted of having] slaughtered or sold [it] on the basis of their testimony, and they turned out to be false witnesses, they pay full restitution. [If] he stole on the evidence of two witnesses, and [was convicted of having] slaughtered or sold it on the basis of the testimony of two other witnesses, [and] these and those turn out to be false witnesses, the first pair of witnesses pays twofold restitution, and the second pair of witnesses pays threefold restitution. [If] the latter pair of witnesses turn out to be false witnesses, he pays twofold restitution, and they pay threefold restitution. [If] one of the latter pair of witnesses turns out to be false, the evidence of the second one is null. [If] one of the first pair of witnesses turns out to be false, the entire testimony is null. For if there is no culpable act of stealing, there is no culpable act of slaughtering or selling.

T. 7:22 [If] two give testimony against a man that he has stolen, and two testify against him that he has slaughtered or sold [the animal], if the two [who testified] concerning his having slaughtered or sold the animal turn out to be perjurers, then he pays twofold restitution, and they pay threefold restitution [M. B.Q. 7:31]. [If] they turned out to be perjurers for both matters, they are liable for both this [form of restitution] as well as that [M. B.Q. 7:3A-D].

T. 7 :23 If two give testimony against a man that he has stolen, and two testify against him that he has slaughtered or sold [the animal], and the two [who testified] concerning his having stolen the animal turn out to be perjurers [M. B.Q. 7:3], he pays twofold damages, and they pay threefold damages.

T. 7:24 "Give me back my ox!" And that one said, "I have only the money [paid for it]" — "Give me the money!" "I have only the beast [I purchased with that money]" — "Give me fourfold or fivefold compensation!" And that one said, "I have only enough for a single ox" — if it was worth, in fact, the value of all [fivefold restitution], they make an estimate of its value [and it is paid over as acceptable restitution].

T. 8:1 He who steals a soul from among his brethren, the children of Israel — it is all the same if the thief is a man, a woman, a proselyte, a freed slave — it is all the same if it is a man, woman, proselyte, or freed slave whom they have stolen — lo, these [who do so] are liable. [If] one has sold him, whether

to his father, brother, or any one of his relatives, he is liable. If]
he stole him but did not sell him, or [if] he sold him and he is
standing there in the market [not yet taken away], he is exempt.
He who steals slaves is exempt. [If] two give testimony against
a thief that he has stolen, and two give testimony against him
that he has sold [a sheep or ox], and they are found to be perjurers
in connection with the theft, he and they are exempt [M. B.Q.
7:3K-L]. [If] they turn out to be perjured as to the sale, he is
exempt, and they are exempt. [If] they turn out to be perjurers
for both this and that [both the stealing and the selling], in such
a case as this does [Scripture] say, "Then you shall do to him as
he had meant to do to his brother" (Deut. 19:19).

**M. 7:4 [If] one stole [an ox or a sheep] [and was so accused]
on the evidence of two witnesses and [was accused of having]
slaughtered or sold [the ox or sheep] on the basis of only
one, or on the basis of the evidence of his own [confession],
he pays twofold restitution and does not pay fourfold or
fivefold restitution. 1) [If] he stole and slaughtered on the
Sabbath, (2) stole and slaughtered for idolatrous purposes,
3) stole from his father's [herd of oxen or sheep] and then
his father died and afterward he slaughtered or sold [the
beast], (4) stole and then consecrated [the animal] and
afterward slaughtered or sold it, he pays twofold restitution
and does not pay fourfold or fivefold restitution.**

B. 7:4 I.4/75B IF TWO WITNESSES GAVE TESTIMONY THAT HE HAD
STOLEN, AND THERE WERE TWO OTHERS WHO GAVE TESTIMONY THAT HE
HAD SLAUGHTERED AND SOLD THE MEAT, IF THE WITNESSES AS TO THE
THEFT WERE PROVEN TO BE A CONSPIRACY OF PERJURERS, THEN
TESTIMONY PART OF WHICH HAS BEEN NULLIFIED IS WHOLLY NULL. IF
THE WITNESSES TO THE SLAUGHTER WERE PROVED TO BE A CONSPIRACY
OF PERJURERS, THEN HE HAS TO PAY THE DOUBLE INDEMNITY, AND THEY
HAVE TO PAY THE INDEMNITY OF THREE TIMES THE VALUE OF THE BEAST.

**M. 7:5 (1) [If] one sold [all] but one hundredth part of [a
stolen ox or sheep], (2) or if [the thief already] owned a share
of it, (3) he who slaughters [an ox or a sheep] and it turns
out to be made into carrion by his own hand, (4) he who
pierces [the windpipe], (5) and he who tears out [its gullet]
pays two fold restitution and does not pay four fold or five
fold restitution. [If] (1) he stole it in the owner's domain but
slaughtered or sold it outside of his domain, or (2) [if] he
stole it outside of his domain and slaughtered or sold it in
his domain, or (3) if he stole and slaughtered or sold it outside**

of his domain, he pays fourfold or fivefold restitution, But if he stole and slaughtered or sold it [wholly] in his domain, he is exempt.

M. 7:6 [If the thief] was dragging [a sheep or ox] out [of the owner's domain], but it died in the domain of the owner, he is exempt. [If] he lifted it up or removed it from the domain of the owner and then it died, he is liable. If] he handed it over for (1) the firstborn offering at the birth of his son, or (2) to a creditor, to (3) an unpaid bailee, or (4) to a borrower, or (5) to a paid bailee, or (6) to a renter, and [one of these] was dragging it away, and it died in the domain of the owner, he is exempt. [If] he raised it up or removed it from the domain of the owner and then it died, he is liable.

T. 7:20 [If] he handed over [an ox or a sheep which he had stolen] for the redemption of his firstborn son, or to his creditor, or to a woman for payment of her marriage-settlement, he has done nothing of effect. [If, however,] he raised it up and then handed it over for the redemption of his firstborn son, or to his creditor, or to a woman for payment of her marriage-settlement, what he has done is entirely valid.

T. 8:2 "Where is my ox, which you stole?" And the other said to him, "You sold it to me," or, "You gave it to me as a gift!" "Your father sold it to me!" or, "Your father gave it to me as a gift!" and witnesses bear testimony against him that he stole it [and] slaughtered or sold it — he pays fourfold or fivefold restitution. But if he confessed to the matter before witnesses gave testimony against him, he pays only the principal. [If he did so] after the witnesses gave testimony against him, he pays fourfold or fivefold restitution.

T. 8:3 "Where is my ox, which you stole?" He said to him, "I found it wandering around and I slaughtered it!" "It came to me of its own accord, and I slaughtered it" "It came to me of its own accord and I slaughtered it!;' "It was standing around in the market and I slaughtered it!" [the plaintiff then says], "I impose an oath upon you to that effect," and he says, "Amen" — and then witnesses come along and testify against him that he had stolen and slaughtered or sold [the sheep or the ox] — he pays fourfold or fivefold restitution. But if he confessed to the matter, whether this is after the witnesses came upon the scene or even before the witnesses came upon the scene, he pays only the principal.

T. 8:4 "Where is my ox, which I left under your guardianship?" He said to him, "I don't know what in the world you're talking about!" or if he said to him, "It disappeared," and then witnesses came along and testified against him that he had eaten it — he pays only the principal. And if he confessed to the accusation, whether this was after the witnesses came along or before the witnesses came along, he pays only the principal.

T. 8:5. "Where is my ox, which you stole?" [if] he said to him, "You sold it to me!" or, "You gave it to me as a gift!" "Your father sold it to me!" Your father gave it to me as a gift!" [and the plaintiff responds], "I impose an oath upon you," [and the defendant said,] "Amen" — and then witnesses come along and testify against him that he had stolen and slaughtered or sold [the sheep or the ox], he pays fourfold or fivefold restitution. But if he had confessed to the matter after the taking of the oath, if this was before the witnesses came along, he pays the principal and an added fifth, as well as a guilt-offering. Now if this was after the witnesses came along, he pays fourfold or fivefold restitution.

T. 8:6 "Where is my ox, which you stole?" He said to him, "I found it wandering around and I slaughtered it!" "On its own it came to me and I slaughtered it!" "I impose an oath upon you [that you are telling the truth]," and he said, "Amen" — then witnesses come along and give testimony against him that in fact he had stolen and slaughtered or sold it — he pays fourfold or fivefold restitution. [If] he confessed after the taking of an oath, whether this is after the witnesses had come along or before the witnesses had come along, he has to pay the principal, an added fifth, and a guilt-offering.

T. 8:7 "Where is my ox, which I left under your guardianship?" He said to him, "I haven't got the slightest idea what you're talking about!" or if he said to him, "It got lost," "I impose an oath on you," and he said, "Amen," then witnesses come along and give testimony against him that he had in fact eaten it — he pays only the principal. [If] he confessed after the taking of the oath, whether this was before the witnesses came along or after the witnesses came along, he pays the principal, the added fifth, and a guilt-offering.

T. 8:8 "Where is my ox?" He said to him, "It was stolen." "I impose an oath on you!" And he said, "Amen." Then witnesses come along and give testimony concerning him that he had stolen it — he pays twofold restitution.

B. PENALTIES FOR ABUSE OF THE LAND

M. 7:7 They do not rear small cattle in the Land of Israel, but they do rear them in Syria and in the wastelands which are in the Land of Israel. They do not rear chickens in Jerusalem, on account of the Holy Things, nor do priests [rear chickens] anywhere in the Land of Israel, because of the [necessity to preserve] the cleanness [of heave offering and certain other foods which are handed over to the priests]. They do not rear pigs anywhere. A person should not rear a dog, unless it is kept tied up by a chain. They do not set traps for pigeons, unless they are thirty ris from a settlement.

T. 8:17 Just as they do not raise small domesticated cattle, so they do not raise small wild beasts.

B. 7:7 I.1/79B THEY DO NOT REAR SMALL CATTLE IN THE LAND OF ISRAEL, BUT THEY DO REAR THEM IN WOODLANDS IN THE LAND OF ISRAEL, AND IN SYRIA, EVEN IN INHABITED AREAS, AND ONE NEED NOT SAY OUTSIDE OF THE LAND OF ISRAEL ALTOGETHER. THEY DO NOT REAR SMALL CATTLE IN THE LAND OF ISRAEL, BUT THEY DO REAR THEM IN THE WILDERNESS OF JUDAH AND IN THE WILDERNESS AT THE BORDER OF AKKO. AND EVEN THOUGH SAGES HAVE SAID, "THEY DO NOT RAISE SMALL CATTLE," THEY MAY IN ANY EVENT RAISE LARGE CATTLE, FOR A DECREE MAY NOT BE ISSUED FOR THE COMMUNITY THAT THE MAJORITY OF THE COMMUNITY CAN CARRY IT OUT. IN THE CASE OF SMALL CATTLE, IT IS POSSIBLE TO IMPORT THEM FROM ABROAD; IN THE CASE OF LARGE CATTLE, IT IS NOT POSSIBLE TO IMPORT THEM FROM ABROAD. AND EVEN THOUGH SAGES HAVE SAID, "THEY DO NOT RAISE SMALL CATTLE," ONE MAY NONETHELESS HOLD ON TO THEM FOR THIRTY DAYS PRIOR TO A FESTIVAL, OR FOR THIRTY DAYS PRIOR TO THE CELEBRATION OF A WEDDING OF ONE OF HIS SONS. BUT HE MAY NOT HOLD ON TO AN ANIMAL BOUGHT FOR THIRTY DAYS, IF THE THIRTY DAYS EXPIRE AFTER THE FESTIVAL. BUT A BUTCHER MAY PURCHASE AND SLAUGHTER, PURCHASE AND HOLD A BEAST, SO LONG AS HE DOES NOT HOLD ON FOR MORE THAN THIRTY DAYS TO AN ANIMAL THAT HE HAS BOUGHT.

B. 7:7 I.16/80B-81A THERE WERE TEN STIPULATIONS THAT JOSHUA MADE WHEN THE ISRAELITES ENTERED THE LAND: [1] THAT CATTLE MAY BE ALLOWED TO PASTURE IN FORESTS; [2] THAT WOOD MAY BE GATHERED FREELY IN PRIVATE FIELDS; [3] THAT GRASS MAY BE GATHERED FREELY IN PRIVATE PROPERTY, EXCEPT FOR A FIELD WHERE FENUGREC IS GROWING; [4] THAT SHOOTS MAY BE CUT OFF FREELY IN ANY PLACE, EXCEPT FOR STUMPS OF OLIVE TREES; [5] THAT A SPRING EMERGING EVEN TO BEGIN WITH MAY BE USED BY TOWNSFOLK; [6] THAT IT IS

PERMITTED TO FISH AT AN ANGLE IN THE SEA OF TIBERIAS, SO LONG AS
NO SAIL IS SPREAD OUT, SINCE THIS WOULD DETAIN THE BOATS; [7]
THAT IT IS PERMITTED TO TAKE A CRAP AT THE BACK OF ANY FENCE,
EVEN IN A FIELD FULL OF SAFFRON; [8] THAT IT IS PERMITTED TO USE
PATHS IN PRIVATE FIELDS UNTIL THE TIME THAT THE SECOND RAINS ARE
ANTICIPATED; [9] THAT IT IS PERMITTED TO TURN ASIDE TO PRIVATE
PATHS TO AVOID ROAD PEGS; [10] THAT SOMEONE WHO IS LOST IN
VINEYARDS IS PERMITTED TO CUT THROUGH GOING UP OR CUT THROUGH
GOING DOWN; [11] THAT A DEAD BODY THAT SOMEONE FINDS NEGLECTED
AND SUBJECT TO IMMEDIATE BURIAL ACQUIRES THE SPOT ON WHICH IT IS
FOUND.

C. PENALTIES FOR ASSAULT

**M. 8:1 He who injures his fellow is liable to [compensate]
him on five counts: (1) injury, (2) pain, (3) medical costs, (4)
loss of income [lit.: loss of time], and (5) indignity For injury:
How so? [If] one has blinded his eye, cut off his hand, broken
his leg, they regard him as a slave up for sale in the market
and make an estimate of how much he was worth beforehand
[when whole], and how much he is now worth. Pain: [If] he
burned him with a spit or a nail, and even on his fingernail,
a place in which [the injury] does not leave a lasting wound,
they assess how much a man in his status is willing to take to
suffer pain of that sort. Medical costs: If] he hit him, he is
liable to provide for his medical care. [If] sores arise on him,
if [they are] on account of the blow, he is liable; [but if] they
are not on account of the blow, he is exempt. [If] the wound
got better and opened up again, got better and opened up
again, he remains liable to provide for his medical care. [If
the wound] properly healed, he is no longer liable to provide
medical care for him. Loss of income: They regard him [in
estimating income] as if he is a keeper of a cucumber field,
for [the defendant] already has paid off the value of his hand
or his leg. Indignity: All [is assessed] in accord with the status
of the one who inflicts the indignity and the one who suffers
the indignity. He who inflicts indignity on one who is naked,
he who inflicts indignity on one who is blind, or he who
inflicts indignity on one who is asleep is liable. But one who
is sleeping who inflicted indignity is exempt [on that count].
[If] he fell from the roof and did injury and also inflicted
indignity, he is liable for the injury [he has inflicted] but
exempt from the indignity. One is liable on the count of
indignity only if he intended [to inflict indignity].**

T. 9:1 There are thirteen generative causes [categories] of damages: ox, pit, destroying beast, conflagration [M. B.Q. 1:1A], unpaid bailee, borrower, paid bailee, renter, injury, pain, medical costs, loss of income, indignity [M. B.Q. 8:1B]. [If] one has inflicted on another person all five [kinds of damage], he pays him for all five. [If he inflicted] only four kinds, he pays him for four. [If he inflicted] only three kinds, he pays him for three. [If he inflicted] only two kinds, he pays him for two. [If he inflicted] only one kind, he pays him for one.

Y. 8:1 I:1 How so? [If] he hit him on his hand and cut it off, he pays all five kinds of compensation: for injury, pain, medical costs, loss of income, and indignity. [If] he hit him on his hand and it swelled up, he pays him four: pain, medical costs, loss of income, and indignity. [If] he hit him on his head and it swelled up, he pays him three: pain, medical costs, and loss of income. If] he hit him on a part of the body which is not visible, he pays him two: pain and medical costs. In the case of hitting his book which is in his hand, he pays him only compensation for the humiliation.

T. 9:2 For injury: How so? [If] he hit him and cut off his hand, hit him and cut off his leg [M. B.Q. 8:1D], they do not regard him as if he makes a sela a day, or as if he makes a maneh a day. But they regard him as if he is a cripple who serves as a watchman for a cucumber-field. And if you say that this smites the rule of justice, the rule of justice indeed has not been smitten. For in any event they pay off the value of the hand or the value of the leg [M. B.Q. 8:1P].

T. 9:3 But [if] he hit him and his hand dried up [and withered], or he hit him and his leg dried up, they do regard him as if he makes a sela a day, and they pay him compensation of a sela a day, or they do regard him as if he makes a maneh a day and pay him off a maneh a day. And they pay him all the compensation for damages. And all of them do they estimate and pay off forthwith. Therefore if he continues to fail, even for five years he has a claim only on the [original] estimate they made for him. How long do they continue to pay him off? Until he returns to health.

T. 9:4 If ulcers grew up on the body because of the wound, and the wound broke open again, he still has to heal him and pay for loss of time, but if it was not because of the wound, he does not have to pay for the healing or the loss of time.

T. 9:5 He who hit his fellow — [if] they formed a prognosis that he would die, they again assess that he would live. [If they formed a prognosis] that he would live, they do not again assess that he would die. [If] they assessed that he would die, then the defendant is liable to the death penalty but exempt from having to pay monetary compensation. [If] they made an estimate as to the monetary compensation, the defendant is liable to pay monetary compensation and exempt from the death penalty. [If] they assessed that he would die, and he got better, they make an estimate of the monetary compensation to be paid a second time. From what point does he pay him off? From the point at which he hit him.

T. 9:6 [If] they assessed that he would live and he died, [the defendant] pays compensation for injury, pain, medical costs, loss of income, and indignity, to the estate of the deceased. [If] they assessed that he would die and he got somewhat better and then got somewhat worse and finally died, they make an estimate of the matter. If on account of the original injury he died, he is liable. [If this] was not the case, lo, this one is exempt.

B. 8:1 V.2/86A IF ONE CUT OFF THE OTHER'S HAND, HE PAYS HIM THE VALUE OF HIS HAND, AND, AS TO LOSS OF TIME FROM WORK, THEY REGARD HIM AS THOUGH HE WERE A WATCHMEN OF A CUCUMBER FIELD. IF HE CUT OFF HIS LEG, HE PAYS HIM FOR THE DEPRECIATION TO HIS WORTH CAUSED BY THE LOSS OF THE LEG, AND, AS TO LOSS OF TIME FROM WORK, THEY REGARD HIM AS THEY HE WERE A DOORKEEPER. IF HE PUT OUT HIS EYE, HE PAYS HIM FOR THE DEPRECIATION OF HIS VALUE BECAUSE OF THE LOSS OF THE EYE, AND AS TO THE LOSS OF TIME FROM WORK, HE IS REGARDED AS IF HE WERE PUSHING THE GRINDING WHEEL IN A MILL. BUT IF HE MADE THE OTHER PARTY DEAF, HE PAYS THE ENTIRE VALUE OF THE PERSON, PURE AND SIMPLE [SINCE HE IS WORTH NOTHING]

T. 9:12 He who inflicts indignity on his fellow when he is naked, lo, he is liable. But it is not the same thing to inflict indignity upon him when he is naked as it is to inflict indignity on him when he is clothed. If he inflicted indignity on him when he was in the bathhouse, lo, this one is liable. But it is not the same thing to inflict indignity upon him when he is in the bathhouse as it is to inflict indignity on him when he is in the market. [And it is not the same thing to receive an indignity from an honored person as it is to receive an indignity from a worthless person. And the indignity inflicted upon a great person who is humiliated is not equivalent to the indignity inflicted upon an unimportant person who is humiliated, or the child of important parents who is subjected to an indignity to the child of unimportant parents who is subjected to an indignity].

M. 8:2 This rule is more strict in the case of man than in the case of an ox. For a man pays compensation for injury, pain, medical costs, loss of income, and indignity; and he pays compensation for the offspring [Ex. 21:22]. But [the owner of] an ox pays compensation only for the injury. And he is exempt from liability to pay compensation for the offspring. M. 8:3 He who hits his father or his mother but did not make a wound on them, or he who injures his fellow on the Day of Atonement is liable on all counts. He who injures a Hebrew slave is liable on all counts, except for loss of time when he belongs to him [who did the damage]. He who injures a Canaanite slave belonging to other people is liable on all counts. M. 8:4 A deaf-mute, idiot, and minor — meeting up with them is a bad thing. He who injures them is liable. But they who injure other people are exempt. A slave and a woman — meeting up with them is a bad thing He who injures them is liable. And they who injure other people are exempt. But they pay compensation after an interval: [if] the woman is divorced, the slave freed, they become liable to pay compensation.

T. 9:8 He who injures his adult sons or daughters is liable under all counts. If he injured a Hebrew boy-slave or girl-slave belonging to other people, they collect from him. And [as to what he owes] his daughter, he pays her off immediately. [As to what he owes] his son, he sets it aside for him [in trust]. [If he injured] his minor sons or daughters, he is exempt on all counts. He who injures his minor daughter — the compensation for her injury belongs to her, and for all other forms of compensation lo, he is exempt.

T. 9:9 [If] others injured her, compensation for her injury belongs to her. And as to the rest of the compensation, he sets it aside for her [in trust]. And if she dies, he inherits her estate.

9:10 He who injures his minor son is liable on all counts. [If he injured] his Canaanite boy-slave or girl-slave, he is liable on all counts, but exempt on the count of compensation for the loss of time, for compensation for loss of time in any event belongs to him [the owner] [M. B.Q. 8:3D-E]. [If] he beat them more than is appropriate, he is liable.

T. 9:11 A father who hits his son, and a teacher who smites his disciple, who smote and did damage — lo, these are exempt. [If] they beat them more than is appropriate, lo, these are liable. A court-officer who administered a blow at the behest of the court and did injury is exempt. [If] he beat the criminal more than is appropriate, lo, this one is liable. A qualified physician who administered a remedy at the behest of a court and did damage is exempt. [If] he did more damage than was appropriate for this case, lo, this one is liable.

T. 9:13 He who inflicts injury on a deaf-mute, idiot, or minor, is liable on four counts, but exempt on the count of indignity, because they are not subject to indignity.

T. 9:14 He who inflicts injury upon his wife — whether he injured her or whether others injured her — they collect [damages] from him. With the compensation, a field is purchased, and he enjoys the usufruct thereof.

Y. 8:4 I:1 [With reference to Ex. 21:26-27: "When a man strikes the eye of his slave,...and destroys it, he shall let the slave go free for his eye's sake. If he knocks out the tooth of his slave,...he shall let the slave go free for the tooth's sake."] Witnesses who stated, "We testify concerning Mr. So-and-so, that he has blinded both eyes of his slave simultaneously," "he has knocked out two of his teeth simultaneously," — the master pays nothing to the slave at all [but sends him forth free]. [If they testified that he had done so] one after another, the slave goes forth to freedom on account of the first, and the master pays him compensation for the loss of the second. The witnesses who testified, "We give evidence that Mr. So-and-so blinded the eye of his slave and afterward he knocked out his tooth," and so the master says, and who turned out to be perjurers — they pay compensation to the slave. [If they said,] ". . . he knocked out his tooth and afterward he blinded his eye," And so the slave says, and they turned out to be perjurers, they pay to the master. [If they said,] "He blinded both of them at once," or "He knocked out both of them at once," and others came and said, "Not so, but it was two of them in succession," and they turned out to be perjurers — they pay to the slave. [If they said,] "He blinded both of them one after the other, or knocked out both of them one after the other," and others came along and said, "Not so, but he did both of them at once," and they turned out to be perjurers — they pay to the master. He blinded the eye of his slave, and lo, he is yet subject to him and working for him—

*and they turn out to be perjurer, they pay both the value of the
slave and of the blinding to the master [=T. Mak. 1:4-5].*

**M. 8:5 He who hits his father or his mother and did make a
wound on them, and he who injures his fellow on the Sabbath
is exempt on all counts, for he is put on trial for his life. And
he who injures a Canaanite slave belonging to himself is
exempt on all counts.**

T. 9:17 [If someone] killed him and killed his beast
simultaneously, killed him and cut off his hand simultaneously,
killed him and blinded his eye simultaneously, [the killer] is
exempt [from having to pay monetary compensation], since it
is said, "when men strive together and hurt a woman with child
so that there is a miscarriage] and yet no harm follows, the one
who hurt her shall be fined" (Ex. 21:22) if there is harm, then
there is no penalty. But if [the defendant] killed his beast and
then killed him, cut off his hand and then killed him, blinded
his eye and killed him, he is liable, since it is said, "He shall
make restitution" (Ex. 22:5). This is the governing principle:
Anyone who is subject to both the death penalty and civil
damages simultaneously is exempt. [But if he is subject to] the
death penalty and afterward to civil damages, or to civil damages
and afterward to the death penalty, lo, this person is liable [for
both].

T. 9:19 He who steals the purse of his fellow and took it out [of
his domain] on the Sabbath, lo, this person is liable, for he
already had become obligated on account of the theft of the
wallet before it had gone forth. If he was dragging it along and
so removed it from the domain of the other, he is exempt [since
he did not make acquisition of the purse before he had also and
simultaneously violated the Sabbath].

T. 9:21 He who does injury to his Hebrew boy-slave or girl-
slave, when they are by themselves [so there are no witnesses]
— lo, these are subjected to an oath and collect [damages]. He
who does injury to his Canaanite boy-slave or girl-slave, when
they are by themselves — is exempt [from paying damages],
for [compensation for injury] is a fine, [and a fine is not imposed
upon the confession of the defendant alone].

T. 9 :22 He who hits his slave — [and then] sold him to someone
else, and [the slave] died — is exempt, since it says, "And he
died under his hand" (Ex. 21:20) — [meaning that one is
punished only] when the act of hitting the slave and the death
of the slave take place while the slave is in the master's domain.
A slave who inflicted injury upon himself goes forth to freedom

and pays off his master. And a woman who inflicted injury on her husband does not lose any of the value of her marriage settlement on that account. And just as she cannot sell off her marriage-settlement while she is subject to him, so she cannot lose a penny of the value of her marriage-settlement while she is subject to him [cf. M. B.Q. 8:4G-H].

T. 9:28 He who injures his fellow, and the one who did the injury died — the heirs must pay compensation. [If] the one who was injured died, [the defendant] pays the estate of the one who was injured. Whether there is a claim or not, this one would take an oath and collect [what was coming to him].]

M. 8:6 He who boxes the ear of his fellow pays him a sela. [If] he smacked him, he pays him two hundred zuz. [If] it is with the back of his hand, he pays him four hundred zuz. [If] he (1) tore at his ear, (2) pulled his hair, (3) spit, and the spit hit him, (4) pulled off his cloak, (5) pulled apart the hairdo of a woman in the marketplace, he pays four hundred zuz.

M. 8:7 Even though [the defendant] pays off [the plaintiff], he is not forgiven until he seeks [forgiveness] from [the plaintiff]. He who says, "Blind my eye," "Cut off my hand," "Break my leg" — [the one who does so] is liable. [If he added,] ". . . on condition of being exempt," [the one who does so] is liable [anyhow]. "Tear my cloak," "Break my jar," [the one who does so] is liable. [If he added,] ". . . on condition of being exempt," [the one who does so] is exempt. "Do it to Mr. So-and-so, on condition of being exempt," he [who does so] is liable, whether this is to his person or to his property.

T. 9:32 He who says, "Blind my eye, which is doing me harm," "Chop off my hand, which is doing me harm," — he is exempt [cf. M. B.Q. 8:7E-I].

T. 9:33 [If] gentiles forced a person and he took away the possessions of his fellow in his very presence, he is exempt. [But if on his own volition] he took them and handed them out, lo, this person is liable [cf. M. B.Q. 8:7N-O].

B. 8:7 I.1/92A ALL OF THESE SUMS THAT ARE SPECIFIED REPRESENT THE MONETARY COMPENSATION FOR HUMILIATION, BUT AS TO THE ANGUISH, EVEN IF THE OFFENDER BROUGHT ALL OF THE FINEST RAMS IN THE WORLD, THE MAN IS NOT FORGIVEN UNTIL HE ASKS FORGIVENESS FROM HIM, AS IT IS SAID, "NOW RESTORE THE MAN'S WIFE...AND HE WILL PRAY FOR YOU" (GEN. 20:7).

D. PENALTIES FOR DAMAGES DONE BY PERSONS TO
    PROPERTY; RESTORING WHAT IS STOLEN

**M. 9:1 [If] he stole a pregnant cow and it gave birth, a ewe
heavy with wool [needing shearing], and he sheared it — he
pays the value of a cow which is about to give birth, or of a
ewe which is about to be sheared. [If] he stole a cow, and it
got pregnant while with him and gave birth, a ewe, and it
became heavy [with wool] while with him, and he sheared,
he pays [compensation in accord with the value of the cow
or ewe] at the time of the theft. This is the governing
principle: all robbers pay compensation [in accord with the
value of the stolen object] at the time of the theft.**

T. 10:1 He who steals a cow and it became pregnant while in
his domain, and did so a second, a third, and even a fourth and
fifth time and so too, he who steals a ewe, and it grows a full
crop of wool while in his domain, even four or five times, a
goat, and he milks it, even four or five times — he pays
compensation lin accord with the value of the stolen beast] at
the time of the theft.

T. 10:2 [If] he stole wool and bleached it, thread and he bleached
it, flax and he washed it, stones and he smoothed them down,
he pays compensation [in accord with their value] at the time
of the theft. [M. B.Q. 9:1A-C].

**M. 9:2 [If] he stole a beast and it got old, slaves and they got
old, he pays [compensation for them in accord with their
value] at the time of the theft. [If] he stole (1) a coin and it
got cracked, (2) pieces of fruit and they turned rotten, (3)
wine and it turned into vinegar, he pays [compensation for
them in accord with their value] at the time of the theft. [If
he stole] (1) a coin, and it was declared invalid, (2) heave
offering, and it became unclean, (3) leaven, and the festival
of Passover passed [making it no longer available for Israelite
use], (4) a beast, and a transgression was committed upon
it, or (5) [a beast] which was invalidated for use on the altar,
or (6) which was going forth to be stoned, [the robber] says
to him, "Here is what is yours right in front of you!"**

T. 10:4 This is the governing principle: Anything which is stolen,
which is available, and [the thief] in no way has changed it
from its original condition — [the thief may] say to him, "Lo,
there is your property before you." But if he changed it in some
way from its original condition, he pays [compensation in accord
with the value] at the time of the robbery. The thief under all

circumstances pays compensation in accord with the value at the time of the theft.

T. 10:7 He who goes down into the ruin which belongs to his fellow and builds it up without permission — they make an estimate [of the matter], and his hand is underneath. He who goes down with permission — they make an estimate [of the matter], and his hand is now on top. How is it that his hand is on the top? If the increase in value is greater than the outlay, he pays him off the increase in value. If the outlay is greater than the increase in value, he pays him what he has laid out.

B. 9:2 IV.1/98A AN OX THAT KILLED SOMEONE — IF THE OWNER SOLD IT BEFORE THE COURT DECREE WAS ISSUED, IT IS DEEMED TO HAVE BEEN VALIDLY SOLD. IF THE OWNER SANCTIFIED IT TO THE TEMPLE, IT IS VALIDLY SANCTIFIED. IF HE SLAUGHTERED IT, ITS MEAT IS PERMITTED. IF THE BAILEE RETURNED IT TO THE HOUSEHOLD OF THE OWNER, IT IS VALIDLY RETURNED [AND THE BAILEE HAS NO FURTHER OBLIGATION]. IF AFTER THE COURT DECREE WAS ISSUED, THE OWNER SOLD IT, IT IS DEEMED NOT TO HAVE BEEN VALIDLY SOLD. IF THE OWNER SANCTIFIED IT TO THE TEMPLE, IT IS NOT VALIDLY SANCTIFIED. IF HE SLAUGHTERED IT, ITS MEAT IS NOT PERMITTED. IF THE BAILEE RETURNED IT TO THE HOUSEHOLD OF THE OWNER, IT IS NOT VALIDLY RETURNED.

M. 9:3 [If] one gave [something] to craftsmen to repair, and they spoiled [the object], they are liable to pay compensation. [If] he gave to a joiner a box, chest, or cupboard to repair, and he spoiled it, he is liable to pay compensation. A builder who took upon himself to destroy a wall, and who smashed the rocks or did damage is liable to pay compensation. [If] he was tearing down the wall on one side, and it fell down on the other side, he is exempt. But if it is because of the blow [which he gave it], he is liable.

T. 10:8 A carpenter who drove a nail into a box, chest, or cupboard, and it broke [M. B.Q. 9:3B], is liable to pay compensation, because he is tantamount to a paid bailee. [If] one handed [wood] over to a joiner to make a chair for him, and he made a bench, a bench, and he made a chair, the hand of the owner is on top. If he gave [wood] to a carpenter to make him a nice chair, and he made him an ugly one, a nice bench, and he made him an ugly one [M. B.Q. 9:3A], the hand of the owner is on top.

9:4 He who hands over wool to a dyer, and the [dye in the] cauldron burned it, [the dyer] pays the value of the wool. [If] he dyed it in a bad color, if [the wool] increased in value

more than the outlay [of the dyer], [the owner of the wool] pays him the money he has laid out in the process of dyeing. But if the outlay of the dyer is greater than the increase in value of the wool, [the owner] pays him back only the value of the improvement.

T. 10:9 He who brings wheat to be ground, and [the miller] did not moisten it, but made it into coarse bran or second-rate flour, or flour to a baker, and he made it into crumbly bread, or meat to a butcher, and he burned it, he is liable to pay damages, because he is in the status *of* a paid bailee.

T. 10:10 He who hands over his beast to a butcher, and it is made into carrion [by the butcher's error], [if he was] a professional, he is exempt. [If he was] an ordinary person, he is liable. [If] he was a paid bailee, one way or the other, he is liable. He who shows a denar to a money-changer and it turns out to be bad is liable to pay [a good denar], because he is in the status of one who is a paid bailee.

M. 9:5 He who stole something from his fellow worth only a perutah, and took an oath to him [that he had stolen nothing, but then wants to make restitution], must take it to him, even all the way to Media. He should not give it to his son or his agent, but he may hand it over to an agent appointed by a court. And if [the victim] died, [the robber] restores [the object] to his estate.

M. 9:6 [If the thief] paid him back the principal but did not pay the added fifth, [if the victim] forgave him the value of the principal but did not forgive him the value of the added fifth, [if] he forgave him for this and for that, except for something less a perutah out of the principal, he need not take it back to him. [If] he [the thief] gave him back the added fifth and did not hand over the principal. [If the victim] forgave him the added fifth but did not forgive him the principal, forgave him for this and for that, except for an amount of the principal that added up to a perutah, then he has to go after him [to make restitution, wherever he may be].

M. 9:7 [If] he paid him back the principal but swore [falsely] to him about the added fifth [and then confessed], lo, this one pays back an added fifth for the added fifth, [and so is the rule] until the value of the principal [of the added fifth] becomes less than a perutah in value. And so [is the rule] in the case of a bailment. If this one pays back the principal,

an added fifth, and a guilt offering. [If one said], "Where is my bailment?" he said to him, "It got lost." "I impose an oath on you!" and he said, "Amen," then witnesses come along and give testimony against him that he had eaten it up — he pays back the principal. [If] he had confessed on his own, he pays back the principal, the added fifth, and a guilt offering.

M. 9:8 "Where is my bailment?" He said to him, "It was stolen." "I impose an oath on you!" And he said, "Amen," — Then witnesses come along and testify against him that he stole it, he pays twofold restitution. [If] he had confessed on his own, he pays the principal, an added fifth, and a guilt offering.

M. 9:9 He who steals from his father and takes an oath to him, and then [the father] dies — lo, this one pays back the principal and an added fifth to his [father's other] sons or brothers [and brings the guilt offering]. But if he does not want to do so or does not have what to pay back, he takes out a loan, and the creditors come along and collect what is owing.

M. 9:10 He who says to his son, "Qonam! You will not derive benefit from anything that is mine!" — if the father died, the son may inherit him. [But if he had specified that the vow applied] in life and after death, if the father died, the son may not inherit him. And he must return [what he has of the father's] to his sons or to his brothers. And if he does not have that to repay, he takes out a loan, and the creditors come along and collect what is owing.

M. 9:11 He who steals from a proselyte and takes a [false] oath to him, and then [the proselyte] dies — lo, this person pays the principal and added fifth to the priests, and the guilt offering to the altar. [If the thief] was bringing up the money and the guilt offering and he died, the money is to be given to his [the thief's] sons. And the guilt offering is set out to pasture until it suffers a disfiguring blemish, then it is sold, and the money received for it falls to the chest for the purchase of a freewill offering.

M. 9:12 If he [who had stolen from a proselyte] had paid over the money to the men of the priestly watch on duty, and then [the thief] died, the heirs cannot retrieve the funds from their possession. [If] he gave the money to the priestly watch of Jehoiarib [which is prior], and the guilt offering to

the priestly watch of Jedaiah [which is later], he has carried out his obligation. If he gave] the guilt offering to the priestly watch of Jehoiarib and the money to the priestly watch of Jedaiah, if the guilt offering is yet available, the family of Jedaiah should offer it And if not, he should go and bring another guilt offering. For he who brings back what he had stolen before he brought his guilt offering has fulfilled his obligation. But if he brought his guilt offering before he brought back what he had stolen, he has not fulfilled his obligation. [If] he handed over the principal but did not hand over the added fifth, the added fifth does not stand in the way [of offering the guilt offering and so completing his obligation].

T. 10:14-15 He who robs the public is liable to restore [what he has stolen] to the public. A more strict rule applies to robbing the public than to robbing an individual. For he who robs from an individual can appease him and restore to him what he has stolen. But he who robs from the public cannot appease all of them and restore to them what he has stolen. He who robs from a gentile is liable to restore to the gentile [what he has stolen]. A more strict rule applies to robbing from a gentile than to robbing from an Israelite, because of the profanation of the Divine Name [involved in robbing from a gentile].

M. 10:1 He who steals [food] and feeds [what he stole] to his children, or left it to them — they are exempt from making restitution. But if it was something which is subject to a mortgage, [that is, real estate] , they are liable to make restitution. They do not change money from the chest of the excise collectors or from the fund of the tax farmers. And they do not take from them contributions to charity. But one may take [from them contributions for charity] when the funds are] from [the collector's] own home or from the marketplace.

T. 5:25 An Israelite who lends money to his fellow on interest and then repented is liable to return [to him the interest he has collected]. [If] he died and left [the money] to his children, the children do not have to return [the money he collected at interest]. And in such a case it is said, "[Though he heap up silver like dust, and pile up clothing like clay;] he may pile it up, but they just will wear it, and the innocent will divide the silver" (Job 27:17). But if their father had left them a cow, a field, a cloak or any sort of object for which he bore responsibility [for replacement, should the object be lost], they are liable to return such an object, for the honor of their father. T. 10:20 If one has stolen and exchanged stolen and consecrated [the object], stolen and given the object as a gift, stolen and placed the object out on loan, stolen and paid a debt, stolen and sent gifts to the house of his father-in-law — lo, this one is liable. But the one who receives the object from him is exempt/ T. B.M. 2:25-6 If the father died and left money gained on interest to his children, even if the heirs know that it was money paid as interest, the children do not have to return the money collected as interest. [But if the father had left them a cow, field, cloak, or any sort of object for which he bore responsibility for replacement, should the object be lost, they are liable to return such an object for the honor of their father].

Y. 10:1 II.4 He who robs and feeds his minor children [cf. M. 10:lA], his Canaanite boy-slave or girl-slave — they are exempt from paying restitution. [Yerushalmi's version: He who robs and feeds his children, whether adult or minor, they are exempt from having to pay restitution. If he left it to them, whether adult or minor, they are liable to do so. Sumkhos says, "The elders are liable, the minors are exempt."] [If] he left them something which is subject to a mortgage, they are liable to make restitution. But if they said, "We do not know what reckoning father made with you [at the hour of his death]," they are exempt from liability to make restitution.

B. 10:1A-C I.1/111B IF ONE STOLE SOMETHING [SUCH AS AN ANIMAL], AND, BEFORE THE OWNER HAD DESPAIRED OF GETTING IT BACK [AT WHICH POINT THE THIEF ACQUIRES TITLE TO THE OBJECT], SOMEONE ELSE CAME ALONG AND ATE UP WHAT HE STOLE, THE OWNER HAS THE CHOICE OF COLLECTING THE PAYMENT FROM THE ONE OR THE OTHER.

M. 10:2 [If] excise collectors took one's ass and gave him another ass, [if) thugs took his garment and gave him another garment, lo, these are his, because the original owners have given up hope of getting them back. He who saves something from a river, from a raid, or from thugs, if the owner has given up hope of getting them back, lo, these belong to him. And so a swarm of bees: If the owner had given up hope of getting it back, lo, this belongs to him. And one may walk through the field of his fellow to get back his swarm of bees. But if he did damage, he pays compensation for the damage which he did. But he may not cut off a branch of his tree [to retrieve the swarm, even] on condition that he pay damages for it.

T. 10:23 A thief who took from this one and gave to that one —
what he has given he has given, and what he has taken he has
taken. A robber who took from this one and gave to that one —
what he has given he has given, and what he has taken he has
taken [cf. M. B.Q. 10:2A-C]. The Jordan [river] which took [a
piece of ground] from this one and [by changing its course]
gave it to that one — what it has taken it has taken, and what it
has given, it has given.

T. 10:24 [If] the river swept away wood, stones, and beams,
from this one, and gave them to that one, if the owner has given
up hope of recovering [what he has lost], lo, these belong to
him [on whose property they were deposited] [M. B.Q. 10:2E-
F]. If the owner continued to go looking for them, or if they
were in some other place, lo, these remain [the possession] of
the owner.

T. 10:27 At what point does a man acquire possession of a
swarm of bees? Once it enters his own enclosed yard. Lo, this
one, whose swarm of bees has gone down into the garden of his
fellow, but the owner of the garden will not let him go in, so
that he will not break down the greens of his vegetables — lo,
this one goes down against the will of the other, and saves his
swarm of bees [M. B.Q. 10:2J]. But if he did damage, he pays
compensation for the damage which he did.

**M. 10:3 He who recognizes his utensils or his books in
someone else's possession, and a report of theft had gone
forth in the town — the purchaser takes an oath to him
specifying how much he had paid and takes [the price in
compensation from the original owner, and gives back the
property] — And if not, [the original owner] has not got the
power [to get his property back]. For I say, "[The original
owner] sold them to someone else, and this one [lawfully]
bought them from that other person."**

**M. 10:4 This one is coming along with his jar of wine, and
that one is coming along with his jug of honey — the jug of
honey cracked — and this one poured out his wine and saved
the honey in his jar, he has a claim only for his wages. And if
he said, "I'll save yours if you pay me back for mine," [the
owner of the honey] is liable to pay him back. [If] the river
swept away his ass and the ass of his fellow, his being worth
a maneh and his fellow's worth two hundred [zuz] [twice as
much], [if] he then left his own and saved that of his fellow,
he has a claim only for his wages. But if he said, "I'll save**

yours, if you pay me back for mine," [the owner of the better ass] is liable to pay him back.

T. 10 :26 [If] this one unloaded his pieces of wood and saved the flax of his fellow, [the latter] pays him his wages, calculated as the value of returning a lost object. If he had said to him, ". . . on condition that he [I] may collect the value of mine [which I shall lose] out of yours," he is liable to pay it to him.

T. 10:28 Two who were in the wilderness, and in the hand of one of them was a jar of water, while in the hand of the other was a jar of honey, [if] the jar of water cracked, it is a condition imposed upon the court that this one should pour out his honey and save the water of his fellow. And when he reaches a settled area, he pays him back the value of his honey. For water preserves life in the wilderness, and honey does not preserve life in the wilderness.

T. B.M. 7:13 A caravan that was passing through the wilderness, and a band of thugs fell on it and seized it for ransom — they make a reckoning in accord with the property loss and not in accord with the number of people. But if they sent out a pathfinder before them, they also make a reckoning of the number of people. But in any event they do not vary from the accepted practice governing those who travel in caravans.

T. B.M. 11:25 The ass drivers have the right to declare, "Whoever loses an ass will be given another ass." But if the loss is caused by negligence, they would not have to meet that stipulation, and if it was not on account of negligence, he is given another ass. And if he said, "Give me the money and I'll watch out for it as a paid bailee," they do not listen to him.

T. B.M. 7:14 A boat that was coming along in the sea and got hit by a storm, so they had to toss some cargo overboard — they make a reckoning in accord with the property loss and not in accord with the number of people. But in any event they do not vary from the accepted practice of sailors.

T. B.M. 11:26 And the sailors have the right to declare, "Whoever loses a ship — we'll provide him with another ship." If it was lost through flagrant neglect, they do not have to provide him with another ship. If it was lost not through flagrant neglect, they do have to provide him with another ship. But if he set sail for a place to which people do not prudently set sail, they do not have to provide him with another ship if he loses his on the perilous voyage.

M. 10:5 He who stole a field from his fellow, and bandits seized it from him — if it is a blow [from which the whole]

district [suffered], he may say to him, "Lo, there is yours before you." But if it is because [of the deeds] of the thief [in particular], he is liable to replace it for him with another field. [If] a river swept it away, he may say to him, "Lo, there is yours before you."

Y. 10:5 If he left his own to save that of his fellow, but his fellow's property emerged on its own [without the help of the other], the fellow does not owe him a thing. But if he left his own property to save that of his fellow, and his own property emerged on its own, what is the law governing his claim, "I had given up hope of saving my property," [and since it therefore was lost to me, you owe me compensation for it]? [The stipulated payment must be given.

M. 10:6 He who (1) stole something from his fellow, or (2) borrowed something from him, or (3) with whom the latter deposited something, in a settled area — may not return it to him in the wilderness. [If it was] on the stipulation that he was going to go forth to the wilderness, he may return it to him in the wilderness.

T. 10:32 [If] one handed over to another a house as a pledge [for a loan], or a field as a pledge, and he saw a brush-fire coming toward his property, and he said to him, "Come and save these, which I owe you," if the other accepted, [the former] is exempt. And if not, he is liable [cf. M. B.Q. 10:6D-E].

M. 10:7 He who says to his fellow, "I have stolen from you...," "You have lent something to .me..."You have deposited something with me...," "and I don't know whether or not I returned [the object] to you"' is liable to pay him restitution. But if he said to him, "I don't know whether I stole something from you," ". . . whether you lent me something," ". . . whether you deposited something with me," he is exempt from paying restitution.

M. 10:8 He who steals a lamb from a flock and [unbeknownst to the owner] returned it, and it died or was stolen again, is liable to make it up. [If] the owner did not know either that it had been stolen or that it had been returned, and he counted up the flock and it was complete, then [the thief] is exempt.

T. 10:33 He who steals a lamb from the flock and returned it to the flock, and afterward the entire flock was stolen, if he had informed the owner, or they had counted [the sheep], he is exempt. And if not, he is liable [M. B.Q. 10:8]. He who steals a jug from a cellar and returned it to the cellar, and afterward all the jugs in the cellar were stolen, if he had informed the owner [that he had returned the jug], he is exempt. And if not, he is liable.

T. 10 :35 He who steals a *sela* from a purse and put it back into the purse, and afterward the entire purse was stolen, if he had informed the owner, he is exempt. And if not, he is liable.

T. 10 :36 He who steals the purse of his fellow and returned it to him while he was asleep, and he woke up, and lo, his purse is in his hand, if [the victim] recognizes it as his, [the other] is exempt. And if not, he is liable. He who steals a *sela* without the knowledge of the owner that it has been stolen, and then [to return it] included it into the reckoning [of what he owed the owner], has fulfilled his obligation.

T. 10:39 Thieves who snuck in by stealth and then did repent — all of them are liable to restore what they have stolen. [If] only one of them repented, he is liable to restore only his share [of the theft] alone. [If] he had been taking out what was in the house and placing it before the others, then he is liable to make restitution of all that had been stolen.

T. 11:1 They do not accept bailments from women, slaves, or minors. [If] one has accepted a bailment from a woman, he must return it to the woman. [If the woman] died, he must return it to her husband. [If] he accepted a bailment from a slave, he must return it to the slave. [If the slave] died, he must return it to his master. [If] he accepted a bailment from a minor, he sets up a trust for him. [If] he died, he returns it to his father. And in all of these cases, [if] they said at the moment of death, "Let my bailment be given to so-and-so, to whom they belong," let that which has been spelled out be done in accord with the stipulation thereby given.

T. 11:2 A son who does business with what belongs to his father, and so too a slave who does business with what belongs to his master, lo, [the goods] are deemed to belong to the father, [or] lo, they are deemed to belong to the master. If they said at the moment of death [however], "Let such-and-such an object be given to So-and-so, to whom they belong," let that which has been spelled out be done in accord with the stipulation thereby given.

M. 10:9 They do not purchase from herdsmen wool, milk, or kids, or from watchmen of an orchard wood or fruit. But they purchase clothing of wool from women in Judah, flax

clothing in Galilee, and calves in Sharon. And in all cases in which [the sellers] say to hide them away, it is prohibited [to make such a purchase]. They purchase eggs and chickens in every locale.

T. 11:9 They do not purchase from shepherds either goats or shearings, or bits of wool. But they purchase from them [garments] which have been sewn. For the ones which have been sewn belong to them. And they purchase from them milk and cheese in the wilderness, but not in settled country In any place at all they purchase from them four or five sheep, four or five bundles of fleece. but not two sheep or two bundles of fleece.

T. 11:11 They do not purchase from a weaver either "thorns," remnants of wool, threads of the bobbin, or remnants of the coil. But they purchase from them a checkered web, spun wool, warp, or woof (woven stuff).

T. 11:12 They do not purchase from a dyer either test-pieces, samples, or wool which has been pulled out. But they purchase from him dyed wool, spun wool, warp, or woof. And they do not buy flocking from the fuller, because they do not belong to him. In a place in which they are usually his, lo, these are assumed to be his land may be purchased from him].

B. 10:9 III.1/119A THEY PURCHASE FROM HOUSEWIVES CLOTHING OF WOOL IN JUDEA AND OF FLAX IN GALILEE, BUT NOT WINE NOR OIL NOR FLOUR; NOR DO THEY MAKE PURCHASES FROM SLAVES OR CHILDREN. BUT IN ALL CASES IN WHICH THEY SAID TO HIDE THE GOODS AWAY, IT IS FORBIDDEN TO DO SO. CHARITY COLLECTORS ACCEPT FROM THEM SOME SMALL THING FOR THE PHILANTHROPIC FUND, BUT NOT A LARGE EXPENSIVE GIFT. THEY DO NOT PURCHASE FROM WORKERS AT THE OLIVE PRESS A SMALL AMOUNT OF OIL OR A SMALL QUANTITY OF OLIVES, BUT THEY PURCHASE FROM THEM OIL BY MEASURE AND OLIVES BY MEASURE.

M. 10:10 Shreds of wool which the laundryman pulls out — lo, these belong to him. And those which the wool comber pulls out — lo, they belong to the householder. The laundryman pulls out three threads, and they are his. But more than this — lo, they belong to the householder. If they were black [threads] on a white [surface], he takes all, and they are his. A tailor who left over a thread sufficient for sewing, or a piece of cloth three by three fingerbreadths — lo, these belong to the householder. What the carpenter takes off the plane — lo, these are his. But [what he takes off] with a hatchet belongs to the householder. And if he was

working in the household of the householder, even the
sawdust belongs to the householder.

11:13 They purchase flocking from laundrymen, because they belong to him. And he should not comb the garment along its warp but along its woof. And he should not place in the garment more than three fuller's hooks [for stretching the garment], and the two upper threads — lo, these are his.

T. 11:16. He who hands over hides to a tanner — the scrapings and the bits pulled up — lo, they belong to the householder. And what comes out with the rinse-water — lo, these belong to him.

T. 11:17 A tailor who left over a thread shorter than the length of a hem, or a piece of cloth three by three fingerbreadths — and he who hands over hides to a tanner — all of them, [when working] in the house of the householder — lo, they belong to the householder.

T. 11:18 Stone-cutters, vine-trimmers, shrub-trimmers, and weed-cutters, when the householder is supervising them, are subject to prohibition on account of thievery. He who hires a worker to trim shrubs with him, or to cut vines — in a locality where it is customary for them to belong to him, lo, they are his. And in a locality where it is customary for them to belong to the householder, lo, they belong to the householder. And they do not vary from the local custom.

II. ANALYSIS: THE PROBLEMATICS OF THE TOPIC, BABA QAMMA

While it is fair to say that Baba Qamma takes as is task the exposition of how the victim of assault or robbery is to be returned to his prior condition, the thug or thief not gaining, it is not particularly interesting to say so. That is for three reasons.

First, the same governing consideration — preserving the status quo in a world of perfect order — characterizes many of the native categories of the halakhah. Most of them turn out to provide occasions for realizing the same goal of restoration and stasis. So while true, that statement of the problematics does not pertain in particular to Baba Qamma and explains little about that corpus of halakhah in particular. More seriously, it does not help us identify the hermeneutics that sustains the exegetics of the halakhic statement on the assigned topic. We should find it difficult to build a bridge to the systematic exposition and exegesis of the law from the general problem of how to restore the status quo and preserve it.

Second and concomitantly, that particular thesis on the topical problematics does not permit us to predict how a given sub-topic will be treated, or, indeed, even to anticipate the division of the topic into sub-topics. It is, once more, much too general to help. To explain what I mean, I point to the topic, Shebi'it, the Sabbatical year. Simply stating the topic, we are able to predict the subdivisions thereof. For Shebi'it it is [1] ceasing work at the advent of the seventh year, [2] prohibited work during the seventh year, [3] restrictions on the use of the produce of the seventh year, [4] remission of debts. The logic of the topic dictates the character and even the order of the first three sub-topics. And that is how the topic is expounded by the Oral Torah, following the structure imposed by the Mishnah-tractate upon the Tosefta, Yerushalmi, and Bavli. Not only so, but the generative problematic emerges. For once we know that we are going to discuss the (known) topic, the Sabbatical year, with the further facts, supplied by the Written Torah, that agricultural labor ceases, then we have solid reason to predict the unfolding of a systematic inquiry into the process of shutting down labor, the prohibition of labor during the designated span of time, and the disposition of what grows on its own, without human intervention, in that period. Even changing the order would introduce confusion. As to the fourth topic, Scripture has dictated its facts, and the halakhah added thereto by the Oral Torah simply amplifies the same facts and refines them. It follows that inherent in the topic is the logic that dictates what sages are going to want to know about the topic, on the one side, and the order in which they will set forth their knowledge, on the other. But by the same criterion — the logical necessities inherent in the stated topic and their consequences for the orderly division and articulation of the facts sages select for exposition — no equivalent answer emerges here. For how are we to make sense of the exposition of the topic, damages inflicted by chattel and persons? The subject treated in the present category does not contain within itself an explanation for why damages done by chattels takes priority over damages done by persons, as though the former contains information necessary for understanding the latter. Any other order would work just as well. But knowing the general theme does not even tell us what topics will, or will not, present themselves for analysis.

Third, if we adopt as our theory of the generative problematics the concern to restore order and attain stasis, we cannot explain how specific cases identify the problems that concern them. The opening propositions, which attain a high level of abstraction and generalization, take as their problem the organization of received data, the comparison and contrast of species of a single genus. They do not undertake to propose and demonstrate propositions, formulating new facts out of received givens, such as we see is the case in Shebi'it (among numerous tractates). Indeed, it is the speciation of the components of the genus, causes of damages, that defines the problematics of Mishnah-, Tosefta-, and Bavli-tractate Chapter One. Taking as our criterion for a valid problematics the capacity to predict the division of the topic into sub-topics (or to explain, after the fact, why the topic is treated as it is), we have to reject the proposed theory of the problematics of the topic. It is not only too general. It proves implausible, because it does not even account for the data at hand.

If we work back from the portrait of the halakhah in the Mishnah to the concerns that shape that portrait, we can move from the particular to the general. The Mishnah's exposition of its topic yields a clear picture of the generative problematics discerned by sages in that particular topic. We can even specify why a given topic served as an ideal medium for exploring a given range of questions that yield concrete cases of abstract conceptions, why sages could make the statement that they wished to make only, or particularly well, through said topic. Now using as our exemplary case Shebi'it, we recall that time and again the law wanted to know how intentionality, encompassing human will and perception, affected the concrete and material working of the law of the Sabbatical year. These define the governing variable, the source of unclarity and confusion; these, too, define the medium for clarification and sorting out disorder. The problematics of the halakhah generates small-scale inquiries into large-bore principles. As is my way, I try to work from the little to the large. In Shebi'it the cases yielded a recurrent question, the question exposed an inherent problematics. But here I find it difficult to answer the question, what statement do sages wish to make through their analysis of the law of Baba Qamma, and why does this particular category of halakhah serve as the chosen medium for making that statement?

For to the question, are we able to ask the cases of Baba Qamma to exemplify a recurrent and deeper question treated in them *in nuce* ? the answer is negative. Neither the order of the topics nor the character of the problems worked out in connection therewith provides a positive response. Ox, pit, crop-destroying beast, fire — why that order and not pit, fire, ox, crop-destroying beast? When it comes to damages done by persons, what logic inherent in the topic tells me that consideration of penalties for the theft of an ox or a sheep comes prior to assessing damages for assault? And, further, we move from the remarkably specific to the very general, treating the theft of an ox or a sheep as a category equivalent in exegetical challenge to penalties for assault. So the order of analysis is not cumulative and tells us nothing of an inner, governing logic. When it comes to identify recurrent questions brought to bear upon diverse data, the picture changes only a little. The framers of the halakhah clearly intend an orderly exposition, which accounts for the character, e.g., of Chapter One and Chapter Eight. In both expositions they clarify by classifying, then comparing and contrasting the taxa. The exercise in the former case exemplifies sages' power of hierarchical classification, the skill with which the manipulate the principles of natural history, so far as comparison and contrast of categories is made to yield new insight. But that banality about a generative interest in hierarchical classification of types of damages and torts serves no better than the consequential observation concerning a paramount interest that the halakhah in general aims at restoration and stabilization of the social order.

Consider, rather, what question common to a range of sub-topics precipitates inquiry of a uniform character among those diverse sub-topics? By way of experiment, let us simply review a sequence of topical sentences of the several sub-divisions of the halakhah and see whether we can identify a type of question that recurs, now dividing the sub-divisions between injury and misappropriation. This we do so as to ask whether a uniform program of analysis or exegesis governs:

INJURY

1. There are four generative causes of damages.
2. A beast is an attested danger to go along in the normal way and to break something. But if it was kicking, or if pebbles were scattered from under its feet and it thereby broke utensils — the owner pays half of the value of the damages caused by his ox.
3. He who leaves a jug in the public domain, and someone else came along and stumbled on it and broke it — the one who broke it is exempt. He who pours water out into the public domain, and someone else was injured on it, is liable to pay compensation for his injury.
4. Two oxen generally deemed harmless which injured one another — the owner pays half-damages for the excess of the value of the injury done by the less injured to the more injured ox.
5. He who digs a pit in private domain and opens it into public domain, or in public domain and opens it into private domain, or in private domain and opens it into private domain belonging to someone else, is liable for damage done by the pit.
6. He who brings a flock into a fold and shut the gate before it as required, but the flock got out and did damage, is exempt. If he did not shut the gate before it as required, and the flock got out and did damage, he is liable.
7. He who causes a fire to break out through the action of a deaf-mute, idiot, or minor, is exempt from punishment under the laws of man, but liable to punishment under the laws of heaven. If he did so through the action of a person of sound senses, the person of sound senses is liable.

MISAPPROPRIATION

8. More encompassing is the rule covering payment of twofold restitution than the rule covering payment of fourfold or fivefold restitution. For the rule covering twofold restitution applies to something whether animate or inanimate. But

the rule covering fourfold or fivefold restitution applies
only to an ox or a sheep alone

9. He who injures his fellow is liable to compensate him on
five counts: (1) injury, (2) pain, (3) medical costs, (4) loss
of income [lit.: loss of time], and (5) indignity

10. He who steals wood and made it into utensils, wool and
made it into clothing, pays compensation in accord with
the value of the wood or wool at the time of the theft.

What do we not find here? Issues common elsewhere, such as intentionality, on
the one side, potentiality vs. actuality, on the other, never occur when we deal
with the matters at hand. So far as intentionality or human perception serves as
a criterion of classification in Kilayim and Shebi'it, we find no counterpart at all.
Clearly, Nos. 1-7 in treating injury all work on assessing culpability and assigning
responsibility. If a question recurs, it concerns how we sort out that mishap
against which we can take precautions from what cannot ordinarily be foreseen
and prevented. But a variety of givens predominate, and those givens involve
facts, not principles of general intelligibility such as might pertain in other halakhic
categories altogether; the givens seem remarkably particular to their context.
And the facts on the face of matters scarcely can be said to inhere in the topic at
hand. Nos. 8-10 in addressing misappropriation want to know how we assess
damages and pay for them. Here too, responsibility to restore the status quo
defines the recurrent question.

Then, to return to our basic problem, what, exactly, concerning Nos. 1-
7, do the framers of the problems that are solved want to know, and why do they
want to know it? If the topic itself does not supply compelling answers to those
questions, and the characteristics of the on-going analysis yield no uniformities,
what is left as source for sages' exegetical program? Absent traits of the topic on
the one side, and a prevailing logical problematics (e.g., the taxonomic power of
intentionality) on the other, only one other source of explanation serves to explain
the exegetical program of the sages at hand, and that is Scripture. Sages located
their exegetical problem in Scripture's rules on the chosen categories — there
alone. What we shall now see is that the halakhah categorized as Baba Qamma
— the halakhah of injury and misappropriation — systematizes facts supplied by
Scripture, identifying the general principles and utilizing those general principles
as the basis for the orderly recapitulation of the established facts, now in an
improved formulation. Not only so, but that work of secondary amplification of
facts of Scripture encompasses nearly the entire tractate; I see little in the halakhah
that aims at more than to articulate what is implicit in facts set forth by the
Written Torah. No halakhic problematic deriving from the Oral Torah dictates
the course of the presentation of the topic. And, a survey of the preceding section
indicates, that work of systematization is complete in the Mishnah; the Tosefta
does not recapitulate the exercise and also does not vastly contribute to it.

To show that that is the case, let me return to the repertoire of topics given just now ask these specific questions and answer them. I ask the question required by the rough reprise given above, and I answer by a systematic demonstration that the halakhah finds in the Written Torah not only its facts but also such a generative problematics as pertains.

1. How do sages know that there are four generative causes of damages [covering Nos. 1, 3, 5, 6, 7)?

> Ox (No. 1): *"When one man's ox hurts another's, so that i t dies, then they shall sell the live ox and divide the price of it; and the dead beast also they shall divide. Or if it is known that the ox has been accustomed to gore in the past, and its owner has not kept it in, he shall pay ox for ox, and the dead beast shall be his"* (Ex. 21:35-6)

> Pit (No. 5): *"When a man leaves a pit open or when a man digs up a pit and does not cover it, and an ox or an ass falls into it, the owner of the pit shall make it good; he shall give money to its owner and the dead beast shall be his"* (Ex. 21:33)

> Crop-destroying beast (No. 6): *"When a man causes a field or vineyard to be grazed over or lets his beast loose and it feeds in another man's field, he shall make restitution from the beast in his own field and in his own vineyard"* (Ex. 22:5)

> Fire (No. 7): *"When fire breaks out and catches in thorns so that the stacked grain or the standing grain or the field is consumed, he that kindled the fire shall make full restitution"* (Ex. 22:6)

The secondary amplification of these generative causes, so elegantly carried forward by the Tosefta's and Bavli's exegesis of the Mishnah's statement, leaves no doubt that, within the prevailing hermeneutics of the native category at hand, the sole task is to articulate the givens of Scripture. That fact becomes more blatant at the next stage.

2. Where do sages learn the distinction between a beast that is deemed harmless and one that is an attested danger [covering Nos. 2, 4, inclusive of [1] half-damages paid in the case of the goring of the former, full damages of the latter; and [2] of selling an ox and dividing the proceeds?

> *"When one man's ox hurts another's, so that it dies, then they shall sell the live ox and divide the price of it; and the dead beast also they shall divide. Or if it is known that the ox has been accustomed to gore in the past, and its owner has not kept it in, he shall pay ox for ox, and the dead beast shall be his"* (Ex. 21:35-6)

> *"When an ox gores a man or woman to death, the ox
> shall be stoned and its flesh shall not be eaten; but the owner
> of the ox shall be clear. But if the ox has been accustomed to
> grow in the past, and its owner has been warned but has not
> kept it in, and it kills a man or a woman, the ox shall be stoned,
> and the owner also shall be put to death. If a ransom is laid on
> him, then he shall give for the redemption of his life whatever
> is laid upon him. If it gores a man's son or daughter, he shall
> be dealt with according to this same rule. If the ox gores a
> slave, male or female, the owner shall give to their master thirty
> shekels of silver, and the ox shall be stoned"* (Ex. 21:28-32)

The entire program of the specified chapters of the Mishnah's presentation of the
halakhah derives from Scripture; the exegesis of the implications of the facts, the
invention of illustrative problems for solution, and the specification of theorems
for demonstration — all depend upon the factual postulates supplied by Scripture.

3. Whence the distinction between the rule covering payment of twofold
restitution than the rule covering payment of fourfold or fivefold restitution (No.
7)?

> *"If a man steals an ox or a sheep and kills it or sells it,
> he shall pay five oxen for an ox and four sheep for a sheep. He
> shall make restitution; if he has nothing, then he shall be sold
> for his theft. If the stolen beast is found alive in his possession,
> whether it is an ox or an ass or a sheep, he shall pay double"*
> (Ex. 22:1-3).

> *"If a man delivers to his neighbor money or goods to
> keep and it is stolen out of the man's house, then if the thief is
> found, he shall pay double"* (Ex. 22:7).

The specified chapter does nothing more than take up Scripture's distinctions
and explore their implications.

4. How do we know that one compensates a person whom he has injured
(No. 9)?

> *"When men quarrel and one strikes the other with a
> stone or with his fist and the man does not die but keeps his
> bed, then if the man rises again and walks abroad with his
> staff, he that struck him shall be clear; only he shall pay for the
> loss of his time and shall have him thoroughly healed"* (Ex.
> 21:18-19).

> *"When men strive together and hurt a woman with
> child so that there is a miscarriage and yet no harm follows,
> the one who hurt her shall be fined, according as the woman's
> husband shall lay upon him; and he shall pay as the judges
> determine. If any harm follows, then you shall give life for life,*

> *eye for eye, tooth for tooth, hand for hand, foot for foot, burn*
> *for burn, wound for wound, stripe for stripe"* (Ex. 21:22-25).

Sages derive the laws of misappropriation and torts from Scripture, the categories being defined out of the passage at hand.

5. What is the basis for requiring compensation for what one has stolen (No. 10)?

> *"If any one sins and commits a breach of faith against*
> *the Lord by deceiving his neighbor in a matter of deposit or*
> *security or through robbery, or if he has oppressed his neighbor*
> *or has found what was lost and lied about it, swearing falsely,*
> *in any of all the things that men do and sin therein, when one*
> *has sinned and become guilty, he shall restore what he took by*
> *robbery or what he got by oppression or the deposit that was*
> *committed to him or the lost thing that he found or anything*
> *about which he has sworn falsely; he shall restore it in full"*
> (Lev. 5:20-24).

Here again, it is not the topic and its inherent logic but Scripture that has dictated the character of the halakhah, within the obvious proviso that, both Scripture's and the Oral Torah's halakhah concur on the justice of restoring stolen property as a principle of the ordering of society. The upshot is that we may account by reference to the Written Torah's laws for nearly the entire exegetical program brought by sages to the halakhic topic of Baba Qamma. Sages chose as their question — the problematic they discerned in the topic at hand — how to organize and systematize Scripture's facts.

Given these facts, what have sages contributed to their elucidation? They clarified details and worked out the secondary and tertiary implications thereof. They spelled out the full range of responsibility ("In the case of anything of which I am liable to take care, I am deemed to render possible whatever damage it may do. [If] I am deemed to have rendered possible part of the damage it may do, I am liable for compensation as if [I have] made possible all of the damage it may do"). They defined the specifics required for applying Scripture's general rules ("a tooth is deemed an attested danger in regard to eating what is suitable for eating"). In the manner of geometry, they showed how, within a given set of postulates, a range of problems was to be solved to yield a proof of a set of theorems. In other words, they did everything but the main thing, which in the case of other native categories is, make a powerful, consequential statement of their own. And yet, the native category delineated by Baba Qamma (along with the other two Babas) takes the primary position in the curriculum of the classical academies where the halakhah is studied. So the native speakers of the halakhah have made known their statement and set down their judgment. And, the repertoire of the halakhah by its documents of origin indicates, it is in the Mishnah that they have recorded their definition of what matters in the topic at hand. The

Tosefta's contribution of cases and examples is subordinate and derivative, to be understood *in context* only by reference to the Mishnah's component of the halakhah.

5

The Tosefta in Halakhic Context:
Tractate Shabbat

I. An Outline of the Halakhah of Shabbat

The lines of structure and order that organize the Israelite household's interior construction mark the confluence of time, space, and circumstance. At a particular time, the space encompassed by the household is demarcated, closed off entirely so that the circumstance of the conduct of life therein is deeply affected. At that point the Israelite household comes to spatial realization, keeping within all who belong, walling off the rest. In concrete terms, on the Sabbath, an invisible wall descends to differentiate the private domain of the household from public domain and to close off the one from the other. And, at that time, in that space, the ordinary foci of workaday activities — cooking and eating, working and resting — become radically re-configured: no cooking, no working, only eating and resting in perfect repose.

The Israelite household at rest recapitulates the celebration of God at the moment of the conclusion and perfection of creation. Then the Israelite household, like creation at sunset marking the end of the sixth day of creation, is sanctified: separated from the profane world and distinguished as God's domain. With all things in place and in order, at the sunset that marks the advent of the seventh day, the rest that marks the perfection of creation descends. The sanctification takes place through that very act of perfect repose that recapitulates the one celebrated at the climax of creation. Like God at the celebration of creation, now man achieves perfect, appropriate rest. That takes place when time, circumstance, but space too, come together. The advent of the Sabbath marks the time, the household, the space, and the conduct of home and family life, the circumstance.

Here, within the interiorities of the Israelite household, in the system of the halakhah, therefore, is where time counts, where we take the measure of space, and where the particularities of private conduct behind the household walls make all the difference. As the advent of the Sabbath, holy time, requires preparation in the Temple, so the same time imposes upon the household a set of rules of sanctification. The Written Torah has set the stage. The Sabbath marks the celebration of creation's perfection (Gen. 2:1-3). Food for the day is to be prepared in advance (Ex. 16:22-26, 29-30). Fire is not to be kindled on that day, thus no cooking (Ex. 34:2-3). Servile labor is not to be carried on on that day by the householder and his dependents, encompassing his chattel (Ex. 20:5-11, Ex. 23:13, 31:12-17, 34:21). The where matters as much as the when and the how: people are supposed to stay in their place: "Let each person remain in place, let no one leave his place on the seventh day" (Ex. 16:29-30), understanding by place the private domain of the household (subject to further clarification in due course).

Sages then make of the Sabbath the first and most important statement of their system, celebrating the stasis of creation, the perfection of the Creator's work, all evoked every time the word "Sabbath" resonated with the sounds of the beginnings, the melodies of the restoration. What the halakhah of the Oral Torah has to contribute to the topic, the Sabbath and its sanctification, emerges in the tractates of Shabbat and Erubin, the former devoted to all matters except remaining in place, the latter dedicated to the rule that each person is to remain in place. These represent some of the most profound and probing reflections of the entire corpus of the halakhah of the Oral Torah. The depths that the plumb, the problems they probe — these remain to be exposed, first within the halakhah, then beneath its surface, in the problematics. And, for the last time, we shall ask where we find a statement of the deep structures of tension and the resolution of tension that animate the halakhah. And the answer, as the following reprise of the halakhah shows, is, in the Mishnah; little if anything first surfaces in the Tosefta, nothing beyond the Tosefta.

I. DIMENSIONS: SPACE, TIME AND THE SABBATH

A. SPACE

M. 1:1 [Acts of] transporting objects from one domain to another [which violate] the Sabbath (1) are two, which [indeed] are four [for one who is] inside, (2) and two which are four [for one who is] outside. How so? [If on the Sabbath] the beggar stands outside and the householder inside, [and] the beggar stuck his hand inside and put [a beggar's bowl] into the hand of the householder, or if he took [something] from inside it and brought it out, the beggar is liable, the householder is exempt. [If] the householder stuck his hand outside and put [something] into the hand of the beggar, or

**if he took [something] from it and brought it inside, the
householder is liable, and the beggar is exempt. [If] the
beggar stuck his hand inside, and the householder took
[something] from it, or if [the householder] put something
in it and he [the beggar] removed it — both of them are
exempt. [If] the householder put his hand outside and the
beggar took [something] from it, or if [the beggar] put
something into it and [the householder] brought it back
inside, both of them are exempt.**

T. 1:1 Four domains are [constituted by] private domain and
public domain. What is private domain? A ditch ten
[handbreadths] deep and four wide, and so too: a wall ten
handbreadths high and four wide — this constitutes absolutely
private domain.

1:2 What is public domain? A high road or a larger public square,
and alleyways which open out [at both ends] — this constitutes
absolutely public domain.

T. 1:3 They do not transport an object from this private domain
into that public domain, and they do not transport an object
from this public domain into that private domain. And if one
transported an object or brought an object in — [if he did so]
inadvertently, he is liable for a sin offering. [If he did so]
deliberately, he is subject to the punishment of extirpation, and
he is stoned. All the same are the one who takes out and the one
who brings in, the one who stretches [something] out and the
one who throws [something] in — [in all such cases] he is liable.

T. 1:4 But the sea, plain, *karmelit* [neutral domain], colonnade,
and a threshold are neither private domain nor public domain.
They do not carry or put [things] in such places. But if one
carried or put [something into such a place], he is exempt [from
punishment]. They do not transport an object either from them
to public domain, or from public domain into such areas as
these. And they do not bring something in either from such
areas as these to private domain or from private domain to such
areas as these. But if one took something out or brought
something in [as specified], he is exempt [from punishment].

T. 1:5 [In the case of] a courtyard belonging to public domain
and of alleyways which do not open out, [if] they prepared an
erub, they are permitted [to carry in the court yard or alleyway,
across the boundaries from one domain to the other]. [If] they
did not prepare an *'erub*, they are prohibited [from doing so].

T. 1:6 [If] man stands on the threshold [of a house] [and] hands
something over to the householder, or the householder hands

something over to him, [if] he hands something over to a beggar, or the beggar hands something over to him, [if] he takes something from the householder and gives it to the beggar, [or] from the beggar and gives it over to the householder, all three of them are exempt [from liability to punishment].

B. 1:1 IV.13/5B IF WITHIN FOUR CUBITS ONE STOPS TO REST, HE IS EXEMPT; IF IT IS TO SHOULDER THE BURDEN, HE IS LIABLE; BEYOND FOUR CUBITS OF THE STARTING POINT, IF HE STOPPED TO CATCH HIS BREATH, HE IS LIABLE; IF IT WAS TO SHOULDER THE BURDEN, HE IS EXEMPT. [ONE IS LIABLE FOR CARRYING AN OBJECT FOUR CUBITS OVER PUBLIC GROUND — IF HE HIMSELF REMOVED IT FROM THE FIRST SPOT AND PUT IT DOWN IN THE OTHER, IN AN INTENTIONAL, SINGLE ACTION. STOPPING TO REST CONSTITUTES AN ACT OF DEPOSIT; WHEN HE RESTARTS, THERE IS A NEW REMOVAL; SO IF HE STOPS TO REST WITHIN FOUR CUBITS OF THE STARTING POINT, HE IS NOT LIABLE, SINCE HE HASN'T CARRIED THE OBJECT FOUR CUBITS. BUT STOPPING TO REARRANGE THE BURDEN DOESN'T CONSTITUTE AN ACT OF DEPOSIT; HENCE WHEN HE DOES EVENTUALLY STOP AFTER FOUR CUBITS, HE HAS EFFECTED REMOVAL AND DEPOSITING IN A SINGLE ACTION, AND IS LIABLE; SO HE WOULD NOT BE LIABLE WHEN STOPPING TO REST THE FIRST TIME, FOR THE FOOD HE CARRIED IN AND OUT WAS NOT CARRIED IN A SINGLE ACT OF REMOVAL AND DEPOSIT; BUT HE WOULD BE LIABLE IF HE WENT IN AND OUT AFTER HIS REST.]

B. TIME

M. 1:2 A man should not sit down before the barber close to the afternoon [prayer], unless he has already prayed. Nor [at that time] should a man go into a bathhouse or into a tannery, nor to eat, nor to enter into judgment. But if they began, they do not break off [what they were doing]. They do break off [what they were doing] to pronounce the recitation of the *Shema.* But they do not break off [what they were doing] to say the Prayer.

M. 1:3 A tailor should not go out carrying his needle near nightfall, lest he forget and cross [a boundary]; nor a scribe with his pen. And [on the Sabbath] one should not search his clothes [for fleas], or read by the light of a lamp. Nonetheless they state: [On the Sabbath] a teacher sees [by the light of a lamp] where the children are reading, but he does not read.

T. 1:8 A tailor should not go out carrying his needle on the eve of the Sabbath near nightfall, lest he forget and cross a boundary [M. Shab. 1:3A B], nor a carpenter with the beam on his shoulder, nor a dyer with the color sample behind his ear, nor a money changer with the denar behind his ear, nor a wool corder with a cord around his neck.

T. 1:10 A man should not go out into the public domain with his coins tied up in a kerchief. And if he went forth [in such wise], lo, this one is liable.

T. 1:11 They go out wearing phylacteries at twilight. And they read in Holy Writ at twilight. But they do not read on Sabbath nights by the light of a lamp, even if it is above him, even if it is in another room, even if it is inside the tenth of ten rooms, one inside another. But he may make use of a light which is located inside a cup or inside a dish, and he need not scruple about the matter.

M. 1:10 They do not roast meat, onions, and eggs, unless there is time for them to be roasted while it is still day. They do not put bread into an oven at dusk, nor cakes on the coals, unless there is time for them to form a crust [even] on the top surface while it is still day.

T. 1:23 They open the irrigation channel for a vegetable patch on the eve of the Sabbath at dusk, and the patch may continue to absorb water through the Sabbath day. They put a perfume brazier under clothing, which continues to absorb the perfume all day long. They put sulphur under silver dishes on the eve of the Sabbath at dusk, and they continue to be sulphured on the Sabbath. They put eye salve on the eye or a poultice on a sore on the eve of the Sabbath at dusk, and these continue to provide healing throughout the entire Sabbath day. But they don't put wheat into the water driven wheels unless there is sufficient time for the wheat to be ground into flour while it is still day.]

M. 1:11 They lower the Passover-offering into an oven at dusk [when the fourteenth of Nisan falls on a Friday]. And they light the fire in the fireplace of the House of the Hearth. But in the provinces, [they do so only if] there is sufficient time for the flame to catch over the larger part of [the wood].

Y. 2:1 IX:3 All those who are liable to immerse do so under ordinary circumstances by day, except for the menstruating woman and the woman after childbirth, who immerse only by night. A menstruating woman whose time had passed may immerse whether by day or by night [on the eighth or successive days, after the onset of her period].

II. PREPARING FOR THE SABBATH: LIGHT, FOOD, CLOTHING

    A. THE SABBATH LAMP

M. 2:1 With what do they kindle [the Sabbath light] and with what do they not kindle [it]? They do not kindle with (1) cedar fiber, (2) uncarded flax, (3) raw silk, (4) wick of bast, (5) wick of the desert, (6) or seaweed; or with (1) pitch, (2) wax, (3) castor oil, (4) oil [given to a priest as heave-offering which had become unclean and must therefore be] burned, (5) [grease from] the fat tail, or (6) tallow.

T. 2:1 They kindle [the Sabbath light] with a wick which is singed [cf. M. Shab. 2:3C E], but not with rags, and even though they are singed. [As to] all those things concerning which they said, "They do not kindle [the lamp with them] on the Sabbath," they do kindle with them on the festival day, except for [heave offering] oil [which has become unclean and is to be] burned [M. Shab. 2:1C4].

T. 2:2 All those things [wicks] concerning which they said, "They do not kindle [the lamp] with them on the Sabbath," it is permitted to make into a fire, whether on the ground or in a candelabrum, whether to get warm by them, or to use their light. And they have stated [the prohibition] only in connection with making them into a wick for a lamp, that alone.

M. 2:2 All kinds of oils are permitted: (1) Sesame oil, (2) nut oil, (3) fish oil, (4) colocynth oil, (5) tar, and (6) naphtha.

M. 2:3 With nothing which exudes from a tree do they light [the Sabbath light], except for flax. And nothing which exudes from a tree contracts uncleanness [as a tent] through overshadowing [a corpse] except for flax.

M. 2:4 A person should not pierce an eggshell with oil and put it on the opening of a lamp so that [the oil] will drip [out and sustain the lamp], even if it is made out of earthenware, But if the potter joined it to begin with [to the lamp], it is permitted, because it is one utensil. A person may not fill a dish with oil and put it beside a lamp and place the head of the wick into it, so that it will draw [oil from the dish of oil].

M. 2:5 He who puts out a lamp because he is afraid of gentiles, thugs, a bad spirit, or if it is so that a sick person might sleep, is exempt [from liability to punishment]. [If he did so], to spare the lamp, the oil, the wick, he is liable.

T. 2:7 They put mud and chips [to keep the flame cool and slow its burning] under the flame on the eve of Sabbath at dusk, so that it will continue to burn throughout the Sabbath night. They put a lump of salt or a split bean on the light on the eve of the Sabbath at dusk, so that it will continue to burn brightly throughout the Sabbath night. They bring up water with a siphon, and they drip drops of water from a perforated vessel for a sick person on the Sabbath [M. Shab. 2:5B].

M. 2:7 Three things must a man state in his house on the eve of Sabbath at dusk: (1) "Have you tithed?" (2) "Have you prepared the symbolic meal of fusion [to unite distinct domains for purposes of carrying on the Sabbath]?" (3) "[Then] kindle the lamp [for the Sabbath]."

M. 2:7 [If] it is a matter of doubt whether or not it is getting dark, (1) they do not tithe that which is certainly untithed, (2) and they do not immerse utensils, (3) and they do not kindle lamps. (1) But they do tithe that which is doubtfully tithed produce, (2) and they do prepare the symbolic meal of fusion [to unite distinct domains for purposes of carrying on the Sabbath], (3) and they do cover up what is to be kept hot.

B. 2:7 I.4/34A IF TWO PERSONS SAID TO SOMEONE, 'GO AND PREPARE FOR US A SYMBOLIC FUSION MEAL,' AND FOR ONE PARTY HE PREPARED THE MEAL WHILE IT WAS CLEARLY STILL DAY, BUT FOR THE OTHER HE PREPARED THE FUSION MEAL AT DUSK [SO WE DON'T KNOW WHETHER OR NOT IT WAS THE SABBATH, IN WHICH CASE THE MEAL IS NULL], AND THE MEAL OF HIM FOR WHOM HE SET FORTH THE FUSION MEAL BY DAY WAS EATEN AFTER NIGHTFALL, THEN BOTH ACQUIRE THE RIGHTS THAT THE MEAL IS SUPPOSED TO CONFER." [THE MEAL MUST BE PREPARED BY DAY AND ALSO MUST STILL BE IN EXISTENCE WHEN THE SABBATH STARTS. THE FIRST HAD THE MEAL PLACED BY DAY BUT IT WAS EATEN AT TWILIGHT; IT IS REGARD AS NIGHT, SO WHEN THE SABBATH STARTED, THE MEAL STILL EXISTED; AS TO THE SECOND, TWILIGHT IS ASSIGNED TO THE DAY, SO IT WAS PLACED BY DAY, AND IT ALSO IS VALID.]

B. FOOD FOR THE SABBATH

M. 3:1 A double stove that [people] have heated with stubble or straw – they put cooked food on it. [But if they heated it] with peat or with wood, one may not put [anything] on it until he has swept it out, or until he has covered it with ashes.

T. 2:16 In the case of something on account of the deliberate doing of which one is liable to extirpation and on account of the in advertent doing of which one is liable for a sin offering, which one did on the Sabbath, whether one did so inadvertently or deliberately — it is prohibited both for him and for others [i.e., if it involves food, he may not eat it]. But in the case of something on account of which people are not liable for the deliberate doing of which to extirpation and on account of the inadvertent doing of which to a sin offering, which one did on the Sabbath inadvertently — it may be eaten at the end of the Sabbath by other others, but not by him. [If] he did so deliberately, it may not be eaten.

M. 3:2 An oven which [people] have heated with stubble or with straw — one should not put anything either into it or on top of it. A single stove which [people] have heated with stubble or with straw, lo, this is equivalent to a double stove. [If they heated it] with peat or with wood, lo, it is equivalent to an oven.

T. 2:11 A double stove which [people] have heated with peat or with wood — they put down [on it] a pot [on the eve of the Sabbath] on the sides of the stove, even though it has not been swept out and had its ashes covered. But they do not keep anything on it unless it is swept out and will have had its ashes covered.

T. 2 12 Coals which have died down or on which one has set thoroughly — lo, they are tantamount to having been covered.

T. 2 :13 Two double stoves which are paired, one of them having been swept out and had its ashes covered, and one of them not having been swept out and had its ashes covered — they keep something on the one which has been swept out and had its ashes covered, and they do not keep anything on the one which has not been swept out and had its ashes covered.

B. 3:2 I.2/38B AN OVEN THAT PEOPLE HEATED WITH STUBBLE OR WITH STRAW — THEY DO NOT LEAN A POT UP AGAINST IT, AND IT GOES WITHOUT SAYING, OR ON TOP OF IT, AND, IT GOES WITHOUT SAYING, INSIDE OF IT, AND, IT GOES WITHOUT SAYING, IF IT WAS HEATED WITH PEAT OR WOOD. IF A SINGLE STOVE IS HEATED WITH STUBBLE OR RAKINGS, ONE MAY LEAN A POT AGAINST IT, BUT NOT PUT A POT ON TOP; IF IT WAS HEATED WITH PEAT OR WOOD, ONE MAY NOT LEAN A POT AGAINST IT.

M. 3:3 They do not put an egg beside a kettle [on the Sabbath] so that it will be cooked. And one should not crack it into [hot] wrappings. And one should not bury it in sand or in road dirt so that it will be roasted.

M. 3:4 A *miliarum* which is cleared of ashes — they drink from it on the Sabbath. An antikhi [boiler], even though it is clear of ashes — they do not drink from it.

T. 3:1 A woman should not fill a pot with peas and pulse and put it into the oven on the eve of the Sabbath at dusk. If she put them in, at the end of the Sabbath they are forbidden, for as long as they take to prepare.

T. 3:2 A baker should not fill a jug with water and put it into the oven on the eve of the Sabbath at dusk. If he put it in, at the end of the Sabbath it is prohibited for as long as it takes to heat up [on its own, after the Sabbath, and not from the heat derived on the Sabbath itself].

T. 3:3 A bath, the holes of which one stopped up on the eve of the Sabbath [to preserve the steam] — at the end of the Sabbath one may wash therein forthwith. [If] one stopped up the openings on the eve of the festival, one may go in on the festival itself and perspire, then go out and take a bath in cold water.

M. 3:5 A kettle [containing hot water] which one removed [from the stove] — one should not put cold water into it so that it [the cold water] may get warm. But one may put [enough cold water] into it or into a cup so that [the hot water] will cool off. The pan or pot which one has taken off the stove while it is boiling — one may not put spices into it. But he may put [spices] into [hot food which is] in a plate or a dish.

T. 3:5 A person may fill a jug of water and put it near a bonfire, not to warm it, but so that its chill may be eased. A man may fill a flask with oil and put it near a fire, not to warm it, but so that its chill may be eased.

T. 3:7 A man may warm a sheet and put it on his belly. But he should not put a hot water bottle on his belly. A man may fill a cup of wine and put it on the kettle, not to heat it up, but to ease its chill.

T. 3:8 A man may fill a cup with water and put it into a basin, whether to heat up cold water, or to cool off hot water.

T. 3:9 He who empties from one kettle to another, or from one pan to another, or from one pot to another, is permitted to put [spices] into the second, but prohibited to put [spices] into the first [cf. M. Shab. 3:5D-G]. A jug [of liquid] from which tithes have not been removed which broke — one brings a utensil and puts it under it. Once it is filled up, it is prohibited to carry it [cf. M. Shab. 3:6A]. A.jar of grapes and a pressing of olives which began to flow — they do not make use of them on the festival, and one need not say, on the Sabbath.

M. 3:6 [On the Sabbath] they do not put a utensil under a lamp to catch the oil. But if one put it there while it is still

day, it is permitted. But they do not use any of that oil [on the Sabbath], since it is not something which was prepared [before the Sabbath for use on the Sabbath]. They carry a new lamp, but not an old one. They put a utensil under a lamp to catch the sparks. But [on the Sabbath] one may not put water into it, because he thereby puts out [the sparks].

T. 2:14 He who forgot cooked food on the stove and the Sabbath day was sanctified while it was there — [if this happened] inadvertently, he may eat that food. [If this was done] deliberately, he may not eat that food. In what circumstances? In the case of food which had not been adequately cooked, or hot water which had not been adequately heated. But in the case of food which had been adequately cooked and hot water which had been adequately heated, lo, these are permitted.

T. 2:17 He who slaughters [an animal] on the Sabbath — [if he did so] inadvertently — it may be eaten at the end of the Sabbath. [If he did so] deliberately, it may not be eaten.

T. 2:18 Produce which one gathered on the Sabbath — if he did so] inadvertently, it may be eaten at the end of the Sabbath. [If he did so] deliberately, it may not be eaten.

T. 2:21 He who plants [seed] on the Sabbath — [If he did so] inadvertently, he may preserve [the plants which come up from the seed]. [If he did so] deliberately, he must uproot [the plants which come up from the seed]. On what account did they rule, "He who plants seed on the Sabbath, [if he did so] inadvertently, may preserve [the plants which come up from the seed]. But pf he did so] deliberately, he must uproot [the plants which come up from the seed]. But in the case of [seed planted in] the Seventh Year, whether this is done inadvertently or deliberately, he must uproot [the plants which come up]"? Because they count out the years in the case of plants which come up, e.g., for *'orlah* and for the fourth year produce] in the case of the Seventh Year [so that if he does not uproot the plants, it will be clear even after the Seventh Year that he has planted them in the Seventh Year. But they do not count out [years] for the Sabbath.]

T. 3:10 A barrel which broke on top of the roof — one may bring a utensil and put it under it [the roof] But he may not bring another utensil and collect [what has flowed or bring another utensil and set it [near the roof]. If there are guests present, he may bring another utensil and collect [what has flowed from the barrel] or another utensil and set it [near the barrel].

M. 4:1 With what do they cover [up food to keep it hot], and with what do they not cover up [food to keep it hot]? They do not cover with (1) peat, (2) compost, (3) salt, (4) lime, or (5) sand, whether wet or dry. or with (6) straw, (7) grape skins, (8) flocking [rags], or (9) grass, when wet. But they do cover up [food to keep it hot] with them when they are dry. They cover up [food to keep it hot] with (1) cloth, (2) produce, (3) the wings of a dove, (4) carpenters' sawdust, and (5) soft hatchelled flax.

Y. 4:1 I.3 [They forbade keeping food warm through covering it up on account of the possibility of leaving the food on the stove. [If one is permitted to cover it up, he will assume it is equally permissible to leave food on the stove to keep it hot.] And contrariwise: they have forbidden leaving food on the stove on account of the possibility of covering it up. They forbade using a stove for keeping food warm, in the case of a stove which produces only a small amount of hot air, on account of the possibility of one's then using a stove which produces a great deal of hot air. They forbade keeping warm on the Sabbath itself food that had been thoroughly cooked, because [one might then keep warm] food that had not been thoroughly cooked [with the result that it will be further cooked on the Sabbath]. They forbade keeping water hot because [one might then] keep food hot that had been cooked thoroughly. [L reads: "They forbade keeping food hot that had been cooked thoroughly because (one might then) keep water hot."] Then they retracted and permitted keeping water hot.

M. 4:2 They cover up [food to keep it hot] with fresh hides, and they carry [handle] them; with wool shearings, but they do not carry them. What does one do? He [simply] takes off the cover, and [the wool shearings] fall off [on their own]. [If] he did not cover up [the food] while it is still day, he should not cover it up after dark. [But if] he covered it up and it became uncovered, it is permitted to cover it up again. One fills a jug [on the Sabbath with cold food or liquid] and puts it under a pillow or a blanket [to keep it cool].

T. 3:19 Shearings of wool which are [stored] in the storeroom they do not carry [cf. M. Shab. 4:2B]. If the householder arranged them so as to be able to make use of them, they do carry them.

T. 3:20 They do not cover up hot [food or water] in the first instance on the Sabbath [cf. M. Shab. 4:2H]. But they add objects onto it.

T. 3:21 [If] one stored food and covered it up with something which may be carried on the Sabbath, or stored food to keep it warm with something which is not carried on the Sabbath but covered it with something which is carried on the Sabbath, lo, this person may remove and restore [the covering] [M. Shab. 4:2A].

T. 3:22 [But] if one stored [food to keep it warm] and covered it over with something which is not carried on the Sabbath, or stored it with something which is carried on the Sabbath but covered it over with something which is not carried on the Sabbath, if part of it became uncovered, one may carry it. But if not, he may not carry it.

T. 3.23 They cover up food with a kettle on top of a kettle, and a pot on a kettle on top of a pot, and a pot on top of a kettle. And one plasters their mouth with dough, not so that they may be heated up, but so as to retain [the heat so they do not cover up snow and ice [vs. M. Shab. 4:2J]. They do not shave snow so that its water will exude. But one does shave it into a cup or into a dish, and need not scruple.

C. ORNAMENTS FOR ANIMALS, CLOTHING FOR PERSONS
ANIMALS

M. 5:1 With what does a beast (Ex. 20:10) go out [on the Sabbath], and with what does it not go out? (1) A camel goes out with its curb, (2) a female camel with its nose ring, (3) a Libyan ass with its bridle, (4) and a horse with its chain. And all beasts which wear a chain go out with a chain and are led by a chain, and they sprinkle on the [chains if they become unclean] and immerse them in place [without removing them].

T. 5:8 A beast should not go forth with a bell on its neck. And it does not go forth with a bell on its garment. This and that one both receive uncleanness. This rule is more strict in the case of a beast than it is in the case of a man. A beast should not go forth with a seal on its neck, nor with a seal on its garment. This and that one do not receive uncleanness [as utensils].

M. 5:2 An ass goes out with its saddle cloth when it is tied on to him. Rams go out strapped up [at the male organ]. And female [sheep] go forth (1) strapped over their tails, (2) under their tails, or (3) wearing protective cloths.

M. 5:3 And with what does [a beast] not go out? (1) A camel does not go out with a pad, nor (2) with forelegs bound together [or: hind legs bound together] or (3) with a hoof

tied back to the shoulder. And so is the rule for all other beasts. One should not tie camels to one another and lead them. But one puts the ropes [of all of them] into his hand and leads them, so long as he does not twist [the ropes together].

T. 4 :3 A camel does not go forth with the pad suspended on its hump, so that the wind will not enter it. But it goes forth with its tail tied to its hump, so that the wind will go into it [cf. M. Shab. 5:3B].

M. 5:4 (1) An ass does not go out with its saddle cloth when it is not tied to him, or with a bell, even though it is plugged, or with the ladder yoke around its neck, or with a strap on its leg. And (2) fowl do not go forth with ribbons or straps on their legs. And (3) rams do not go forth with a wagon under their fat tail. And (4) ewes do not go forth protected [with the wood chip in their nose]. And (5) a calf does not go out with its rush yoke. Or (6) a cow with a hedgehog skin [tied around the udder], or with a strap between its horns.

T. 4:5 A horse does not go forth with a fox tail, or with a crimson thread between its eyes. A cow does not go forth with its muzzle, nor foals with their fodder bags. A beast does not go forth wearing a sandal, nor with an amulet, even though it is tested. This rule is more strict for beast than for man. But it does go forth with bandage on a wound, and with splints on a broken bone, and with a dangling afterbirth.

PERSONS

M. 6:1 With what does a woman go out, and with what does she not go out? A woman should not go out with (1) woolen ribbons, (2) flaxen ribbons, or (3) with bands around her head (4) or with a headband, (5) head bangles, when they are not sewn on, (6) or with a hair-net, into the public domain. Nor [should she go out] (1) with a [tiara in the form of] a golden city, (2) a necklace, (3) nose rings, (4) a ring lacking a seal, or (5) a needle lacking a hole. But if she went out [wearing any one of these] she is not liable for a sin-offering.

T. 4:6 A woman should not go out wearing a chaplet. And if she went out [wearing it], lo, this one is liable.

B. 6:1 III.5/58a A SLAVE MAY NOT GO FORTH ON THE SABBATH WITH A SEAL AROUND HIS NECK NOR MAY HE GO FORTH WITH A SEAL ON HIS CLOTHING. NEITHER ONE NOR THE OTHER RECEIVES UNCLEANNESS. [THEY ARE NOT ORNAMENTS NOR USEFUL UTENSILS, BUT MERELY BADGES

OF SHAME.] NOR MAY HE GO OUT WITH A BELL AROUND HIS NECK. BUT HE MAY GO FORTH WITH A BELL ON HIS GARMENT. BOTH THIS BELL AND THAT DO RECEIVE UNCLEANNESS. AND A BEAST SHOULD NOT GO FORTH WITH A SEAL AROUND ITS NECK NOR WITH A SEAL ON ITS COVERING NOR WITH A BELL ON ITS COVERING NOR WITH A BELL AROUND ITS NECK; BUT NONE OF THESE IS SUSCEPTIBLE TO UNCLEANNESS.

M. 6:2 A man should not go out with (1) a nail-studded sandal, (2) a single sandal if he has no wound on his foot, (3) tefillin, (4) an amulet when it is not by an expert, (5) a breastplate, (6) a helmet, or (7) with greaves. But if he went out [wearing any one of these], he is not liable to a sin-offering.

T. 4:8 A man should not put on a nail studded sandal and walk about in it inside the house [cf. M. Shab. 6:2A], even from one bed to another. But he takes it and covers up utensils with it.

T. 4:10 A. As to an amulet which is not made by an expert [tested and found effective], even though they do not go out wearing it on the Sabbath, they carry [handle] it [in the house] on the Sabbath.

M. 6:3 A woman should not go out with (1) a needle which has a hole, (2) with a ring which has a seal, (3) with a cochlae brooch, (4) with a spice box, or (5) with a perfume flask.

M. 6:4 A man should not go out with (1) a sword, (2) bow, (3) shield, (4) club, or (5) spear. And if he went out, he is liable to a sin-offering. A garter is insusceptible to uncleanness, and they go out in it on the Sabbath. Ankle chains are susceptible to uncleanness, and they do not go out in them on the Sabbath.

T. 5:7 A man should not go out with a bell around his neck. But he goes forth with a bell on his garment. And neither this one nor that receives uncleanness. A man should not go forth with a seal around his neck nor with a seal on his garment. This one and that one receive uncleanness.

M. 6:5 A woman goes out in hair ribbons, whether made of her own hair or of the hair of another woman or of a beast; and with (1) headband, (2) head bangles sewn [on the headdress], (3) a hair-net, and (4) wig, in the courtyard; (1) with wool in her ear, (2) wool in her sandals, (3) wool she has used for a napkin for her menstrual flow; (1) pepper, (2) a lump of salt, and (3) anything she puts into her mouth, on condition that she not first put it there on the Sabbath. And if it fell out, she may not put it back.]

T. 4:11 A woman should not go out wearing a key on her finger to the public domain. And if she went out, lo, this one is liable. The governing principle is as follows: In any object which is worn as an ornament, she should not go forth. But if she went forth, she is exempt. In any object which is not worn as an ornament, she should not go forth. And if she went forth, lo, this one is liable. But: She goes forth wearing her gold embroidered hair net, and in its foils, covering, and beads, and in gold plated shoes and slippers.

M. 6:6 She goes out with a sela coin on a bunion. Little girls go out with threads and even ships in their ears. Arabian women go out veiled. Median women go out with cloaks looped up over their shoulders. And [so is the rule] for any person, but sages spoke concerning prevailing conditions.

M. 6:7 She weights her cloak with a stone, a nut, or a coin, on condition that she not attach the weight first on the Sabbath.

T. 4:13 She may wear a cloak thrown over her shoulder for the first time on the Sabbath, with an object which one may handle on the Sabbath [cf. M. 6:6D].

M. 6:8 A cripple's knee pads (1) are susceptible to uncleanness imparted by pressure [to something upon which a Zab may lie or sit], (2) they go forth with them on the Sabbath, and (3) they go into a courtyard with them. His chair and its pads (1) are susceptible to uncleanness imparted by pressure, (2) they do not go out with them on the Sabbath, and (3) they do not go in with them into a courtyard. An artificial arm is insusceptible to uncleanness, and they do not go out in it.

T. 5:2 They go out with wool tuft or a flake of tuft. Under what circumstances? When one has soaked them in oil and tied them with a rope. [If] he did not soak them in oil and tie them with a rope, they do not go forth in them. But if they went forth in them on the eve of the Sabbath, even though one did not soak them with oil and did not tie them with a rope, they do go forth in them [on the Sabbath]

T. 5:3 They go out wearing a bandage or a sponge on a sore, on condition that they not tie them with a string or a rope. They go out with the skin of a garlic or the skin of an onion on a sore. But if it fell out, one does not put it back. And it is not necessary to say that one should not apply it to begin with on the Sabbath.

T. 5:4 They go out with a binding on a sore, and one ties it and unties it on the Sabbath. And a poultice which fell off the binding does one put back.

T. 5:5 They go out with a poultice, a plaster, and a compress on a sore. But if one of these fell off, one does not put it back. And it is not necessary to say that one should not apply it to begin with on the Sabbath.

M. 6:9 Boys go out in garlands, and princes with bells. [And so is the rule] for any person, but sages spoke concerning prevailing conditions.

T. 5:13 Shepherds may go out with their sackcloths, and they did not state this rule for shepherds alone, but any person may do so; but it is ordinarily shepherds who go out with sackcloths; sages speak in terms of prevailing conditions.

III. PROHIBITED ACTS OF LABOR ON THE SABBATH: NOT TRANSPORTING OBJECTS FROM ONE DOMAIN TO ANOTHER

A. THE GENERATIVE CATEGORIES OF PROHIBITED ACTS OF LABOR

M. 7:1 A governing principle did they state concerning the Sabbath: Whoever forgets the basic principle of the Sabbath and performs many acts of labor on many different Sabbath days is liable only for a single sin-offering. He who knows the principle of the Sabbath and performs many acts of labor on many different Sabbaths is liable for the violation of each and every Sabbath. He who knows that it is the Sabbath and performs many acts of labor on many different Sabbaths is liable for the violation of each and every generative category of labor. He who performs many acts of labor of a single type is liable only for a single sin-offering.

T. 8:3 All generative classes of kinds of labor in the Torah — if one did all of them in a single spell of inadvertence, he is liable for each and every one of them [cf. M. Shab. 7:1D].

T. 8:4 All acts of destruction are exempt [when done on the Sabbath], except for him who strikes [another person] and he who kindles a fire on the Sabbath.

B. 7:1 II.5/69A IF ONE WAS UNAWARE OF BOTH THIS AND THAT [THAT THERE IS SUCH A THING AS THE SABBATH AND THAT THIS ACT OF LABOR IS FORBIDDEN ON THE SABBATH], THAT IS A DEFINITION OF AN INADVERTENT SIN OF WHICH THE TORAH SPEAKS. IF ONE WAS FULLY AWARE OF THIS AND OF THAT, THAT IS THE DEFINITION OF A DELIBERATE ACTION OF WHICH THE TORAH SPEAKS. IF ONE WAS UNAWARE OF THE

PRINCIPLE OF THE SABBATH BUT WAS FULLY INFORMED AS TO THE
CLASSIFICATIONS OF FORBIDDEN LABOR, OR IF HE WAS UNINFORMED OF
THE CLASSIFICATIONS OF FORBIDDEN LABOR BUT WAS FULLY INFORMED
ABOUT THE SABBATH, OR IF HE SAID, "I KNOW THAT THIS ACT OF LABOR
IS FORBIDDEN, BUT I DON'T KNOW THAT ON ITS ACCOUNT ONE IS LIABLE
TO AN OFFERING," OR, "NOT LIABLE" — HE IS LIABLE?

B. 7:1 V.6/71A IF ONE REAPED AND GROUND GRAIN TO THE VOLUME
OF A DRIED FIG, IN A SPELL OF UNAWARENESS OF THE SABBATH BUT OF
AWARENESS AS TO THE FORBIDDEN ACTS OF LABOR [AND IS LIABLE ON A
SINGLE COUNT], AND HE AGAIN REAPED AND GROUND GRAIN TO THE
VOLUME OF A DRIED FIG KNOWING THAT IT WAS THE SABBATH BUT
UNAWARE OF THE PROHIBITION AS TO THE VARIOUS ACTS OF LABOR [HE
WAS TOLD IT WAS THE SABBATH BUT FORGOT THESE ACTS ARE FORBIDDEN
THEREON; IN THIS CASE HE IS CULPABLE ON TWO COUNTS], AND THEN
HE WAS INFORMED ABOUT THE MATTER OF THE REAPING AND GRINDING
IN UNAWARENESS OF THE SABBATH BUT WAS AWARE OF THE ACTS OF
LABOR [FREEDMAN: SO HE SET ASIDE A SIN-OFFERING ON ACCOUNT OF
BOTH ACTS OF LABOR, BEFORE HAVING LEARNED OF HIS SECOND SERIES
OF OFFENSES], AND THEN HE WAS INFORMED OF THE REAPING AND
GRINDING PERFORMED WHEN AWARE OF THE SABBATH BUT UNAWARE IN
REGARD TO THE LABORS, THE ATONEMENT FOR THE FIRST ACT OF REAPING
INVOLVES ATONEMENT FOR THE SECOND, AND ATONEMENT FOR THE FIRST
ACT OF GRINDING INVOLVES ATONEMENT FOR THE SECOND. [FREEDMAN:
THIS IS IN RESPECT TO EXPIATION; THE SACRIFICE FOR HIS FIRST TWO
ACTS OF REAPING AND GRINDING IS AN ATONEMENT FOR HIS SECOND
TWO ACTS, SINCE ALL WERE PERFORMED IN ONE STATE OF UNAWARENESS,
WITHOUT ANY INFORMATION IN THE INTERVAL, NOTWITHSTANDING THAT
HIS FIRST UNAWARENESS DIFFERED IN KIND FROM HIS SECOND
UNAWARENESS.] BUT IF HE WAS FIRST INFORMED ABOUT THE REAPING
PERFORMED WHEN HE WAS AWARE OF THE SABBATH BUT UNAWARE OF
THE FORBIDDEN LABOR, THEN ATONEMENT FOR THIS SECOND REAPING
INVOLVES ATONEMENT FOR THE FIRST REAPING AND ITS ACCOMPANYING
GRINDING. [WHEN HE MAKES ATONEMENT FOR HIS SECOND REAPING,
HE AUTOMATICALLY MAKES ATONEMENT FOR THE FIRST AS WELL, AND
SINCE HIS FIRST REAPING AND GRINDING ONLY NECESSITATE ONE
SACRIFICE, HIS FIRST GRINDING, TOO, IS ATONED FOR THEREBY.] BUT
THE CORRESPONDING GRINDING [THE SECOND ONE] STANDS AS BEFORE.
[IT IS UNATONED FOR UNTIL ANOTHER SACRIFICE IS BROUGHT.]. IF ONE
ATE TWO OLIVE'S BULKS OF FORBIDDEN FAT IN A SINGLE SPELL OF
INADVERTENCE AND HE WAS INFORMED CONCERNING ONE OF THEM, AND
THEN HE WENT AND ATE AN OLIVE'S BULK OF FORBIDDEN FAT DURING
THE SPELL OF INADVERTENCE COVERING THE SECOND —IF HE BROUGHT

AN OFFERING COVERING THE FIRST ACTION, BOTH THE FIRST AND THE SECOND ACTS ARE ATONED FOR, BUT THE THIRD IS NOT ATONED FOR. IF HE BROUGHT AN OFFERING FOR THE THIRD, THE THIRD AND SECOND ARE ATONED FOR, BUT THE FIRST IS NOT ATONED FOR. IF HE BROUGHT AN OFFERING FOR THE SECOND ACT, ALL OF THEM ARE ATONED FOR." [SINCE BOTH THE FIRST AND THE THIRD WERE EATEN IN THE STATE OF UNAWARENESS OF THE SECOND, ALL ARE COVERED; BUT THE FIRST TWO RULINGS SHOW HE REJECTS THE THEORY THAT ATONEMENT FOR ONE THING INVOLVES ATONEMENT FOR ANOTHER AS WELL.]

B. 7:1 V.12 THERE IS A MORE STRICT RULE THAT APPLIES TO THE SABBATH THAN APPLIES TO OTHER RELIGIOUS DUTIES, AND THERE IS A MORE STRICT RULE THAT APPLIES TO OTHER RELIGIOUS DUTIES THAT DOES NOT APPLY TO THE SABBATH. FOR IN THE CASE OF THE SABBATH, IF ONE HAS DONE TWO FORBIDDEN ACTIONS IN A SINGLE SPELL OF INADVERTENCE, HE IS LIABLE FOR EACH ONE SEPARATELY, A RULE THAT DOES NOT APPLY TO OTHER RELIGIOUS DUTIES. THE MORE STRICT RULE APPLYING TO OTHER RELIGIOUS DUTIES IS THAT IF ONE HAS PERFORMED A FORBIDDEN ACTION INADVERTENTLY, WITHOUT PRIOR INTENTION, HE IS LIABLE, WHICH IS NOT THE RULE FOR THE SABBATH.

M. 7:2 The generative categories of acts of labor [prohibited on the Sabbath] are forty less one: (1) he who sows, (2) ploughs, (3) reaps, (4) binds sheaves, (5) threshes, (6) winnows, (7) selects [fit from unfit produce or crops], (8) grinds, (9) sifts, (10) kneads, (11) bakes; (12) he who shears wool, (13) washes it, (14) beats it, (15) dyes it; (16) spins, (17) weaves, (18) makes two loops, (19) weaves two threads, (20) separates two threads; (21) ties, (22) unties, (23) sews two stitches, (24) tears in order to sew two stitches; (25) he who traps a deer, (26) slaughters it, (27) flays it, (28) salts it, (29) cures its hide, (30) scrapes it, and (31) cuts it up; (32) he who writes two letters, (33) erases two letters in order to write two letters; (34) he who builds, (35) tears down; (36) he who puts out a fire, (37) kindles a fire; (38) he who hits with a hammer; (39) he who transports an object from one domain to another — lo, these are the forty generative acts of labor less one.

B. 7:2 I.1/73B WHAT'S THE POINT OF THE ENUMERATION? TO TEACH THAT IF SOMEONE DOES THEM ALL IN A SINGLE SPELL OF INADVERTENCE, HE STILL IS LIABLE ON EACH COUNT SEPARATELY.

T. 8:6 He who forgets the details of the Torah and commits many transgressions is liable for each and every one of them. How so? [If] he knew that there is such a thing as forbidden fat, but said, "This is not the sort of fat on account of which people are liable," [if] he knew that there is such a thing as [prohibited] blood, and said "This is not the sort of blood on account of which people are liable," he is liable for each and every [transgression committed by eating the blood or the fat].

T. 9:17 He who digs, ploughs, or cuts a trench — these are deemed a single type of forbidden labor. He who threshes, beats flax, or gins cotton — these are deemed a single type of forbidden labor. He who pulls up, reaps, cuts grapes, harvests olives, cuts dates, or hoes — these are deemed a single type of forbidden labor [cf. M. Shab. 7:2B].

T. 9:18 A. He who launders and he who wrings out — it is a single type of forbidden labor [cf. M. Shab. 7:2C].

B. 4:2 I.4/49B PEOPLE ARE LIABLE ONLY FOR CLASSIFICATIONS OF LABOR THE LIKE OF WHICH WAS DONE IN THE TABERNACLE. THEY SOWED, SO YOU ARE NOT TO SOW. THEY HARVESTED, SO YOU ARE NOT TO HARVEST. THEY LIFTED UP THE BOARDS FROM THE GROUND TO THE WAGON, SO YOU ARE NOT TO LIFT THEM IN FROM PUBLIC TO PRIVATE DOMAIN. THEY LOWERED BOARDS FROM THE WAGON TO THE GROUND, SO YOU MUST NOT CARRY ANYTHING FROM PRIVATE TO PUBLIC DOMAIN. THEY TRANSPORTED BOARDS FROM WAGON TO WAGON, SO YOU MUST NOT CARRY FROM ONE PRIVATE DOMAIN TO ANOTHER.

B. DOMAINS AND THE PROHIBITION OF TRANSPORTING OBJECTS FROM ONE DOMAIN TO ANOTHER

M. 7:3 And a further governing rule did they state: Whatever is suitable for storage, which people generally store in such quantity as one has taken out on the Sabbath — he is liable to a sin-offering on its account. And whatever is not suitable for storage, which people generally do not store in such quantity as one has taken out on the Sabbath – only he is liable on its account who stores it away [and who then takes it out].

B. 7:3 II.1/76A IN THE CASE OF ANYTHING THAT IS NOT REGARDED AS SUITABLE FOR STORAGE, THE LIKE OF WHICH IN GENERAL PEOPLE DO NOT STORE AWAY, BUT WHICH A GIVEN INDIVIDUAL HAS DEEMED FIT FOR STORAGE AND HAS STORED AWAY, AND WHICH ANOTHER PARTY HAS COME ALONG AND REMOVED FROM STORAGE AND TAKEN FROM ONE DOMAIN TO ANOTHER ON THE SABBATH — THE PARTY WHO MOVED THE OBJECT ACROSS THE LINE THAT SEPARATED THE TWO DOMAINS HAS BECOME LIABLE BY REASON OF THE INTENTIONALITY OF THE PARTY WHO STORED AWAY THIS THING THAT IS NOT ORDINARILY STORED.

M. 7:4 He who takes out a quantity of (1) straw sufficient for a cow's mouthful; (2) pea stalks sufficient for a camel's

mouthful; (3) ears of grain sufficient for a lamb's mouthful; (4) grass sufficient for a kid's mouthful; (5) garlic or onion leaves, ([if] fresh, a dried fig's bulk), [and if] dry, sufficient for a kid's mouthful is liable,] and they do not join together with one another [to form a quantity sufficient for culpability], because they are not subject to equivalent measures. He who takes out foodstuffs [for a human being] in the volume of a dried fig is liable. And they do join together with one another [to form a quantity sufficient for culpability], because they are subject to equivalent measures, except for their (1) husks, (2) kernels, (3) stalks, (4) coarse bran, and (5) fine bran.

T. 8:8 He who takes out coarse bran for food, in the volume of a dried fig [is liable] [cf. M. Shab. 7:4H4]. [If he took it out] for a domesticated animal, [the measure for which he is liable] is enough for a mouthful for a lamb. [If he took it out] for dyeing, [the prohibited measure is] enough with which to dye a small garment. As to young sprouts of a service tree and carobs before they have become sweet, [one is liable if he takes out] a volume of dried fig. Once they have grown sweet, [he is liable if he takes out] sufficient for a mouthful for a lamb. But as to arum, mustard, and lupines, and all other things which are pickled, whether or not they have grown sweet [the prohibited measure is] a dried fig.

M. 8:1 He who takes out (1) wine — enough to mix a cup; (2) milk — enough for a gulp; (3) honey — enough to put on a sore; (4) oil — enough to anoint a small limb; (5) water — enough to rub off an eye salve; and (6) of all other liquids, a quarter-log; (7) and of all slops [refuse], a quarter-log.

M. 8:2-4 He who takes out (1) rope — enough to make a handle for a basket; (2) reed cord — enough to make a hanger for a sifter or a sieve — (3) paper — enough to write on it a receipt for a tax collector. And he who takes out (1) a receipt for a tax collector is liable; (2) used paper — enough to wrap around a small perfume bottle. (3) Leather — enough to make an amulet; (4) parchment — enough to write on it a small pericope of the tefillin, which is "Hear O Israel"; (5) ink — enough to write two letters; (6) eye shadow — enough to shadow one eye. (7) Lime — enough to put on the head of a lime twig; (8) pitch or sulphur — enough for making a small hole; (9) wax — enough to put over a small hole; (10) clay — enough to make the [bellow's] hole of the

crucible of a goldsmith. (11) Bran — enough to put on the mouth of the crucible of a goldsmith; (12) quicklime — enough to smear the little finger of a girl.

T. 8:13-14 Bills of purchase and sale, mortgage deeds and pledges, deeds of gift — in any size at all — he is liable. Parchment and inferior parchment — enough to write a *mezuzah* thereon. A piece of vellum — enough to write a small pericope thereon. What is this small pericope? It is the *Shema'*.

M. 8:5 Earth for clay — enough to make a seal for a letter. (2) Manure or (3) fine sand — enough to manure a cabbage stalk, enough to manure a leek. (4) Coarse sand — enough to cover a plasterer's trowel; (5) reed — enough to make a pen. And if it was thick or broken — enough to [make a fire to] cook the smallest sort of egg, mixed [with oil] and put in a pan.

M. 8:6 (1) Bone — enough to make a spoon. (2) Glass — enough to scrape the end of a shuttle; (3) pebble or stone — enough to throw at a bird.

M. 9:5 He who brings out wood — [is liable if he carries out] enough to cook a small egg; spices — enough to spice a small egg; and they join together with one another [to make up the requisite quantity to impose liability]. (1) Nutshells, (2) pomegranate shells, (3) woad, and (4) dyer's madder — enough to dye a garment as small as a hair-net; (5) urine, (6) soda, (7) soap, (8) cimolian earth, or (9) lion's leaf — enough to launder a garment as small as a hair-net.

T. 8:31 He who takes out two planks at once, lo, this one is liable. [He who takes out] kernels of dates — one. A root: for planting — one, for a beast — a lamb's mouthful, for wood — in the measure of wood. Bundles of hyssop, savory, and thyme which one put into storage: for eating — a dried fig [in volume]; for a beast — a lamb's mouthful; for wood — in the measure of wood; for sprinkling — in the measure of [enough for~ sprinkling [purification water on someone made unclean with corpse uncleanness]. Seeds: for planting — two. For a beast — a pig's mouthful. How much is a pig's mouthful? One. Others say, "For counting — five."

T. 8:32 He who takes out some of the stones of a house smitten with *nega'im,* its wood and its dirt, in any amount at all — lo, this one is liable.

T. 9 3 He who takes out a bit of the fluff of cotton, cissaros blossom, a camel, a rabbit, or of a creature of the sea, and all other substances which are spread out, all in the measure of a double sit, lo, this one is liable. In the case of fabric, sacking, or hide, as is the measure which is sufficient to render them unclean, so is the measure sufficient to impose liability for taking them out [from private to public domain].

T. 9:4 He who takes out utensils, whether large or small, lo, this one is liable. He who takes out a coal in any measure at all, lo, this one is liable. A flame in any measure at all — lo, this one is liable.

M. 9:6 (1) Pepper in any quantity at all; (2) tar in any quantity at all; (3) various sorts of spices and metal tools in any quantity at all; (1) stones of the altar, (2) dirt of the altar, (3) worn-out holy books, and (4) their worn-out covers — in any quantity at all. They store them away in order to hide them [for permanent storage].

M. 9:7 He who takes out a peddler's basket, even though there are many different sorts of things in it, is liable only for a single sin-offering. Garden seeds — less than a dried fig's bulk. [The standard measures for the following are:] (1) for cucumber seeds — two, (2) gourd seeds — two, (3) Egyptian bean seeds — two; [the standard measure for] (1) a clean, live locust — in any quantity whatsoever; [the standard measure for] (2) a dead one — the size of a dried fig; [the standard measure for] (3) 'a vineyard bird' [a kind of locust] whether alive or dead — in any quantity at all, for they store it away for [later use as] a remedy.

M. 10:1 He who put [something] away for seed, for a sample, or for a remedy and [then] took it out on the Sabbath is liable in any amount whatsoever. But any [other] person is liable on that same account only in the specified measure pertinent to [that sort of thing]. [If the person] went and put it back, he is liable [should he take it out again] only in the specified measure pertinent to it.

C. THE PROHIBITION OF CARRYING ON THE SABBATH ACROSS THE LINES OF DOMAINS

M. 10:2 He who takes out food and puts it down on the threshold, whether he then went and took it out, or someone else took it out, is exempt [from liability to a sin-offering], for he has not [completely] performed his prohibited act of labor at one time. A basket which is full of produce, which one put on the outer [half of the] threshold, even though the larger quantity of the produce is outside — he is exempt, unless he takes out the entire basket.

M. 10:3 He who takes [something] out, (1) whether in his right hand or in his left, (2) in his lap or (3) on his shoulder, is liable, for so is the manner of carrying [an object] by the children of Kohath (Num. 7:9). [If he takes something out] (1) on the back of his hand, (2) on his foot, (3) in his mouth, (4) in his elbow, (5) in his ear, or (6) in his hair, (1) in his wallet with its mouth downward, (2) between his wallet and his cloak, (3) in the hem of his cloak, (4) in his shoe, (5) in his sandal, he is exempt [from liability to a sin-offering]. For he has not carried [the object] out the way people [generally] carry out [objects].

T. 9:8(9) He who intends to take something out in his wallet with its mouth upward and took it out in his wallet with its mouth downward [M. Shab. 10:3D], inside his wallet and took it out between his wallet and his cloak or in the neck of his cloak [M. Shab. 10:3D2], is exempt [from liability to a sin offering].

M. 10:4 He who intends to take out something before him, and it slipped behind him is exempt. [If he intended to carry it out] behind him and it slipped in front of him, he is liable. Truly did they say, A woman who wore drawers [and took something out in them], whether in front of her or behind her, is liable, for they are likely to be moved around.

T. 9:9 He who intends to take something out in his wallet with its mouth upward and took it out in his wallet with its mouth downward, inside his wallet and took it out between his wallet and his cloak or in the neck of his cloak, is exempt; he who intends to take something out in his wallet with its mouth downward is exempt.

M. 10:5 He who takes out a loaf of bread into the public domain is liable. [If] two people took it out, they are exempt. [If] one person could not take it out, but two people took it out, they are liable. He who takes out food in a volume less than the specified measure in a utensil is exempt even on account of [taking out] the utensil, for the utensil is secondary to it [the food]. [He who takes out] a living person in a bed is exempt even on account of [taking out] the bed, for the bed is secondary to him. [If he took out] a corpse in a bed, he is liable. And so [one who takes out] an olive's bulk of corpse matter and an olive's bulk of carrion and a lentil's bulk of a dead creeping thing is liable.

T. 9:10 Two people holding on to a pitchfork and stacking, to a shuttle and pressing, to a pen and writing, to a reed, and they took it out to the public domain — both of them are exempt [from liability to bring a sin offering]. [If they were holding on to] a wheel of dried figs, and they took it out to the public domain, to a beam, and they took it out to the public domain.

B. 10:5E-K I.1/93B HE WHO TAKES OUT FOOD IN A VOLUME SUFFICIENT TO MEET THE SPECIFIED MEASURE — IF HE DOES SO IN A UTENSIL, HE IS LIABLE FOR TAKING OUT THE FOOD BUT EXEMPT FOR TAKING OUT THE UTENSIL. BUT IF THE UTENSIL WAS NECESSARY FOR CARRYING OUT THE FOOD, HE IS LIABLE ALSO FOR THE UTENSIL [SO HE IS LIABLE ON TWO COUNTS].

M. 10:6 He who pares his fingernails with one another, or with his teeth, so, too, [if he pulled out the hair of] his (1) head, (2) moustache, or (3) beard — and so she who (1) dresses her hair, (2) puts on eye-shadow, or (3) rouges her face — these acts are prohibited because of [the principle of] Sabbath rest. He who picks [something] from a pot which has a hole [in the bottom] is liable. [If he picks something from a pot] which has no hole [in the bottom], he is exempt.

T. 9:11 [If] one took out a half dried fig's bulk [of food] and went and took out a half dried fig's bulk [of food] in a single spell of inadvertence, he is liable. [If he did so] in two spells of inadvertence, he is exempt. [If] the first [which was taken out] was eaten before the second was put down, whether this was in a single spell of inadvertence or in two spells of inadvertence, he is exempt. [If~ he took out a half dried fig's bulk [of food] and put it down in one area of four cubits [of the doorway], and went and took out another dried fig's bulk [of food] and put it down in another area of four cubits [of the doorway], if he brought [the second] by the way [of the first], he is liable. And if not, he is exempt.

T. 9:14 He who plucks up [a plant], whether with his right hand or his left, lo, this one is liable. [If he did so] with one of his hands, with his foot, with his mouth with his elbow, or if he was walking along on the ground and pebbles were kicked up from under his feet and fell on pieces of grass and pulled them up, he is exempt.

D. THROWING OBJECTS FROM ONE DOMAIN TO ANOTHER

M. 11:1 He who throws [an object] from private domain to public domain, [or] from public domain to private domain, is liable. [He who throws an object] from private domain to

private domain, and public domain intervenes is exempt from penalty. How so? Two balconies opposite one another [extending] into the public domain — he who stretches out or throws [an object] from this one to that one is exempt. [If] both of them were [different private domains on the same side of the street and] at the same story, he who stretches [an object over] is liable, and he who throws from one to the other is exempt. For thus was the mode of labor of the Levites: Two wagons, one after the other, in the public domain — they stretch beams from this one to that one, but they do not throw [them from one to the other].

T. 10:1 He who throws an object from private domain to private domain and public domain intervenes [M. Shab. 11:1B] — [if he throws to a distance of less than] four cubits, he is exempt [If he throws] beyond four cubits, he is liable. Two promenades, one above the other [if] one threw from the top to the bottom one, beyond a distance of four cubits, he is liable. [If this was] within a distance of four cubits, he is exempt. [If] he threw from a promenade to a shed, a stable, a storage area, or a courtyard, even though they are in a valley, lo, this one is liable. He who throws from a store through a stoa to the plaza is liable. [If he threw an object] from the store to the stoa, and from the stoa to the plaza, he is exempt.

T. 10:2 Two fields, one above the other — [if] one threw [an object] from the lower to the upper, or from the upper to the lower, he is exempt. A promenade above a field — and one threw from the promenade to the valley, he is exempt.

T. 10:3 An alley at the level of private domain and sloping down to the public domain — if there is an area at a height of ten handbreadths within a space of four cubits, it does not require side-beams and a top beam [to close it off]. Public domain which slopes down to private domain, lo, it is equivalent to private domain. [If] it is at the level of public domain and slopes down to private domain, if there is an area at a height of ten handbreadths in a space of four cubits, it does not require side-beams and a top beam to close it off. Private domain which slopes down to public domain, lo, it is equivalent to public domain. [If] it is at the same level on all sides and high in the middle, if there is in the high area a space of ten handbreadths in height within four cubits, it does not require side-beams and a cross beam. Private domain which slopes down into private domain, lo, it is equivalent to private domain. If it slopes down] to public domain, lo, it is equivalent to public domain.

T. 10:5 A roof in public domain ten handbreadths high and four broad — [if] one took something from it or put something onto it, he is liable. [If it is] less than the specified area, [if he put an object on it] within a space of four cubits, he is exempt. [If he did so] outside of four cubits, he is liable.

T. 10:6 A pillar in the public domain ten handbreadths high and four cubits broad — [if] one took something from it or put something onto it, he is liable. [If it is] less than the specified area, [if he put an object on it] within a space of four cubits, he is exempt. [If he did so] outside of four cubits, he is liable.

T. 10:7 A candelabrum in the public domain ten handbreadths high, and the cup on top is four cubits broad — [if] one took something from it or put something onto it, he is liable. [If it is] less than the specified area, pf he put an object on it] within a space of four cubits, he is exempt. [If he did so] outside of four cubits, he is liable.

M. 11:2 The bank of a cistern and the rock ten handbreadths high and four broad — he who takes [something] from that area or who puts something onto that area is liable. [If they were] less than the stated measurements, he is exempt [from any penalty for such an action].

M. 11:3 He who throws [something from a distance of] four cubits toward a wall — [if he throws it] above ten handbreadths, it is as if he throws it into the air [which is public domain]. [If it is] less than ten handbreadths, it is as if he throws an object onto the ground [which is private domain]. He who throws [an object to a distance of] four cubits on the ground, is liable. [If] he threw [an object] within the space of four cubits and it rolled beyond four cubits, he is exempt. [If he threw an object] beyond four cubits and it rolled back into four cubits, he is liable.

T. 10:8 A wagon in the public domain ten handbreadths high — lo, all the same is the one who unloads it and the one who loads it up — lo, this person is liable.

T. 10:9 He who tosses [an object] against a wall above ten handbreadths,and it went and landed in a hole four by four handbreadths, lo, this person is liable [cf. M. Shab. 11:3A B].For they do not move objects from one domain to another.

T. 10:10 In a case of those who play ball in public domain,if the ball went from the hand of one of them beyond a distance of four cubits,he is liable [cf. M. Shab. 11:3D].A large basket in public domain, ten handbreadths high,and so a deep hole —

they do not carry an object from inside them to the public domain, nor from the public domain to them.But one may climb down inside of them and eat a meal.[If they are] less than the specified dimensions, [if he throws something] within a range of four cubits, he is exempt; [if he did so] beyond four cubits, he is liable.

B. 11:3A-D I.3/100A AN ALLEYWAY THAT IS LEVEL INSIDE BUT SLOPES DOWNWARD TOWARD PUBLIC DOMAIN, OR THAT IS LEVEL IN PUBLIC DOMAIN BUT THAT SLOPES DOWNWARD INSIDE — THAT ALLEYWAY [TO BE MARKED OFF AS PRIVATE DOMAIN FOR PURPOSES OF CARRYING THEREIN ON THE SABBATH] REQUIRES NEITHER CROSSBEAM NOR SIDEBOARDS [TO MAKE IT INTO PRIVATE DOMAIN; THE SLOPE ITSELF IS THE PARTITION].

M. 11:4 He who throws [an object to a distance of] four cubits into the sea is exempt. If it was shallow water and a public path passed through it, he who throws [an object for a distance of] four cubits is liable. And what is the measure of shallow water? Less than ten handbreadths in depth. [If there was] shallow water, and a public path goes through it, he who throws into it to a distance of four cubits is liable.

M. 11:5 He who throws [an object] (1) from the sea to dry land or (2) from dry land to the sea, or (3) from the sea to a boat, or (4) from a boat to the sea, or (5) from one boat to another, is exempt. [If] boats are tied together, they move [objects] from one to the next. If they are not tied together, even though they lie close together, they do not carry [objects] from one to the other.

T. 10:11 A. tongue of the sea which goes into a courtyard — they do not draw water from it on the Sabbath,unless they made for it a partition ten handbreadths high.Under what circumstances?When it flows in through a breach more than ten handbreadths.But if [the breach through which the sea flows is less than ten handbreadths and is] equivalent to a doorway, it requires nothing.

T. 10:12 A rock in the sea ten handbreadths high — they do not carry anything from it to the sea or from the sea to it. [If it is] less than the specified dimensions, lo, this is permitted.[The rule applies] so long as it is equivalent in area [no more than] to a space of sufficient for the sowing of two *seahs* of seed.

T. 10:14 A boat in the sea ten handbreadths high — they do not carry from the boat to the sea or from the sea into it. [If] they were untied, they go back to their status of being prohibited [so that one may not carry from one to the next] [cf. M. Shab.

11:5E F]. [If] they went and tied them together again, whether constrainedly or inadvertently, or deliberately or in error, they go back to their status of being permitted [so that one may now carry from one to the next]. For any sort of partition made on the Sabbath, whether those who make it are constrained, do so inadvertently, do so deliberately, or do so in error — lo, this is a valid partition.

T. 10:15 Boats tied together are deemed to have been formed into a single courtyard by an *'erub,* and they carry from one to the next. [If] they were untied, they go back to their status of being prohibited [so that one may not carry from one to the next] [cf. M. Shab. 11:5E F]. [If] they went and tied them together again, whether constrainedly or inadvertently, or deliberately or in error, they go back to their status of being permitted [so that one may now carry from one to the next]. For any sort of partition made on the Sabbath, whether those who make it are constrained, do so inadvertently, do so deliberately, or do so in error — lo, this is a valid partition.

M. 11:6 He who throws [an object] and realizes [remembers what he has done] after it leaves his hand, [if] another person caught it, [if] a dog caught it, or [if] it burned up in a fire [intervening in its flight path] — he is exempt. [If] he threw it intending to inflict a wound, whether at a man or at a beast, and realizes [what he has done] before it inflicted the wound, he is exempt. This is the governing principle: All those who may be liable to sin-offerings in fact are not liable unless at the beginning and the end, their [sin] is done inadvertently. [But] if the beginning of their [sin] is inadvertent and the end is deliberate, [or] the beginning deliberate and the end inadvertent, they are exempt — unless at the beginning and at the end their [sin] is inadvertent.

T. 10:20 If there is in the inadvertent deed of one of them sufficient time to perform a complete act of forbidden labor, he is liable. How so? [If] he knew that it was Sabbath and he deliberately performed a forbidden act of labor, this is the deliberate sort of commission of a forbidden act of labor referred to in the Torah. If he was engaged in that act, he is exempt. [If] he was unaware that it was the Sabbath but deliberately performed a forbidden act of labor, or [if] he knew that it was Sabbath and intended to do a forbidden act of labor on it, but did not know that on account of the commission of that particular act of labor, he is liable to a sin offering — this is an inadvertent violation referred to in the Torah.

IV. PROHIBITED ACTS OF LABOR

A. WHAT CONSTITUTES A WHOLE ACT OF LABOR

M. 12:1 He who builds — how much does he build so as to be liable [on that count]? He who builds — in any measure at all. He who hews stone, hits with a hammer or adze, bores — in any measure at all is liable. This is the governing principle: Whoever on the Sabbath performs a forbidden act of labor and [the result of] his act of labor endures is liable.

M. 12:2 He who ploughs — in any measure whatsoever, he who (1) weeds, he who (2) cuts off dead leaves, and he who (3) prunes — in any measure whatsoever, is liable. He who gathers branches of wood — if [it is] to improve the field — in any measure at all; if [it is] for a fire — in a measure [of wood] sufficient to cook a small egg, [is liable]. He who gathers herbs if [it is] to improve the field — in any measure at all; if it is for cattle [to eat] — in the measure of a lamb's mouthful, [is liable].

T. 9:15 He who pulls up endives for eating [is liable if he takes up] the bulk of a dried fig: [if it is] for a beast, a kid's mouthful; [if it is] to improve the ground, any amount at all. If he intends [to pull it up] for all of these [purposes], he is liable on two counts. If he was engaged in this matter and pulled it up, he is exempt.

T. 9:16 He who prunes [leaves] for eating is liable if he pruned] the bulk of a dried fig, [if it is] for a beast, a lamb's mouthful; [if it is] to improve the tree, any amount at all [cf. M. Shab. 12:2B3]. If he intends [to prune] for all of these [purposes], he is liable on two counts. If he was engaged in pruning, he is exempt.

T. 9:19 He who selects, grinds, sifts, kneads, bakes for food [is liable if what is produced is] of the volume of a dried fig; [if this is] for a beast, a lamb's mouthful; [if this is] for dyeing, enough to dye a small garment; and for all other purposes, as is the measure for them to be susceptible to uncleanness, so is the measure for [liability for] the one who takes them [cf. M. 7:2, 12:2].

T. 9:20 He who pulls a wing from a bird, trims it, and plucks the down, is liable for three sin offerings.

T. 11:4 He who puts out a fire and he who kindles a fire [in any measure at all], lo, this one is liable.He who puts oil into a

lamp, even though there already is oil in the lamp,lo, this one
is liable.[If] one moved it from one place to another, he is
exempt. [If] he tilted it on its side, lo, this one is liable.

T. 11:5 [If] there were before him two burning lamps,[and] he
intended to put out this one but put out the other,lo, this one is
liable. [If there were before him] two unlit lamps, [if] he
intended to light this one and lit that one, he is liable. [If] one
was unlit and one was burning, [if] he intended to put out the
one which was burning and instead he lit the one which was
unlit, to light the one which was unlit and instead he put out the
one which was burning, lo, this one is exempt. [If] he
intentionally put out the one which was lit and kindled the one
which was unlit in a single gesture, he is liable for two sin
offerings. [If] one person provides the fire, another the wood,
another the pot, another the water, another the meat, another
the spices, and finally someone came along and stirred the pot,
all of them are liable. [If] one provided the pot, one the water,
one the meat, one the spices, one the fire, one the wood, and
one came along and stirred, only the last two [who participated]
are liable.

B. 12:2 II.1/103A He who picks endives and cuts greens, if this
is for human consumption — one is liable for doing so on the
Sabbath and cutting a volume of a dried fig; if it is for animal
food, one is liable for cutting or picking enough for a kid's
mouthful; if it is for fuel, it must be enough fuel to boil an
egg lightly; if it is to improve the soil [leaving room for other
plants], it is however little.

M. 12:3 He who writes two letters, whether with his right
hand or with his left, whether the same letter or two different
letters, whether with different pigments, in any alphabet, is
liable.

M. 12:4 He who writes two letters during a single spell of
inadvertence is liable. [If] he wrote with (1) ink, (2) caustic,
(3) red dye, (4) gum, or (5) copperas, or with anything which
leaves a mark, on two walls forming a corner, or on two
leaves of a tablet, which are read with one another, he is
liable. He who writes on his flesh is liable.

T. 11:8 He who traces something on a hide like the shape of
writing is exempt. He who makes a mark on a hide like the
shape of writing is liable. [If] he wrote with nut shells,
pomegranate shells, congealed blood, or congealed milk, on an
olive leaf, a carob leaf, or a gourd leaf, on anything which lasts

[M. Shab. 12:4C], he is liable. [If he wrote] on a lettuce leaf, a leek leaf, an onion leaf, a vegetable leaf, on anything which does not last [M. Shab. 12:5B], or with something which does not last on something which lasts, he is exempt — unless he wrote in something which lasts on something which lasts.

T. 11:9 He who writes one large letter, [even] if it is of the same size as two regular letters, is exempt.

T. 11:10 He who erases one large letter, if it is of the same size as two regular letters, is liable.

T. 11:11 [If] ink fell on a book and he erased it, wax on a pad and he removed it, if there is in the place in which it fell sufficient space for the writing of two letters, he is liable. He who erases in order to spoil is exempt. You have none who is liable except for one who erases in order to write. He who erases in order to correct, in any measure at all, lo, this one is liable.

T. 11:12 He who [intends to] write one letter and made it two letters, two letters and made them one letter, lo, this one is liable. [If] he intended to write one letter and they came out at his hand in the form of two letters, two letters and one letter came out, lo, this one is liable.

11:13 [If] he wrote two dots, and someone else came along and finished them and made them into two letters, the latter person is liable. [If] he wrote on the corner inside, he is liable [M. Shab. 12:4D]. [If he did so] on the outside, he is exempt.

T. 11:16 [If] one person holds on to the pen, and another takes his hand and guides it in writing, the one who holds the pen is liable. The one who guides his hand in writing is exempt. [But] if he intended to help the other to write, then the one who holds the pen is exempt, and the one who guides his hand in writing is liable. [If] the one who holds the pen [writes] inadvertently, but the one who guides his hand in writing does so deliberately, [the former] is liable [to a sin offering]. [If] the one who holds the pen [writes] deliberately, and the one who holds his hand and guides it in writing does so inadvertently [e.g., not knowing that it is the Sabbath, or that it is prohibited to do so on the Sabbath], [the former] is exempt [from liability to a sin offering].

T. 11:17 [If] a minor holds the pen and an adult holds his hand and guides it in writing, he [the minor] is liable. [If] the adult holds the pen and a minor holds his hand and guides it in writing, he [the adult] is exempt.

T. 11:18 [If] one person puts in the ink, one the water, and one the gum, the last two are liable. [If] one puts in the gum, one the water, and one the ink, the last two are liable. [If] one puts in the ink, one the gum, and one the water, the last one is liable. [If] one puts in the gum, one the ink, and one the water, the last is liable. [If] one puts in the water, one the ink, and one the ink and one the water, one puts in the water and one the flour, one the flour and one the water, one puts in the water and one the dirt, one the dirt and one the water, the last one is liable.

M. 12:5 If] one wrote with (1) fluids [blood, water, milk, honey, (2) fruit juice, (3) dirt from the street, (4) writer's sand, or with anything which does not leave a lasting mark, he is exempt. (1) [If he wrote] with the back of his hand, with his foot, mouth, or elbow, (2) [if] he wrote one letter alongside a letter already written, (3) [if] he wrote a letter on top of a letter [already written], (4) [if] he intended to write a het and wrote two zayins, (5) [if he wrote] one on the ground and one on the beam, (6) [if] he wrote [two letters] on the two walls of the house, on the two sides of a leaf of paper, so that they cannot be read with one another, he is exempt.

T. 11:7 [If] one wrote at the head of one writing sheet on one side, and one writing sheet on the other side, (even though) [if] one joins them to one another, they appear to be a single [letter], he is liable [cf. M. Shab. 12:5]. But if not, he is exempt. [If] he wrote one letter, and someone else came along and wrote one letter, and someone else came along and wrote one letter, even if [all together there is written] an entire name, even an entire book, [each one of them] is exempt. [If] he wrote one letter and [thereby] completed the [whole] name, or one letter and completed the writing of the book, he is liable [cf. M. Shab. 12:5E].

M. 13:2 He who makes two meshes for the heddles or the sley [of a loom], [or two meshes] in a sifter, sieve, or basket, is liable. He who sews two stitches [is liable]. And he who tears in order to sew two stitches [is liable].

T. 12:1 He who weaves two threads on the thick part of the web or on the border — lo, this one is liable [cf. M. Shab. 13:1C]. He who weaves two threads on the hem along the breadth of three loops, lo, this one is liable. He who weaves three threads at the beginning ~of the process of weaving] — lo, this one is liable [M. Shab. 13:1A]. To what is this likened? To [weaving] a small belt two threads over the breadth of three meshes [in size]. He who weaves three threads at the outset, lo, this one is liable [M. Shab. 13:1A] .

M. 13:3 He who tears [his clothing] because of his anger or on account of his bereavement, and all those who effect destruction, are exempt. But he who destroys in order to improve — the measure [for] his [action] is the same as for him who improves.

M. 13:4 The measure for one who bleaches, hackles, dyes, or spins is a double sit. And he who weaves two threads — his measure is a sit.

M. 13:5 [He who drives] a bird into a tower trap, or a deer into a house, into a courtyard, or into a corral is liable. This is the governing principle: [If] it yet lacks further work of hunting, he [who pens it in on the Sabbath] is exempt. [If] it does not lack further work of hunting, he is liable.

M. 13:6 A deer which entered a house, and someone locked it in — he [who locked it in] is liable. [If] two people locked it in, they are exempt. [If] one person could not lock the door, and two people did so, they are liable.

M. 13:7 [If] one of them sat down at the doorway and did not completely fill it [so that the deer could yet escape], but a second person sat down and finished filling it, the second person is liable. [If] the first person sat down at the doorway and filled it up, and a second one came along and sat down at his side, even though the first one got up and went along, the first remains liable, and the second exempt. lo, to what is this equivalent? To one who locks his house to shut it up [and protect it], and a deer turns out to be shut up [and trapped] inside.

T. 12:2 Two who [on the Sabbath] hunted a deer — both of them are exempt. For two individuals are not culpable for a single prohibited act of labor [completed] by both of them together] [cf. M. Shab. 13:6]. [If] the first one hunted it and left it, the second hunted it and left it, both of them are liable. [If] the first one hunted it and gave it over to the second, the first is liable, and the second is exempt.

T. 12:3 He who hunts [traps] a deer in a courtyard which has two doorways is exempt. [If] the first one locked one door, and a second person came along and locked the second door, the second is liable, and the first is exempt. [If] the first one went and opened the door and locked it again, the first is liable on account of a second prohibited act of hunting.

T. 12 :4 He who hunts a lame deer, a sick one, or a young one, is exempt. He who hunts an old one is liable. He who hunts doves of a dovecot or doves kept in an upper room or birds which make their nest in pitcher shaped nests, or anything which yet lacks [the completion of the process of] hunting, is liable. [He who hunts] ducks, chickens, Herodian pigeons, or anything which yet lacks no [further act of] hunting, is exempt [cf. M. Shab. 13:5F]. He who hunts flies and mosquitos is liable.

T. 12 :5 He who hunts locusts in the time of dew is exempt. [If he does so] in the time of heat, he is liable. He who hunts a domesticated beast, a wild beast, or fowl, on ground which is not the domain of a human being, if they yet lacked further work of hunting, is liable. [If he hunted them] on ground which is the domain of a human being, even though they yet lack further work of hunting, he is exempt. He who spreads out a trap for a domesticated beast, a wild beast, or a bird [not present at the time], even though they enter into it, is exempt. [If he spread it] for a domesticated beast, a wild beast, or a bird [present at the time], if they then went into it, he is liable. He who releases a domesticated beast, a wild beast, or a bird from a trap is exempt.

T. 12 :6 Two who sat down [and filled up] a doorway — both of them are exempt, for it is not known which of them got there first [M. Shab. 13:7A]. [If] this one sat down first and that one sat down second, the first is liable, and the second is exempt. [If] one person sat down at the doorway, and another person came along and hunted [a deer] inside the courtyard, the one who sits down at the doorway is liable, and the one who hunted it inside is exempt. [If] one person sat down at the doorway, and someone else came along and sat down inside, and someone else came along and sat down outside, the one who is sitting at the doorway is liable. And the latter two are exempt.

T. 12:7 [If] one person sat at the doorway, and a deer turned out to be inside [the house], even though the one sitting at the doorway plans to stay there until dark, he is exempt [from punishment on the grounds of hunting]. For the [unintentional] act of hunting came before the intention to accomplish the act. You have none who is liable except one who actually intends to carry out an act of hunting. If the act of hunting came before the intention to hunt, the man is therefore exempt [cf. M. Shab. 13:7F].

M. 14:1 The eight creeping things mentioned in the Torah [the weasel, mouse, great lizard, gecko, land crocodile, lizard, sand lizard, and chameleon] — he who hunts them or wounds them is liable. And as to all other abominations and creeping

things, he who wounds them is exempt. He who hunts them
for use is liable. [He who hunts them] not for use is exempt.
A wild beast and a bird which are in his domain — he who
hunts them is exempt. He who wounds them is liable.

**M. 14:2 They do not make pickling brine on the Sabbath.
But one makes salt water and dips his bread in it and puts it
into cooked food.**

T. 12:17 They crack nuts, scrape pomegranates, and cut figs on
the Sabbath for use on that same Sabbath, but not on the Sabbath
for use after the Sabbath. For in the latter case he is as one who
gets things ready on the holy day for an ordinary day's use.
They rinse utensils on the Sabbath for use on that same Sabbath,
but not on this Sabbath for use on some other Sabbath. How
so? [If] one ate in some of them on the night of the Sabbath, he
may rinse them to eat in them in the morning. [If he ate in
some of them] in the morning, he rinses them to eat in them for
the main meal. [If he ate in some of them] for the main meal,
he rinses them to eat in some of them at the afternoon meal. [If
he ate in some of them] at the afternoon meal, he may not rinse
them from that time forth. The cups does he rinse all the day,
for there is no time limit. They may rinse ten cups, since if he
wants, he may drink out of any one. They set ten beds, for if he
wants, he may lie down in any one of them.

B. HEALING ON THE SABBATH

**M. 14:3 They do not eat Greek hyssop on the Sabbath,
because it is not a food for healthy people. But one eats
pennyroyal or drinks knot grass water. All sorts of foods a
person eats [which serve for] healing, and all such drinks he
may drink, except for palm tree water [purgative water] or
a cup of root water, because they are [solely] for jaundice.
But one may drink palm tree water [to quench] his thirst.
And one anoints with root oil, [if it is] not for healing.**

**M. 14:4 He who has tooth problems may not suck vinegar
through them. But he dunks [his bread] in the normal way,
and if he is healed, he is healed. He who is concerned about
his loins [which give him pain], he may not anoint them
with wine or vinegar. But he anoints with oil — not with
rose oil. Princes [on the Sabbath] anoint themselves with
rose oil on their wounds, since it is their way to do so on
ordinary days.**

T. 12:10 He who is concerned about his throat should not keep
oil in the throat for a lubricant. But he puts a good quantity of
oil into a sauce of oil and arum and swallows it.

T. 12:11 He who is concerned about his head, and so too, he on whom sores came up, anoints with oil, but does not anoint with wine or vinegar. For it is usual to anoint with oil, but it is not usual to anoint with wine or vinegar.

T. 12:12 A person anoints oil on a wound, on condition that he not take it with a cloth or a rag. They prepare a wine potion for a sick person on the Sabbath. Under what circumstances? When it was mixed on the eve of the Sabbath. [But if] it was not mixed on the eve of the Sabbath, it is prohibited to do so. For they do not mix to begin with on the Sabbath. They do not mix wine and oil for a sick person on the Sabbath.

12:13 A. They drink manure water, palm tree water, and a cup of root-water [vs. M. Shab. 14:3F]. And one may rinse off his hands, face, and feet with them. One may not rinse off his sandal with them. A person may bathe in the baths of Tiberias or in the Great Sea, but not in a pond for steeping flax nor in the Sea of Sodom. Under what circumstances? When he does so intending it as a remedy. But if it is to emerge from uncleanness to cleanness, lo, this is permitted.

T. 12 :14 A. One may not put water onto a sponge and place it on his wound. But he may put [water] on his feet, and it then rolls down onto the sponge [located on the wound]. A person may put a dry cloth or a dry sponge on his wound, but not dry reed grass or a dry compress of rags on his wound. They put water into parched wheat, on condition that one not knead. They put sesame and nuts into honey, on condition that one not scramble it. They grind fine olives for a sick person on the Sabbath, on condition that he not knead them, but he may scramble them in cooked food and eat.

C.   KNOT-TYING, CLOTHING AND BEDS

M. 15:1 On account of [tying] what sorts of knots [on the Sabbath] are [people] liable? (1) A camel driver's knot, and (2) a sailor's knot. And just as one is liable for tying them, so he is liable for untying them.

M. 15:2 You have knots on account of which they are not liable, like a camel driver's knot and a sailor's knot. A woman ties (1) the slit of her shift, (2) the strings of her hair-net and of her belt, (3) the thongs of a shoe or sandal, (4) [leather] bottles of wine or oil, and (5) a cover over meat. They tie a bucket with a belt but not with a rope.

M. 15:3 They fold up clothing even four or five times. And they spread beds on the night of the Sabbath for use on the Sabbath, but not on the Sabbath for use after the Sabbath.

T. 12:15 Fish or cheese which is laid out [and tied to] reeds or leaves one unties and eats, on condition that he not put it back. A woven basket of palm leaves and a basket for dried figs does one tear apart [so as to] eat [the contents], on condition that he not repair the basket [cf. M. Shab. 15:1C]. This is the governing principle: On account of any knot which lasts and which one can untie with one hand, or which does not last but which one cannot untie with one hand, they are not liable — unless it is a knot which lasts and which one cannot untie with one hand. A rope tied onto a cow one may tie onto the crib, and one tied onto the crib one may attach onto the cow.

T. 12:16 A rope which is in the house they carry about. One which is in the store room they do not carry about. If the householder so arranged it as to be able to make use of it, they do carry it about. A rope of a bucket which snapped — they do not tie it, but they loop it [cf. M. Shab. 15:2D].

T. 12:17 They rinse cups, dishes, and plates [T.'s version: utensils on the Sabbath for use on that same Sabbath but not on one Sabbath for use on some other Sabbath. How so? [If] one ate in them] on the night of the Sabbath, he may rinse them to eat in them in the morning. [If he ate in them] in the morning, he may rinse them so to eat in them for the main meal. If he ate in them for the main meal, he may rinse them to eat in them at the afternoon meal. If he ate in them at the afternoon meal, he may not rinse them from that time forth. The cups does he rinse all the day, for there is no time as to drinking.

V. ACTIONS THAT ARE PERMITTED ON THE SABBATH

A. SAVING OBJECTS FROM A FIRE ON THE SABBATH

M. 16:1 All Holy Scriptures — do they save from fire, whether they read in them or do not read in them. And even though they are written in any language [besides Hebrew], [if they become useless] they require storage [and are not to be burned]. And on what account do they not read in [some of] them? Because of the neglect of the [proper study of the Torah in the] study house.hey save the case of the scroll with the scroll and the case of the phylacteries with the phylacteries, even though there is money in them. And where do they [take them to] save them? To a closed alley [which is not open as a thoroughfare and so is not public domain].

T. 13:4 [If] they were written in paint, red ink, gum ink, or calcanthum, they save them and store them away. As to scrolls containing blessings [e.g., amulets], even though they include the letters of the Divine Name and many citations of the Torah, they do not save them, but they are allowed to burn where they are. On this basis they have stated, Those who write blessings are as if they burn the Torah.

T. 13 :6 A scroll which has caught fire at the top — one takes hold of it and reads in it. If the fire goes out, it goes out. A cloak which has caught fire at the top — one takes it and puts it on. If the fire goes out, it goes out. A utensil which has caught fire at the top — one takes it and makes use of it. If the fire goes out,it goes out. A scroll which fell into an oven — one imparts uncleanness to heave-offering [located therein, in order to save the scroll]. They put out a fire in order to save Holy Scriptures, but not [to save] heave offering. Greater is the power of Holy [Scriptures] than the power of heave-offering. For in the case of [a fire endangering] Holy [Scriptures] one saves the whole thing. But in the case of [a fire endangering] heave offering, one saves [only enough food for three meals], just as one saves food in an unconsecrated state. They save food from the festival day for the Sabbath, but not on this Sabbath for use on some other Sabbath, nor on the Sabbath for a festival, nor on the Sabbath for the Day of Atonement, nor on the Day of Atonement for the Sabbath, and, it goes without saying, not on the festival for an ordinary day [cf. M. Shab. 15:3].

T. 13:7 One should not save [food from a fire on the Sabbath] and afterward call [guests to join in], but he should first call [guests to join in] and afterward should save [the food] [cf. M. Shab. 16:3D]. [If~ one has saved a loaf of bread of fine flour, he is not permitted to save a loaf of bread of coarse flour. If he saved a loaf of bread of coarse flour, he is permitted to save a loaf of bread of fine flour. And they do not practice deception in this matter.

M. 16:2 They save food enough for three meals — [calculated from] what is suitable for human beings for human beings, what is suitable for cattle for cattle. How so? [If] a fire broke out on the night of the Sabbath, they save food for three meals. [If it broke out] in the morning, they save food for two meals. [If it broke out] in the afternoon, [they save food for] one meal.

M. 16:3 They save a basket full of loaves of bread, even if it contains enough food for a hundred meals, a wheel of pressed

figs, and a jug of wine. And one says to others, "Come and save [what you can] for yourselves [as well]." Now if they were intelligent, they come to an agreement with him after the Sabbath. Where do they [take them to] save them? To a courtyard which is included within the Sabbath limit that fuses the area into a single domain [erub].

M. 16:4 And to that place [M. 16:3F-H] one takes out all his utensils. And he puts on all the clothing which he can put on, and he cloaks himself in all the cloaks he can put on. And he goes back, puts on clothing, and takes it out, and he says to others, "Come and save [the clothing] with me."

M. 16:6 A gentile who came to put out a fire — they do not say to him, "Put it out," or "Do not put it out," for they are not responsible for his Sabbath rest. But a minor [Israelite child] who came to put out a fire — they do not hearken to him [and let him do so], because his Sabbath rest is their responsibility.

M. 16:7 They cover a lamp with a dish so that it will not scorch a rafter; and the excrement of a child; and a scorpion, so that it will not bite.

M. 16:8 A gentile who lit a candle — an Israelite may make use of its light. But [if he did so] for an Israelite, it is prohibited [to do so on the Sabbath]. [If a gentile] drew water to give water to his beast, an Israelite gives water to his beast after him. But [if he did so] for an Israelite, it is prohibited [to use it on the Sabbath]. [If] a gentile made a gangway by which to come down from a ship, an Israelite goes down after him. But [if he did so] for an Israelite, it is prohibited [to use it on the Sabbath].

T. 13 :10 They do not rent utensils to a gentile on Friday. But on Wednesday or Thursday it is permitted to do so.

T. 13:11 They do not send letters with a gentile on Friday, but on Wednesday or Thursday it is permitted.

13:12 [If] a gentile drew water to give to his beast, an Israelite gives water to his beast after him. But [if the gentile did sol for the Israelite, it is prohibited [M. Shab. 16:8D E]. [If a gentile] gathered hay to feed his beast, an Israelite feeds his beast after him. But [if he did so] for the Israelite, it is prohibited. Under what circumstances [is it permitted]? In the case of a gentile who does not know him. But in the case of a gentile who does know him, lo, this is prohibited. For he grows accustomed to this practice, and will work for him on another Sabbath. And in all cases in which an Israelite has done such deeds as these, whether he did so inadvertently, deliberately, or in error, lo, this is prohibited [for another Israelite to benefit from the violation of the Sabbath performed by this Israelite].

B. <u>HANDLING OBJECTS ON THE SABBATH IN PRIVATE DOMAIN</u>

M. 17:1 All utensils are handled on the Sabbath, and their [detached] doors along with them, even though they were detached on the Sabbath. For they are not equivalent to doors of a house, for the [latter] are not prepared [in advance of the Sabbath to be used].

M. 17:2 One handles (1), a hammer to split nuts, (2) an ax to chop off a fig, (3) a saw to cut through cheese, (4) a shovel to scoop up dried figs, (5) a winnowing shovel or (6) a fork to give something thereon to a child, (7) a spindle or (8) a shuttle staff to thrust into something, (9) a sewing needle to take out a thorn, (10) a sack maker's needle to open a door.

T. 13:15 The frame of a bed and a cradle, the poles of a bed and the boards of a mattress, the leg of a bed, and the handle of a knife — lo [if one of these should come out], one may not put it back. But if he put it back, he is exempt, on condition that he not fix it firmly. But if he fixed it firmly, he is liable for a sin offering.

T. 13:16 They move about a horn to give drink to an infant. They handle a rattle, a notebook, and a mirror to cover utensils with them [cf. M. Shab. 17:2]. And they do not look into a mirror on the Sabbath. But if it was affixed to the wall, it is permitted.

T. 13:17 They do not rattle either a bell or a clapper for an infant on the Sabbath. They do not handle a mallet, a plane, a borer, or a chisel. One should not smite with a mallet on a plane, nor should one open [a cask of dates] with a chisel the way one does so on an ordinary day. Utensils made of hardened dung and stone and dirt, lo, they are deemed equivalent to all other utensils and they handle them. A ball, whether it is hollowed out or not hollowed out, do they handle on the Sabbath. They referred to its being hollowed out only in respect to uncleanness. A mortar, if there is garlic in it, do they handle, and if not, they do not handle it.

Y. 17:2 I.2 A utensil which serves a distinctive purpose prohibited on the Sabbath may be handled only in the case of a need [appropriate to the Sabbath], while one which serves a distinctive purpose permitted on the Sabbath may be handled both in the case of a need appropriate to the Sabbath and otherwise.

M. 17:3 A reed for olives, if it has a knot on its top, receives uncleanness. And if not, it does not receive uncleanness. One way or the other, it is handled on the Sabbath.

M. 17:4 All utensils are handled in case of need and not in case of need.

T. 14:1 At first they ruled: Three utensils may be moved about on the Sabbath: a fig cake knife, a pot soup ladle, and a small table knife. They went and continued to add to the list, until they came to rule: All utensils are moved about on the Sabbath, except for a large saw or plowshare [M. Shab. 17:4A B].

T. 14:2 A bed which broke — it and its fragments are permitted to be handled on the Sabbath. A hammock which broke — it and its fragments may be handled on the Sabbath. The stopper of a jug which broke — it and its fragments may be handled on the Sabbath. And one should not trim the fragment or support the legs of a bed in it. And one should not cover utensils with it. [If] one tossed it into the garbage, it and its parts are not handled on the Sabbath.

B. 17:4A-B I.3/123B THEY PERMITTED HANDLING AN ARTICLE THE FUNCTION OF WHICH WAS FOR A PERMITTED PURPOSE, ON CONDITION THAT IT WAS REQUIRED FOR ITS OWN PURPOSE [NOT BECAUSE THE PLACE WHERE IT WAS SITUATED WAS REQUIRED]; THEN THEY WENT AND PERMITTING HANDLING SOMETHING THAT SERVED A PERMITTED PURPOSE MERELY BECAUSE THE SPACE WHERE IT WAS LOCATED WAS NEEDED; AND THEN THEY WENT AND PERMITTED HANDLING SOMETHING THE USUAL USE OF WHICH WOULD BE PERMITTED ON THE SABBATH, SO LONG AS IT WAS REQUIRED FOR ITSELF [FOR USE IN A FORM OF LABOR THAT IS PERMITTED], BUT NOT MERELY BECAUSE THE SPACE WHERE IT WAS LOCATED WAS NEEDED. AND STILL, THESE COULD BE HANDLED ONLY WITH ONE HAND, BUT NOT WITH TWO [SO THAT AN OBJECT, TOO, HEAVY FOR A SINGLE HAND COULD NOT BE HANDLED], UNTIL, FINALLY, THEY SAID, ALL UTENSILS MAY BE HANDLED ON THE SABBATH, AND EVEN WITH TWO HANDS.

M. 17:5 All utensils which are handled on the Sabbath — fragments deriving from them may be handled along with them, on condition that they perform some sort of useful work [even if it is not what they did when they were whole]: [So how large must these fragments be to be regarded as useful for some work, if not the work they originally did?]

(1) fragments of a kneading trough — [must be sufficiently large on their own] to cover the mouth of a barrel, (2) glass fragments — [must be sufficiently large on their own] to cover the mouth of a flask.

M. 17:6 A stone in a gourd shell [used for weighting it] — if they draw water in it and it does not fall out, they draw water with it [the gourd shell]. And if not, they do not draw water with it. A branch tied to a pitcher — they draw water with it on the Sabbath.

M. 17:7 The window shutter [stopper of a skylight] — they shut the window with it."

M. 17:8 All utensil covers which have handles are handled on the Sabbath.

M. 18:1 They clear away even four or five baskets of straw or grain on account of guests, or on account of [avoiding] neglect of the house of study. But [they do] not [clear away] a storeroom. They clear away (1) clean heave-offering, (2) doubtfully tithed produce, (3) first tithe the heave-offering of which has been removed, (4) second tithe and (5) consecrated produce which have been redeemed; and dried lupine, for it is food for poor people; but [they do] not [clear away] (6) produce from which tithes have not been removed, (7) first tithe the heave-offering of which has not been removed, (8) second tithe and (9) consecrated produce which have not been redeemed; arum, or mustard.

T. 14:4 They do not clear away a store room in the first instance on the Sabbath [M. Shab. 18:1B]. But one may make a path in it, so one may go in and come out. A large courtyard into which rain fell, and in which was a house of mourning, or a house of celebration [so that guests are coming] [cf. M. Shab. 18: 1A] — one may bring straw in a basket and make a path in it, on condition that he not make a path by hand or by using a basket, as he does on ordinary days. Boards which one planed, even though they are smooth, and even though they are made ready — they handle them. A basket of gum, a root of a tree, and a sheaf of papers or hides which have not been worked, if the householder has made them ready [for use], they handle them. And if not, they do not handle them.

T. 14:7 A jug which was opened and a watermelon which was pierced — one takes them and puts them in a covered place.

T. 14:8 They handle cistus, because it is food for gazelles, and mustard, because it is food for doves. This is the governing principle: Whatever is set aside for its distinctive purpose do they handle, and whatever is not set aside for its distinctive purpose they do not handle.

M. 18:2 Bundles of straw, branches, or young shoots — if one prepared them for food for cattle, they handle them, And if not, they do not handle them. They turn up a basket for chickens, so that they may go up [into the hen house] and down on it. A chicken that fled — they drive it along until it goes back [into the chicken yard]. They pull calves or young asses in the public way. A mother drags along her child.

M. 18:3 They do not deliver the young of cattle on the festival, but they help out. And they do deliver the young of a woman on the Sabbath. They call a midwife for her from a distant place, and they violate the Sabbath on her [the woman in childbirth's] account. And they tie the umbilical cord.

T. 14:11 Bundles of hyssop, savory, and thyme, which one brought in for the wood — one may not eat of them on the Sabbath. If he brought them in for food for cattle, he may eat of them. They crush and eat, on condition that one not crush them with a utensil.

T. 14:12 Cress which one chopped up on the eve of the Sabbath — one puts in vinegar and oil but does not chop it up. But he mixes and adds mint and puts it in.

T. 14:13 Mustard which one kneaded on the eve of the Sabbath — one brings honey and puts it into it, and he does not crush but mixes it.

T. 14:14 Garlic which one crushed on the eve of the Sabbath — one brings grits and puts it into it, and he does not chop it up but stirs it.

T. 14:15 They do not crush salt in a wooden crusher, but one chops it with the handle of a knife [or] a wooden pot ladle, and he need not scruple.

T. 14:16 They do not chop pressed figs or dried figs or carobs for elders on the Sabbath. But one chops it with the handle of a knife [or] a wooden pot ladle, and he need not scruple. He who rubs ears of corn on the eve of the Sabbath winnows them from hand to hand and eats them. But [he does] not [do so] with a basket or with a dish. He who rubs ears of corn on the eve of a festival winnows them with a basket or a dish. But [he does] not [do so] with a tray, a sifter, or a sieve, as they do on ordinary days.

T. 15:2 How do they help out in the delivery of the young of cattle on a festival [cf. M. Shab. 18:3A]? They blow into its nose and put a teat into its mouth, and one holds up the offspring so that it not fall down.

C. CIRCUMCISION ON THE SABBATH

M. 18:3 And all things required for circumcision do they perform on the Sabbath.

M. 19:1 Any sort of labor [in confection with circumcision] which it is possible to do on the eve of the Sabbath does not override [the restrictions of] the Sabbath, and that which it is not possible to do on the eve of the Sabbath does override [the prohibitions of] the Sabbath.

M. 19:2 They do prepare all that is needed for circumcision on the Sabbath: they (1) cut [the mark of circumcision], (2) tear, (3) suck [out the wound]. And they put on it a poultice and cumin. If one did not pound it on the eve of the Sabbath, he chews it in his teeth and puts it on. If one did not mix wine and oil on the eve of the Sabbath, let this be put on by itself and that by itself. And they do not make a bandage in the first instance. But they wrap a rag around [the wound of the circumcision]. If one did not prepare [the necessary rag] on the eve of the Sabbath, he wraps [the rag] around his finger and brings it, and even from a different courtyard.

B. 19:2 I.1/133B As to one performing the rite of circumcision, so long as he is engaged in the rite of circumcision, he may return to cut both the shreds of the corona that invalidate the circumcision and those that do not. Once he has completed the rite, he may return to operate on the shreds that invalidate the circumcision but he may not return to cut away those that do not invalidate the circumcision.

M. 19:3 They wash off the infant, both before the circumcision and after the circumcision, and they sprinkle him, [If the sexual traits of the infant are a matter of] doubt, or [if the infant] bears the sexual traits of both sexes, they do not violate the Sabbath on his account.

T.15:4 They remove the shreds of remaining membrane for the circumcision. One wraps on it wool or flax threads, on condition that one not tie them [M. Shab. 19:2F]. And one sprinkles warm water on it [M. Shab. 19:3C]. And not only so, but a man sprinkles hot water on his wound. For so long as one is involved in the rite of circumcision, one may go over even those shreds of flesh which do not invalidate the rite of circumcision. But once he has stopped, he may go back only over those shreds of flesh which invalidate the circumcision alone.

T. 15:5 On account of an infant born at seven months [of pregnancy] they override [the prohibitions] of the Sabbath. On account of an infant born at eight months, they do not override the prohibitions of the Sabbath [cf. M. Shab. 19:3G H]. [If] it is a matter of doubt whether it is born at seven months of pregnancy or eight, they do not override the restrictions of the Sabbath on his account. An infant born after eight months of pregnancy, lo, it is tantamount to a stone. And they do not move him about. But his mother bends over him and gives him suck.

M. 19:4 He who had two infants, one to circumcise after the Sabbath and one to circumcise on the Sabbath, and who forgot [which was which] and circumcised the one to be circumcised after the Sabbath on the Sabbath, is liable. [If he had] one to circumcise on the eve of the Sabbath and one to circumcise on the Sabbath, and he forgot and on the Sabbath, circumcised the one to be circumcised on the eve of the Sabbath,

M. 19:5 An infant is circumcised on the eighth, ninth, tenth, eleventh or twelfth day [after birth], never sooner, never later. How so? Under normal circumstances, it is on the eighth day. [If] he was born at twilight, he is circumcised on the ninth day. [If he was born] at twilight on the eve of the Sabbath, he is circumcised on the tenth day [the following Sunday]. In the case of a festival which falls after the Sabbath, he will be circumcised on the eleventh day [Monday]. In the case of two festival days of the New Year, he will be circumcised on the twelfth day [Tuesday]. An infant who is sick — they do not circumcise him until he gets well.

M. 19:6 These are the shreds [of the foreskin, if they remain] which render the circumcision invalid: flesh which covers the greater part of the corona — and such a one does not eat heave-offering. And if he was fat [so the corona appears to be covered up], one has to fix it up for appearance's sake. [If] one circumcised but did not tear the inner lining [the cut did not uncover the corona, since the membrane was not split and pulled down], it is as if he did not perform the act of circumcision.

T. 15:11 They remove debris for one whose life is in doubt on the Sabbath. And the one who is prompt in the matter, lo, this one is to be praised. And it is not necessary to get permission

from a court. How so? [If] one fell into the ocean and cannot
climb up, or [if] his ship is sinking in the sea, and he cannot
climb up, they go down and pull him out of there. And it is not
necessary to get permission from a court.

T. 15:(12)13 If he fell into a pit and cannot get out, they let
down a chain to him and climb down and pull him out of there.
And it is not necessary to get permission from a court. A baby
who went into a house and cannot get out — they break down
the doors of the house for him, even if they were of stone, and
they get him out of there. And it is not necessary to get
permission from a court. They put out a fire and make a barrier
against a fire on the Sabbath [cf. M. Shab. Chap. 16]. And one
who is prompt, lo, this one is to be praised. And it is not
necessary to get permission from a court.

T. 15:14 He whom a snake bit — they call a doctor for him
from one place to another. And they slaughter a chicken for
him and cut leeks for him, and he eats them and does not have
to tithe them.

T. 15:15 They heat water for a sick person on the Sabbath,
whether to give it to him to drink or to heal him with it. And
they do not say, "Wait on him, perhaps he'll live [without it]."
But a matter of doubt concerning him overrides [the prohibitions
of] the Sabbath. And the doubt need not be about this Sabbath,
but it may be about another Sabbath. And they do not say, Let
the matters be done by gentiles or children, but they should be
done by adult Israelites. And they do not say, Let these matters
be done by the testimony of women, by Samaritans. But they
join the opinion of Israelites with them [to decide to save a life
by violating the Sabbath].

D. PREPARING FOOD FOR MAN AND BEAST

**M. 20:1 (1) On the festival they do not spread out a strainer,
and (2) on the Sabbath they do not pour [wine] into one
which is spread out. But on the festival they pour [wine]
into one which is spread out.**

**M. 20:2 They pour water over wine dregs so that they will
be clarified. And they strain wine in cloths or in a twig basket.
And they put an egg into a mustard strainer. And they
prepare honeyed wine on the Sabbath.**

**M. 20:3 They do not soak asafoetida in warm water. But
one puts it into vinegar. And they do not soak vetches or rub
them. But one puts them into a sieve or a basket. They do
not sift chopped straw in a sifter. Nor does one put it on a**

high place so that the chaff will fall out. But one takes it in a sieve and pours it into the crib.

M. 20:4 They take [fodder] from before one beast and put it before another beast on the Sabbath.

M. 20:5 The straw which is on the bed — One should not shift it with his hand. But he shifts it with his body. And if it was food for a beast, or if there was a cushion or a sheet on it, he may shift it with his hand. A press used by householders do they loosen but do they not tighten. And one of laundrymen one should not touch [at all].

T. 16:5 Straw on which one slept on the eve of the Sabbath one moves about with his hand on the Sabbath. [If] he did not sleep on it on the eve of the Sabbath he should not move it about with his hand on the Sabbath [cf. M. Shab. 20:5A B]. A press of householders which one has loosened to remove clothing from it — one may handle the beam and the sideboards and put them back into a box, for they are utensils [cf. M. Shab. 20:5E F].

M. 21:1 A man takes up his child, with a stone in [the child's] hand, or a basket with a stone in it. And they handle unclean heave-offering along with clean heave-offering or with unconsecrated food.

T. 16:6 A utensil which contains things which may be handled and things which may not be handled — one handles it [the prohibited object] and removes it from it and puts it back in its place [cf. M. Shab. 21:1A C].

M. 21:2 A stone which is over the mouth of a jar — One tilts [the jar] on its side and [the stone] falls off. [If] it [the jar] was among [other] jars, one lifts it [the jar] up and [then] turns it on its side, so that it [the stone] falls off. Coins which are on a pillow — One shakes the pillow, and they fall off. [If] there was snot on it, one wipes it off with a rag. [If] it was made of leather, they pour water on it until it [the snot] disappears.

T. 16:8 They wipe [something] off with the tail of a horse, a cow, or a fox with a napkin [used for picking] thorns and with a hair of a kidney bean — on condition that one not wipe off [the object] with his hand and with a cloth, as they do on ordinary days [cf. M. Shab. 21:2F-G].

T. 16:9 Pieces of fruit which were scattered one gathers up one by one and eats. If one sort of fruit was mixed up with another, one chooses and eats, chooses and leaves them on the table, chooses and throws what he wants before his cattle. [If] he selected these by themselves and those by themselves, or [if] he removed dirt and pebbles from them, lo, this one is liable [by reason of selecting].

T. 16:10 An unripe fig which one stored in straw, and so too a cake which one stored under coals — if part of it is in the open, one may take it. But if not, one may not take it.

M. 21:3 They remove from the table crumbs less than an olive's bulk in size, pods of chick-peas, and pods of lentils, because it is food for a beast. A sponge, if it has a handle — they wipe with it. And if not, they do not wipe with it.

M. 22:1 A jar which broke [on the Sabbath] — they save from it[s wine] enough sustenance for three meals. And one says to others, "Come along and save some for yourself" on condition that one not sponge it up. They do not squeeze pieces of fruit to get out the juice. And if the juice came out on its own, it is prohibited [for use on the Sabbath]. Honeycombs which one broke on the eve of the Sabbath and [their liquids] exuded on their own — they are prohibited.

M. 22:2 Whatever is put into hot water on the eve of the Sabbath — they soak it [again] in hot water on the Sabbath. And whatever is not put into hot water on the eve of the Sabbath — they [only] rinse it in hot water on the Sabbath, except for pickled fish, small salted fish, and Spanish tunny fish, for rinsing them is the completion of their preparation [for eating].

M. 22:3 A person breaks a jar to eat dried figs from it, on condition that he not intend [in opening the jar] to make it into a utensil. And they do not pierce it on the side. And if it was pierced, one should not put wax on it, because he would [have to] spread it over [which is a prohibited act].

M. 22:4 They put a cooked dish in a cistern so that it may be preserved, and [a vessel containing] fresh water into foul water to keep it cool, and cold water into the sun to warm it up. He whose clothing fell into water on the way goes along in them and does not scruple. [When] he reaches the outer courtyard, he spreads them out in the sun. But [this he does not do] in front of people.

M. 22:5 He who bathes in cave water or in the water of Tiberias and dried himself, even with ten towels, may not then carry them in his hand. But ten men dry their faces,

hands, and feet with a single towel and bring it along in their hand.

T. 16:12 Utensils which were made unclean by a primary source of uncleanness — they do not immerse them on the festival, and it is not necessary to say, on the Sabbath. But one fills a cup, a ladle, or a flagon to drink and gives thought to [the water in the cup, that it is intended for drinking] and then he immerses it. One immerses in the normal manner in order to be purified from uncleanness deriving from a major source of uncleanness, and it is not necessary to say, from one deriving from a minor source of uncleanness.

T. 16:13 A person tears the hide which is on a jar of wine or muries on condition that he not have the intention of making it into a spout. They do not crack open closed stew-pots.

T. 16:14 They do not put oil on utensils to beautify them But if it is to make use of them or to preserve [something] in them, it is permitted. A person should not put oil on a table of marble to anoint himself on it, because they do not anoint, blow upon, or rinse the ground on the festival, and it is not necessary to say, on the Sabbath.

T. 16:17 A person brings a good quantity of oil in many towels to the bath [M. Shab. 22:5], and he anoints himself limb by limb, and dries his whole body, limb by limb, and need not scruple.

M. 22:6 They anoint and massage the stomach. But they do not have it kneaded or scraped. They do not go down to a muddy wrestling ground. And they do not induce vomiting. And they do not straighten [the limb of] a child or set a broken limb. He whose hand or foot was dislocated should not pour cold water over them. But he washes in the usual way. And if he is healed, he is healed.

T. 16:23 A beast who ate produce, even all day long, they walk it in the courtyard so that it not die.

T. 16:24 They do not examine blemishes [in sacrificial animals] on the festival, and it is not necessary to say, on the Sabbath. But if it is for that very day [that the sacrificial animal is needed], then they do examine blemishes on the Sabbath, and it is not necessary to say, on a festival.

E.   SEEMLY AND UNSEEMLY BEHAVIOR ON THE SABBATH

M. 23:1 A man [on the Sabbath] asks for jugs of wine or oil from his fellow, provided that he does not say to him, "Lend [them] to me." And so a woman [borrows] loaves of bread

from her neighbor. And if one does not trust the other, he leaves his cloak with him and settles with him after the Sabbath. And so is the case on the eve of Passover in Jerusalem when that day coincides with the Sabbath: One leaves his cloak with him and takes his Passover lamb and settles with him after the festival.

T. 17:1 A. An inscription which runs under pictures or busts [of rulers] — they do not look at it [on the Sabbath]. Not only so, but also on an ordinary day they do not look at busts.

M. 23:2 A man may count the number of his guests and the finger food portions orally, but not by what is written down. And he casts lots with his children and the members of his household at the table [to decide who gets which portion], on condition that he not intend to offset a larger portion, against a small one, because of [the prohibition of playing with] dice [on the Sabbath]. And they cast lots on a festival day for [which priest gets which part of] Holy Things, but not for the portions.

T. 17:5 A man may reckon his expenses — how much he paid out at home, how much he paid his workers, how much he paid for his guests from the wall [on which he wrote] past expenses, but not from the wall on which he writes future expenses [M. Shab. 23:2A].

T. 17:6 A man may count his guests, how many are outside and how many are inside, and how many portions he must prepare for them, from writing which is on the wall, but not from a tray and not from a notebook as he would do on an ordinary day.

T. 17:7 A man may take out part of what he has in his house and set it before guests, for instance nuts, dates, and parched corn.

T. 17:9 Any account which one requires, whether concerning matters in the past or concerning matters in the future, they do not reckon on the Sabbath. Accounts which are of no purpose do they reckon on the Sabbath.

M. 23:3 A man should not hire workers on the Sabbath. And a man should not ask his fellow to hire workers for him. They do not wait at twilight at the Sabbath limit to hire workers, or to bring in produce. But one may wait at the Sabbath limit at twilight to guard [produce, and after nightfall] he brings back the produce in his hand. A governing principle did Abba Saul state, "Whatever I have the right to say [to another person to do], on that account I have the right to wait at twilight at the Sabbath limit."

T. 17:10 A person should not walk along the border of the entire district so that it will grow dark and he may go in and take a bath, or along the Sabbath limit, so that it will get dark and he may get produce [M. Shab. 23:3D]. But he may wait at the Sabbath limit at twilight to guard [produce] and /after nightfall/ he brings back the produce in his hands [M. Shab. 23:3E], and he need not scruple.

T. 17:11 A man may not say to his fellow, "Well, we shall see whether you will join me [to work for me] in the evening."

T. 7:12-13 They do not go to the Sabbath limit to wait nightfall to bring in a beast. But if the beast was standing outside the Sabbath limit, one calls it and it comes on its own. "Whatever I have the right to say [to another person to do], on that account I have the right to wait at twilight at the Sabbath limit." And they wait at the Sabbath limit to supervise the affairs of a bride or those of a corpse, to bring him a bier and shrouds. And they say to a person, "Go to such and such a place, and if you can't get them there, bring them from somewhere else; if you can't get them for a maneh, get them for two."

M. 23:4 They wait at the Sabbath limit at twilight to attend to the business of a bride, and the affairs of a corpse, to bring it a coffin and wrappings. A gentile who brought wailing pipes on the Sabbath — an Israelite should not make a lament with them, unless they came from a nearby place, [If] they made for him [a gentile] a coffin and dug a grave for him, an Israelite may be buried therein. But if this was done for an Israelite, he may not ever be buried therein.

T. 17:14 A gentile who brought wailing pipes on the Sabbath for a particular Israelite — one should not make a lament with them for that particular Israelite [M. Shab. 23:4C], but it is permitted to do so for some other Israelite.

T. 17:15. If they made for him a coffin and dug a grave for him [an Israelite], that particular Israelite is not to be buried therein, but another Israelite is permitted [to be buried therein] [M. Shab. 23:4F].

T. 17:16 Pieces of fruit which went forth outside of the Sabbath limit and came back, [if this happened] inadvertently, may be eaten. [If this happened] deliberately, they may not be eaten.

M. 23:5 They prepare all that is needed for a corpse. They anoint and rinse it, on condition that they not move any limb of the corpse. They remove the mattress from under it.

And they put it on [cool] sand so that it will keep. They tie the chin, not so that it will go up, but so that it will not droop [further]. And so in the case of a beam which broke — they support it with a bench or the beams of a bed, not so that it will go up, but so that it will not droop further. They do not close the eyes of a corpse on the Sabbath, nor on an ordinary day at the moment the soul goes forth. And he who closes the eyes of a corpse at the moment the soul goes forth, lo, this one sheds blood.

M. 24:1 He who was overtaken by darkness on the road gives his purse to a gentile. If there is no gentile with him, he leaves it on an ass. [When] he reaches the outermost courtyard [of a town], he removes [from the ass] those utensils which may be handled on the Sabbath. And [as to] those [utensils] which are not to be handled on the Sabbath, he unloosens the ropes, and the bundles fall by themselves.

M. 24:2 They loosen bundles of hay in front of cattle, and they spread out bunches, but not small bundles. And they do not chop up unripe stalks of corn or carobs before cattle, whether large or small [beasts].

M. 24:3 They do not stuff food into a camel or cram it [into its mouth]. But they put food into its mouth. And they do not fatten calves [with food against their will], but they put food into their mouths [in the normal way]. And they force-feed chickens, They put water into the bran, but they do not knead it, And they do not put water before bees or doves which are in dovecotes. But they do put it before geese, chickens, and Herodian doves.

T. 17:21 What is "stuffing" [fattening calves against their will] [M. Shab. 24:3C]? So long as one forces it down and opens the mouth wide and puts water and vetches in simultaneously.

T. 17:22 What is "putting" [food into the mouth of a camel] [M. Shab. 24:3B]? So long as one feeds it standing and gives it water standing and puts vetches out separately and water separately [into its mouth].

T. 17:23 They strew food before ducks, chickens, and Herodian pigeons and put water before them [M. Shab. 24:3D, G]. And it is not necessary to say that they fatten them. They do not fatten doves of the dovecot and those of the upper room and birds whose nests are in pitcher shaped niches in the wall or in the loft. They do not put water before them [M. Shab. 24:3F]. And it is not necessary to say that they do not force feed them [cf. M. Shab. 24:3D].

M. 24:4 They cut up gourds before cattle, and carrion meat before dogs.

M. 24:5 They abrogate vows on the Sabbath. And they receive questions concerning matters which are required for the Sabbath. They stop up a light hole. And they measure a piece of stuff and an immersion pool.

T. 17:24 Vows made on the Sabbath they abrogate on the Sabbath [in the case of a husband with a wife's vows, or a father and a minor daughter's vows]. On what account did they rule, Vows made on the Sabbath do they abrogate on the Sabbath? Because after dark [at the end of the Sabbath] he no longer has the power to abrogate them [cf. M. Shab. 24:5A].

T. 17:25 He who guards seeds against birds and guards against wild beasts guards them in the normal way on the Sabbath, on condition that he not clap his hands on his hips, stamp his feet, or clap his hands as he does on an ordinary day.

T. 17:26 He who hires a worker to watch his cow or to watch his child should not give him his wage for the Sabbath [labor at all]. Therefore he [the guard] is not responsible to him on the Sabbath [should harm befall].

T. 17:27 If he was hired by the week, by the month, or by the year, or by the septennate, he pays him his salary for the Sabbath [as well]. Therefore he [the guard] is responsible to him on the Sabbath.

T. 17:28 He should not say to him, "Pay me my salary for the Sabbath." But he says to him, "Pay me for ten days."

T. 17:29 They do not climb a tree or ride on a domestic beast or swim in water — and they do not clap hands on thighs or clap hands together or dance — in private property, and it is not necessary to say, in public property.

II. ANALYSIS: THE PROBLEMATICS OF THE TOPIC, SHABBAT

In the setting of its topic, the Sabbath, the halakhah of Shabbat as set forth in the Mishnah and uniquely there articulates in acute detail only a few generative conceptions. But these encompass the whole of the halakhah. The result of the applied reason and practical logic, most, though not all, of the concrete rulings we have surveyed embody those few conceptions. But because of the promiscuous character of the illustrative compositions, the halakhah in its formulation in the Mishnah and the Tosefta appears prolix, when in fact it is intellectually quite economical. As a matter of fact, I shall now show, the presentation of the halakhah serves the dual purpose of setting forth governing conceptions through exemplary cases, on the one side, and supplying information required for the correct observance of the Sabbath, on the other. It is only to the latter project that the Tosefta contributes.

But the former task — instantiating, through exemplary cases, the generative conceptions of a broad and fundamental character — vastly predominates. In my item-by-item survey and classification of the halakhah of Shabbat, with the focus on the Mishnah, I find only the following that fall entirely outside of the few principles that govern throughout: M. 2:1, 3:1, 3:2, 4:1, 20:1-4, 23:1-2 — a negligible proportion of the whole. But my list of cases in which the laws encapsulate in cases all of six governing principles covers nearly the entire Mishnah-tractate, and, it follows, nearly the whole of the halakhah (since the Tosefta mainly amplifies and refines the principles initially stated by the Mishnah, and the Talmuds contribute little halakhah to begin with). The generative problematics of the topic turns out to impart coherence to the presentation of the halakhah of Shabbat. The interesting questions, to which we shall progress, are two. The first is the extent to which the problematics derives from the topic, and the degree to which the problematics in no way is particular to that topic. The second is the character of the halakhic problematics particular to the topic, Shabbat, and the messages concerning Shabbat conveyed in concrete patterns of conduct set forth in the halakhah.

In due course we shall see that the larger part of the halakhah, and much of the expository shank of the tractate of the law we have reviewed, serve to set forth a single, encompassing conception, one that in its way recalls the governing conceptions embodied in the halakhah of Shebi'it, 'Orlah, and (in its odd way) even Kilayim. Israel at home, in its households ("tents"), recapitulates and realizes creation once again. But in so stating, I have gotten far ahead of the story; the interpretive exercise takes up the results of defining the problematics of the halakhah of both Shabbat and Erubin. At this point in the exposition it suffices to state that nearly the whole of the halakhah of Mishnah-tractate Shabbat therefore addresses issues that transcend the cases at hand. For the topic at hand, the halakhah of Shabbat (not merely of Mishnah-tractate Shabbat) serves as a medium for the concretization in normative action of certain large and encompassing conceptions. These emerge when we survey the details of the law, specifying the passages of the Mishnah (and others where important) that through concrete cases work out the requirements of abstract principles that inhere. There are, by my way of seeing things, only six in all, and we find a place among those six generative principles for nearly the whole of the halakhah before us. In my catalogue I specify at the right-hand margin the Mishnah-compositions that recapitulate the problematics under discussion, so readers can test the validity of that claim.

The conceptions are of two types, the one distinctive to the Sabbath, the other pertinent to a broad spectrum of halakhic categories but here illustrated by cases involving the Sabbath. We begin with the more general. The latter type supplies the larger number of generative conceptions, concerning, first, intentionality, second, causality (cause and effect), and, third, how many things are one and one many. These constitute philosophical, not theological problems.

Let us consider the recurrent concerns that transcend the Sabbath altogether, starting with intentionality:

1. INTENTIONALITY: THE CLASSIFICATION OF AN ACTION IS GOVERNED BY THE INTENTION BY WHICH IT IS CARRIED OUT, SO TOO THE CONSEQUENCE:

A. One is not supposed to extinguish a flame, but if he does so for valid reasons, it is not a culpable action; if it is for selfish reasons, it is. If one deliberately violated the Sabbath, after the Sabbath one may not benefit from the action; if it was inadvertent, he may. We consider also the intentionality of gentiles. One may not benefit indirectly from a source of heat. But what happens *en passant,* and not by deliberation, is not subject to prohibition. Thus if a gentile lit a candle for his own purposes, the Israelite may benefit, but if he did so for an Israelite, the Israelite may not benefit.

B. If one did a variety of actions of a single classification in a single spell of inadvertence, he is liable on only one count.

C. In the case of anything that is not regarded as suitable for storage, the like of which in general people do not store away, but which a given individual has deemed fit for storage and has stored away, and which another party has come along and removed from storage and taken from one domain to another on the Sabbath — the party who moved the object across the line that separated the two domains has become liable by reason of the intentionality of the party who stored away this thing that is not ordinarily stored.

D. The act must be carried out in accord with the intent for culpability to be incurred. The wrong intention invalidates an act, the right one validates the same act. Thus a person breaks a jar to eat dried figs from it, on condition that he not intend [in opening the jar] to make it into a utensil.

M. 2:5, T. 2:16, T. 2:14, T. 2:17-18, 21, M. 7:1-2, 10:4, 22:3-4

The principle that we take account of what one plans, not only what one does, and that the intentionality of an actor governs, yields at least four quite distinct results, none of them interchangeable with the others, but all of them subject to articulation in other contexts altogether, besides Shabbat.

To begin with, we deal with a familiar principle. Intentionality possesses taxonomic power. The status of an action — culpable or otherwise — is relative to the intent with which the action is carried out. That encompasses a gentile's action; he may not act in response to the will of an Israelite. But if he acts on his own account, then an Israelite *en passant* may benefit from what he has done. The law of Kilayim, Shebi'it, and and the shank of the Babas, goes over the same ground.

If the intention is improper, the action is culpable, if proper, it is not. But so far as inadvertence is the opposite of intentionality, second, the result of the failure to will or plan is as consequential as the act of will. If one acts many times in a single spell of inadvertence, the acts are counted as one. This too is an entirely familiar notion.

The third entry is the most profound, and it carries us nearest to the particularities of the halakhah of Shabbat. To understand it, we have to know that the halakhah in general takes account of what matters to people but treats as null what does not. Hence a sum of money or a volume of material deemed negligible is treated as though it did not exist.[1] If one deliberately transports a volume of material of such insufficient consequence that no one would store that volume of that material, no violation of the law against transporting objects has taken place. Transporting objects from one domain to the other matters only when what is transported is valued. What, then, about a volume of material that people in general deem null, but that a given individual regards as worth something? For example, people in general do not save a useless sherd or remnant of fabric. But in a given case, an individual has so acted as to indicate he takes account of the sherd. By his action he has imparted value to the sherd, even though others would not concur. If then he has saved the negligible object, he has indicated that the sherd matters. If someone else takes the sherd out of storage and carries it from one domain to another, what is the result? Do we deem the one person's evaluation binding upon everyone else? Indeed we do, and the second party who does so is liable. The reason that ruling is not particular to the Sabbath becomes clear in the exegesis of the law, which carries us to a variety of other halakhic topics altogether, e.g., what is susceptible to uncleanness must be deemed useful, and what is held of no account is insusceptible, and what a given person deems useful is taken into account, and the rest follows.

The fourth matter involving intentionality is a commonplace of the halakhah and recapitulates the principle of the first. If someone acts in such a

---

[1] So too a sherd that can serve some useful purpose is taken into account; it is subject to uncleanness; one that can serve no useful purpose is treated as null, useless and hence not subject to uncleanness. How we assess usefulness is subject to much interesting reflection in other chapters of the halakhah, which need not detain us here. My point is only that the considerations operative here encompass vast areas of halakhah, which, in practical detail, scarcely intersect.

way as to violate the law but the act does not carry out his intent, he is not culpable; if he acts in accord with his intent and the intent is improper, he is culpable. So the match of intention and action serves to impose culpability.

In these ways, the particular law of Shabbat embodies general principles of intentionality that pertain to many other halakhic rubrics. While these four exercises in the practical application of the theory of intentionality encompass the halakhah of the Sabbath, none required the topic at hand in particular to make the point it wished to make; the applied reason and practical logic of intentionality yield only measured insight into the problematics of Shabbat.

The matter of causality produces a number of cases that make the same point, which is, we take account of indirect consequences, not only direct causality. But the consequences that we impute to indirect causality remain to be specified.

2. NOT ONLY DIRECT, BUT INDIRECT CONSEQUENCES ARE TAKEN INTO ACCOUNT.

A.   Since one may not perform an act of healing on the Sabbath, one may not consume substances that serve solely as medicine. But one may consume those that are eaten as food but also heal. One may lift a child, even though the child is holding something that one is not permitted to handle or move about; one may handle food that one may not eat (e.g., unclean) along with food that one may eat. One may not ask gentiles to do what he may not do, but one may wait at the Sabbath limit at twilight to do what one may ask another person to do. Thus: they do not go to the Sabbath limit to wait nightfall to bring in a beast. But if the beast was standing outside the Sabbath limit, one calls it and it comes on its own.

M. 3:3, 4, 5, M. 4:2, M. 14:3-4, 16:7-8, 21:1-3, 23:3-4, 24:1-4

Once we distinguish indirect from direct causality, we want to know the degree to which, if at all, we hold a person responsible for what he has not directly caused; what level of culpability, if any, pertains? The point is that what comes about on its own, and not by the direct action of the Israelite adult, is deemed null. If one is permitted to eat certain foods, then those foods may be eaten on the Sabbath even though they possess, in addition to nourishment, healing powers. Indirect consequences of the action are null. One may carry a child, even though the child is holding something one may not carry. We impose a limit on the effects of causation, taking account of direct, but not indirect, results of one's action. One may make the case that the present principle places limits upon the one that assigns intentionality taxonomic power; here, even though one may will the result, if one has not directly brought about the result, he is still exempt from liability. In no way is this law particular to the Sabbath.

The third generative conception that in no way limits itself to Sabbath law involves assessing the manner in which we classify actions and the definition thereof. It invokes the rules of classification, e.g., when does an action encompass many episodes, and when does a single deed stand on its own? Sages conceive that a single spell of inadvertence, covering numerous episodes or transactions, constitutes one unitary action, the episodes being joined by the inadvertence of the actor, the actions then being treated as indivisible by reason of a single overarching intentionality, as we have already noted. They further conceive that numerous actions of a single type entail a single count of guilt, the repeated actions of the same classification constituting one protracted deed. On the other hand, by reason of consciousness, the performance of many actions entails guilt on each count, for each action on its own carries out the actor's intentionality. The larger problem of the many and the one forms the generative problematic of entire tractates, e.g., tractate Keritot, and enormous, interesting compositions of halakhah are devoted to the way in which many things fall into a single classification, or a single category yields many subdivisions, e.g., tractate Peah (for land). In the present halakhic rubric, the generative conception generates an elegant composition, but not a rich body of exegesis.

> 3. IN ASSESSING CULPABILITY FOR VIOLATING THE HALAKHAH OF THE
> SABBATH, WE RECKON THAT AN ACTION NOT ONLY MAY BE SUBDIVIDED
> BUT IT ALSO MAY BE JOINED WITH ANOTHER ACTION, SO THAT MULTIPLE
> ACTIONS YIELD A SINGLE COUNT OF CULPABILITY.
>
> A. Thus whoever forgets the basic principle of the Sabbath and performs many acts of labor on many different Sabbath days is liable only for a single sin-offering. He who knows the principle of the Sabbath and performs many acts of labor on many different Sabbaths is liable for the violation of each and every Sabbath.
>
> B. He who knows that it is the Sabbath and performs many acts of labor on many different Sabbaths is liable for the violation of each and every generative category of labor. He who performs many acts of labor of a single type is liable only for a single sin-offering.
>
> M. 7:1-2, 22:5

Clearly, the principle that an act on its own is classified, as to culpability, by the considerations of intentionality, on the one side, and the classification of actions, on the other, cannot limit itself to the matter of the Sabbath. And we shall meet it many times in other areas of law altogether, e.g., oaths, acts of the contamination of the Temple (one or many spells of inadvertence, one or many types of action), and so on without limit.

A program of questions of general applicability to a variety of topics of the halakhah clearly shaped the problematics of Shabbat. Intentionality, causality, and classification of the many as one and the one as many — these standard themes of philosophical inquiry turn out to shape the presentation of the halakhah at hand, and, as my references indicate, the exegetical problems deemed to inhere in the topic at hand transform much of the halakhah into an exercise in analytical thinking carried out in concrete terms — applied reason and practical logic of a philosophical character. If we were composing a handbook of halakhic exegesis for a commentator intent on covering the entire surface of the halakhah, the issue of the many and the one would take its place, alongside the issues of causality, direct and indirect, and the taxonomic power of intentionality. But the specificities of the halakhah of Shabbat in no way provided more than the occasion for a routine reprise of these familiar foci of exegesis.

For the religious principles that animate the halakhah and its exposition and exegesis, we shall have to look elsewhere. If we had to stop at this point and generalize upon our results, we should conclude that the halakhah on the Sabbath serves as a mere vehicle for the transmission of philosophical principles of general applicability. Cases of applied reason and practical logic sustain concrete illustration of abstractions, occasions for solution, in detail, of the working of axiomatic givens, governing postulates in the solution of problems of theory set forth in matters of fact. No problematics distinctive to the topic at hand precipitates deep thought that surfaces, in due course, in the formulation of specific problems and cases. Were we to close the matter where we now stand, then, the halakhah of Shabbat would appear to have no bearing upon the theme of the Sabbath, and that theme would appear to be interchangeable with any other for the purposes of the exegesis of abstract principles. Then, if we distinguish the philosophical, deriving from principles of general applicability based on analysis of everyday things, from the theological, deriving from distinctive conceptions based on divinely revealed conceptions, we should consequently assign the halakhah a philosophical, but not a theological, task.

Such a result even merely on the face of things would prove dubious. For we should be left with a body of law disconnected from the religious life that accords to that law origins in revelation and authority in God's will. The halakhah would emerge as the concretization of philosophical reflections bear no consequence for the knowledge of God and what God has in mind for holy Israel. A mere medium of concretization of abstract thought, the halakhah would contain within itself no deep thought upon theological principles, thought deriving from the revealed Torah. But as we shall now see, alongside systematic thinking about philosophical problems subject to generalization throughout the law, the Oral Torah's halakhah of Shabbat states in practical terms a set of conceptions deriving from a close reading of the Written Torah's account of the Sabbath.

These conceptions, framed in the same manner of concretization — practical logic and applied reason — embody deep thought about issues particular to the Sabbath. They yield conclusions that form the foundations of a massive theological structure, one built out of what is conveyed by revelation and implicit in the Torah's account of matters. These conclusions, of a broad and general character, can have emerged only from the topic at hand. And the statement that sages wished to set forth can have come to systematic expression only in the particular setting defined by that topic — and the halakhah required for the concretization of the message deemed to inhere in that topic. I cannot overstate matters. The Sabbath, and only the Sabbath, could produce a suitable statement of the conclusions sages set before us. And once in hand, the same conclusions turn out to delineate a vast world of cogent construction: the rules of creation as God intended it to be, translated into conduct in the here and now. When people study the details of the halakhah, they encounter the concretization of governing conceptions revealed in the Torah in connection with the topic at hand and in no other conception. When people carry out the halakhah of Shabbat, meaning, refrain from the actions deemed improper on that holy day, they realize by what they do not do a conception of such grandeur and profundity as to make of holy Israel God's Sabbath-surrogate in the here and now: people who act like God on the Sabbath. To state the upshot in a simple way: in keeping the halakhah of Shabbat, Israel acts out the logic of creation, and this they do by what they do not do.

Let me specify what I conceive to be the encompassing principles, the generative conceptions that the laws embody and that animate the law in its most sustained and ambitious statements. They concern three matters, [1] space, [2] time, and [3] activity, as the advent of the Sabbath affects all three.

The advent of the Sabbath transforms creation, specifically reorganizing space and time and reordering the range of permissible activity. First comes the transformation of space that takes effect at sundown at the end of the sixth day and that ends at sundown of the Sabbath day. At that time, for holy Israel, the entire world is divided into public domain and private domain, and what is located in the one may not be transported into the other. What is located in public domain may be transported only four cubits, that is, within the space occupied by a person's body. What is in private domain may be transported within the entire demarcated space of that domain. All public domain is deemed a single spatial entity, so too all private domain, so one may transport objects from one private domain to another. The net effect of the transformation of space is to move nearly all permitted activity to private domain and to close off public domain for all but the most severely limited activities; people may not transport objects from one domain to the other, but they may transport objects within private domain, so the closure of public domain from most activity, and nearly all material or physical activity, comes in consequence of the division of space effected by sunset at the end of the sixth day of the week.

1. SPACE: ON THE SABBATH THE HOUSEHOLD AND VILLAGE DIVIDE INTO PRIVATE AND PUBLIC DOMAIN, AND IT IS FORBIDDEN TO TRANSPORT OBJECTS FROM THE ONE DOMAIN TO THE OTHER:

A.   Private domain is defined as at the very least an area ten handbreadths deep or high by four wide, public domain, an unimpeded space open to the public. There one may carry an object for no more than four cubits, which sages maintain is the dimension of man.

B.   The sea, plain, *karmelit* [neutral domain], colonnade, and a threshold are neither private domain nor public domain. They do not carry or put [things] in such places. But if one carried or put [something into such a place], he is exempt [from punishment].

C.   If in public domain one is liable for carrying an object four cubits, in private domain, there is no limit other than the outer boundaries of the demarcated area of the private domain, e.g., within the walls of the household.

D.   What is worn for clothing or ornament does not violate the prohibition against carrying things from private to public domain. If one transports an object from private domain to private domain without bringing the object into public domain, e.g., by tossing it from private to private domain, he is not culpable.

M. 1:1, M. 6:1-9, 11:1-6

The point of the division into private and public domain emerges in the exposition of the distinction; it concerns transporting objects. One may cross the line, but not carry anything in so doing — hence the concern for what may or may not be worn as clothing. The same point emerges in the rule that one may move an object from one private domain to another, so long as public domain does not intervene. Carrying within public domain forms an equally important consideration; one may do so only within the space occupied by his very body, his person. But the four cubits a person occupies in public domain may be said to transform that particular segment of public domain into private domain, so the effect is the same. The delineation of areas that are not definitively public domain but also not private domain — the sea and the plain, which are not readily differentiated, the space within a colonnade, a threshold — simply refines and underscores the generative distinction of the two distinct domains.

So when it comes to space, the advent of the Sabbath divides into distinct domains for all practical purposes what in secular time is deemed divided only as to ownership, but united as to utilization. Sacred time then intensifies the arrangements of space as public and private, imparting enormous consequence to the status of what is private. There, and only there, on the Sabbath, is life to be lived. The Sabbath assigns to private domain the focus of life in holy time: the household is where things take place then. When, presently, we realize that the household (private domain) is deemed analogous to the Temple or tabernacle

(God's household), forming a mirror image to the tabernacle, we shall understand the full meaning of the generative principle before us concerning space on the Sabbath.

Second comes the matter of time and how the advent of sacred time registers. Since the consequence of the demarcation on the Sabbath of all space into private and public domain effects, in particular, transporting objects from one space to the other, how time is differentiated will present no surprise. The effects concern private domain, the household. Specifically, what turns out to frame the halakhic issue is what objects may be handled or used, even in private domain, on the Sabbath.[2] The advent of the Sabbath thus affects the organization of space and the utilization of tools and other objects, the furniture of the household within the designated territory of the household. The basic principle is simple. Objects may be handled only if they are designated in advance of the Sabbath for the purpose for which they will be utilized on the Sabbath. But if tools may be used for a purpose that is licit on the Sabbath, and if those tools are ordinarily used for that same purpose, they are deemed ready at hand and do not require reclassification; the accepted classification applies. What requires designation for Sabbath use in particular is any tool that may serve more than a single purpose, or that does not ordinarily serve the purpose for which it is wanted on the Sabbath. Designation for use on the Sabbath thus regularizes the irregular, but is not required for what is ordinarily used for the purpose for which it is wanted and is licitly utilized on the Sabbath.

2. TIME: WHAT IS TO BE USED ON THE SABBATH MUST BE SO DESIGNATED IN ADVANCE.

A.   For example, on the Sabbath people do not put a utensil under a lamp to catch the oil. But if one put it there while it is still day, it is permitted. But they do not use any of that oil on the Sabbath, since it is not something which was prepared [before the Sabbath for use on the Sabbath.

B.   What one uses on the Sabbath must be designated in advance for that purpose, either in a routine way (what is ordinarily used on the Sabbath, e.g., for food preparation, does not have to be designated especially for that purpose) or in an exceptional manner. But within that proviso, all utensils may be handled on the Sabbath, for a permitted purpose. If something is not ordinarily used as food but one designated it for that

---

[2] That explains, also, the logic of taking up the matter of space before the issue of time, and, as we shall see, a single logic also accounts for situating third in sequence the matter of activity: where, what, and how.

purpose, e.g., for cattle, it may be handled on the Sabbath.

M. 3:6, 17:1-8, 18:2, 20:5, 22:2

The advent of sacred time calls into question the accessibility and use of the objects and tools of the world, but with a very particular purpose in mind. That purpose emerges when we note that if an object is ordinarily used for a purpose that is licit on the Sabbath, e.g., for eating, it need not be designated for that purpose for use on the Sabbath. Since on the Sabbath it is used for its ordinary, and licit, purpose, that suffices. So the advent of the Sabbath requires that things licit for use on the Sabbath be used in the manner that is standard. If one wishes to use those things for a given purpose that is licit on the Sabbath, but that those objects do not ordinarily serve, then in advance of the Sabbath one must designate those objects for that purpose, that is, regularize them. That rule covers whole, useful tools, but not broken ones or tools that will not serve their primary purpose.

The Sabbath then finds all useful tools and objects in their proper place; that may mean, they may not be handled at all, since their ordinary function cannot be performed on the Sabbath; or it may mean, they may be handled on the Sabbath exactly as they are handled every other day, the function being licit on the Sabbath; or it may mean, they must be designated in advance of the Sabbath for licit utilization on the Sabbath. That third proviso covers utensils that serve more than a single function, or that do not ordinarily serve the function of licit utilization on the Sabbath that the householder wishes them to serve on this occasion. The advent of the Sabbath then requires that all tools and other things be regularized and ordered. The rule extends even to utilization of space, within the household, that is not ordinarily used for a (licit) purpose for which, on the Sabbath, it is needed. If guests come, storage-space used for food may be cleared away to accommodate them, the space being conceived as suitable for sitting even when not ordinarily used for that purpose. But one may not clear out a store room for that purpose. One may also make a path in a store room so that one may move about there. One may handle objects that, in some way or another, can serve a licit purpose, in the theory that that purpose inheres. But what is not made ready for use may not be used on the Sabbath. So the advent of the Sabbath not only divides space into public and private, but also differentiates useful tools and objects into those that may or may not be handled within the household.

We come to the third generative problematics that is particular to the Sabbath. The affect upon activity that the advent of the Sabbath makes concerns constructive labor. I may state the generative problematics in a simple declarative sentence: *In a normal way one may not carry out entirely on his own a completed act of constructive labor, which is to say, work that produces enduring results.* That is what one is supposed to do in profane time. What is implicit in that simple statement proves profound and bears far-reaching implications. No prohibition impedes performing an act of labor in an other-than-normal way, e.g., in a way that is unusual and thus takes account of the differentiation of time. Labor in a natural, not in an unnatural, manner is prohibited. But that is not all. A person is not forbidden to carry out an act of destruction, or an act of labor that produces no lasting consequences. Nor is part of an act of labor, not brought to conclusion, prohibited. Nor is it forbidden to perform part of an act of labor in partnership with another person who carries out the other requisite part. Nor does one incur culpability for performing an act of labor in several distinct parts, e.g., over a protracted, differentiated period of time. The advent of the Sabbath prohibits activities carried out in ordinary time in a way deemed natural: acts that are complete, consequential, and in accord with their accepted character.

3. ACTIVITY: ON THE SABBATH ONE IS LIABLE FOR THE INTENTIONAL COMMISSION OF A COMPLETED ACT OF CONSTRUCTIVE LABOR, E.G., TRANSPORTING AN OBJECT FROM ONE DOMAIN TO THE OTHER, IF ONE HAS PERFORMED, IN THE NORMAL MANNER, THE ENTIRE ACTION BEGINNING TO END.

A.   If one has performed only part of an action, the matter being completed by another party, he is exempt. If one has performed an entire action but done so in an-other-than-ordinary manner, he is exempt. If one transports an object only to the threshold and puts it down there, he is exempt, even though, later on, he picks it up and completes the transportation outward to public domain.

B.   He one performed a forbidden action but did not intend to do so, he is exempt. If one performed a forbidden action but in doing so did not accomplish his goal, he is exempt: If one transported an object or brought an object in — if he did so inadvertently, he is liable for a sin offering. If he did so deliberately, he is subject to the punishment of extirpation.

C.   All the same are the one who takes out and the one who brings in, the one who stretches something out and the one who throws [something] in — in all such cases he is liable. By observing Sabbath prohibitions prior to sunset, one takes precautions to avoid inadvertent error.

D.   One is liable for constructive, but not destructive acts of labor, and for acts of labor that produce a lasting consequence but not ephemeral ones.

E.   One is liable for performing on the Sabbath classifications of labor the like of which was done in

the tabernacle. They sowed, so you are not to sow.
They harvested, so you are not to harvest. They lifted
up the boards from the ground to the wagon, so you
are not to lift them in from public to private domain.
They lowered boards from the wagon to the ground,
so you must not carry anything from private to public
domain. They transported boards from wagon to
wagon, so you must not carry from one private domain
to another.

F.   But moving the object must be in the normal manner,
not in an exceptional way, if culpability is to be
incurred.

G.   An entire act of labor must involve a minimum volume,
and it must yield an enduring result. An act of
destruction is not culpable. Thus, as we recall, he
who tears [his clothing] because of his anger or on
account of his bereavement, and all those who effect
destruction, are exempt.

H.   Healing is classified as an act of constructive labor, so
it is forbidden; but saving life is invariably permitted,
as is any other action of a sacred character that cannot
be postponed, e.g., circumcision, saving sacred scrolls
from fire, saving from fire food for immediate use,
and tending to the deceased, along with certain other
urgent matters requiring a sage's ruling.

M. 1:1, 2, 3, 10-11, 2:7, 8, 7:2, M. 7:3-4,

M. :1-6, 9:5-7, 10:1, 10:2-4, 10:5-6, 12:1-5,

M. 13:2-7, 14:1-2, 15:1-3, 16:1-8, 18:3, 19:1-6,

T. 15:11ff., M. 22:1, 22:6, 23:5, 24:5

This systematic, extensive, and richly detailed account of the activity, labor, that
is forbidden on the Sabbath but required on weekdays introduces these
considerations, properly classified:

A. Preconditions

    1. intentionality: the act must carry out the intention of
the actor, and the intention must be to carry out an
illicit act of labor

    2. a single actor: culpability is incurred for an act started,
carried through, and completed by a single actor, not
by an act that is started by one party and completed by
another

    3. analogy: an act that on the Sabbath may be carried out
in the building and maintenance of the tabernacle

(Temple) may not be performed in the household, and
on that analogy the classification of forbidden acts of
labor is worked out

B. Considerations
1. routine character: the act must be done in the manner
    in which it is ordinarily done
2. constructive result: the act must build and not destroy,
    put together and not dismantle; an act of destruction
    if not culpable

C. Consequences
1. completeness: the act must be completely done, in all
    its elements and components
2. permanent result: the act must produce a lasting result,
    not an ephemeral one
3. consequence: to impart culpability, a forbidden act of
    labor must involve a matter of consequence, e.g.,
    transport of a volume of materials that people deem
    worth storing and transporting, but not a negligible
    volume

What is the upshot of this remarkable repertoire of fundamental considerations
having to do with activity, in the household, on the holy day? The halakhah of
Shabbat in the aggregate concerns itself with formulating a statement of how the
advent of the Sabbath defines the kind of activity that may be done by specifying
what may not be done. That is the meaning of repose, the cessation of activity,
not the commencement of activity of a different order. To carry out the Sabbath,
one does nothing, not something. And what is that "nothing" that one realizes
through inactivity? One may not carry out an act analogous to one that sustains
creation. An act or activity for which one bears responsibility, and one that
sustains creation, is [1] an act analogous to one required in the building and
maintenance of the tabernacle, [2] that is intentionally carried out [3] in its entirety,
[4] by a single actor, [5] in the ordinary manner, [6] with a constructive and [7]
consequential result — one worthy of consideration by accepted norms. These
are the seven conditions that pertain, and that, in one way or another, together
with counterpart considerations in connection with the transformation of space
and time, generate most of the halakhah of Shabbat.

This survey of the halakhah of Shabbat suffices to demonstrate that early
the entirety of the halakhic corpus is set forth to show in ordinary time what it
means to sanctify the Sabbath. But while we now can identify the generative
problematics of the halakhah, the religious principles of the halakhah remain to
be seen. These are what a religious commentary to the halakhah claims to state.
At this point it suffices to note a few obvious conceptions that animate the law.
Like God at the completion of creation, the halakhah of the Sabbath defines the

Sabbath to mean to do no more, but instead to do nothing. At issue in Sabbath rest is not ceasing from labor but ceasing from labor of a very particular character, labor in the model of God's work in making the world. Then why the issues of space, time, and activity? Given the division of space into public domain, where nothing much can happen, and the private domain of the household, where nearly everything dealt with in the law at hand takes place, we realize that the Sabbath forms an occasion of the household in particular. There man takes up repose, leaving off the tools required to make the world, ceasing to perform the acts that sustain the world. It is in the halakhah of the Mishnah that these matters are set forth — and to that statement of the halakhah the Tosefta contributes only points of clarification and instantiation and secondary development. So much for what Alberdina Houtman did not notice. That is because — obviously — she did not think to look.

South Florida Studies in the History of Judaism

240164	Approaches to Ancient Judaism, New Series, Volume Thirteen	Neusner
240165	Targum Studies, Volume Two: Targum and Peshitta	Flesher
240166	The Text and I: Writings of Samson H. Levey	Chyet
240167	The Documentary Form-History of Rabbinic Literature: I. The Documentary Forms of Mishnah	Neusner

South Florida Academic Commentary Series

243001	The Talmud of Babylonia, An Academic Commentary, Volume XI, Bavli Tractate Moed Qatan	Neusner
243002	The Talmud of Babylonia, An Academic Commentary, Volume XXXIV, Bavli Tractate Keritot	Neusner
243003	The Talmud of Babylonia, An Academic Commentary, Volume XVII, Bavli Tractate Sotah	Neusner
243004	The Talmud of Babylonia, An Academic Commentary, Volume XXIV, Bavli Tractate Makkot	Neusner
243005	The Talmud of Babylonia, An Academic Commentary, Volume XXXII, Bavli Tractate Arakhin	Neusner
243006	The Talmud of Babylonia, An Academic Commentary, Volume VI, Bavli Tractate Sukkah	Neusner
243007	The Talmud of Babylonia, An Academic Commentary, Volume XII, Bavli Tractate Hagigah	Neusner
243008	The Talmud of Babylonia, An Academic Commentary, Volume XXVI, Bavli Tractate Horayot	Neusner
243009	The Talmud of Babylonia, An Academic Commentary, Volume XXVII, Bavli Tractate Shebuot	Neusner
243010	The Talmud of Babylonia, An Academic Commentary, Volume XXXIII, Bavli Tractate Temurah	Neusner
243011	The Talmud of Babylonia, An Academic Commentary, Volume XXXV, Bavli Tractates Meilah and Tamid	Neusner
243012	The Talmud of Babylonia, An Academic Commentary, Volume VIII, Bavli Tractate Rosh Hashanah	Neusner
243013	The Talmud of Babylonia, An Academic Commentary, Volume V, Bavli Tractate Yoma	Neusner
243014	The Talmud of Babylonia, An Academic Commentary, Volume XXXVI, Bavli Tractate Niddah	Neusner
243015	The Talmud of Babylonia, An Academic Commentary, Volume XX, Bavli Tractate Baba Qamma	Neusner
243016	The Talmud of Babylonia, An Academic Commentary, Volume XXXI, Bavli Tractate Bekhorot	Neusner
243017	The Talmud of Babylonia, An Academic Commentary, Volume XXX, Bavli Tractate Hullin	Neusner
243018	The Talmud of Babylonia, An Academic Commentary, Volume VII, Bavli Tractate Besah	Neusner
243019	The Talmud of Babylonia, An Academic Commentary, Volume X, Bavli Tractate Megillah	Neusner
243020	The Talmud of Babylonia, An Academic Commentary, Volume XXVIII, Bavli Tractate Zebahim A. Chapters I through VII	Neusner

South Florida International Studies in Formative Christianity and Judaism

South Florida-Rochester-Saint Louis
Studies on Religion and the Social Order

HIEBERT LIBRARY

3 6877 00160 3660

BM
508.5
.S33
N48
1998